THE VOICES WITHIN

ALSO BY CHARLES FERNYHOUGH

A Thousand Days of Wonder:
A Scientist's Chronicle of His Daughter's Developing Mind

Pieces of Light:
How the New Science of Memory
Illuminates the Stories We Tell About Our Pasts

THE VOICES WITHIN

THE HISTORY AND SCIENCE
OF HOW WE TALK
TO OURSELVES

CHARLES FERNYHOUGH

BASIC BOOKS
New York

Designed by Trish Wilkinson
Set in 11.5-point Minion Pro

Library of Congress Cataloging-in-Publication Data

Names: Fernyhough, Charles, 1968– author.
Title: The voices within : the history and science of how we talk to
    ourselves / Charles Fernyhough.
Description: New York : Basic Books, [2016] | Includes bibliographical
    references and index.
Identifiers: LCCN 2016012629 (print) | LCCN 2016019777 (ebook) | ISBN
    9780465096800 (hardcover) | ISBN 9780465096817 (e-book)
Subjects: LCSH: Self-talk. | Thought and thinking. |
    Communication—Psychological aspects.
Classification: LCC BF697.5.S47 F47 2016 (print) | LCC BF697.5.S47 (ebook) |
    DDC 153.4/2—dc23
LC record available at https://lccn.loc.gov/2016012629

10 9 8 7 6 5 4 3 2 1

For Jim Russell

We think not in words but in shadows of words.
—Vladimir Nabokov, *Strong Opinions*

CONTENTS

I

FUNNY SLICES OF CHEESE

IT IS AN AUTUMN DAY in the city. I am on a subway train on my way
to a lunch meeting. The midday rush has not yet started, and I have
managed to find a seat in one of those carriages where you sit in two
facing rows, close enough to skim the front page of whatever newspaper is being read opposite you. The train has stopped between sta-
tions and we are waiting for an announcement. People are reading
paperback novels, the junk newspapers, those strange technology
manuals that you only ever see being studied on the underground.
The rest of us are staring at the obscurely color-coded pipes that vein
the tunnel just outside the carriage window. My destination is probably still a quarter of a mile away. I am not doing anything unusual;
in fact, I am not doing anything at all. It is a moment of faintly
self-conscious peacefulness. I am an ordinary man on the wrong side
of forty, in sound mental and physical health. I have had slightly too
much sleep, slightly too little food, and I am looking forward to
lunch in the city with a pleasant sense of appetites not yet satisfied.

Suddenly I burst out laughing. A moment ago I was an anonymous ticket-carrying passenger; now I am blowing my cover with a
more than audible snigger. I am a frequent visitor to the city, but I
am not used to having so many strangers looking at me at the same
time. I have enough presence of mind, and consciousness of my

audience, to rein in my laughter before a private joke turns into a public embarrassment. It is not what I am laughing about that is interesting so much as the fact that I am laughing at all. I have not gate-crashed someone else's joke or overheard a funny snippet of conversation; I have done something much more mundane. You could say that I have just had the most ordinary experience that a person can have on a subway train. I have had a thought.

You GET FUNNY SLICES *of cheese at Wembley Arena.*
    It's not a line that would reduce many to laughter. I still don't know why I was thinking about the football stadium, or what cheese had to do with anything. But I know that this sentence was there in my head, like the utterance of some small internal voice, and that it made me laugh out loud. It didn't have that effect on anyone else in the train compartment, because no one else heard it. My fellow passengers didn't laugh at my mental intrusion (because they couldn't hear it), but they also didn't laugh at me for laughing. They understood that I, like most of the people there, was busy with thoughts, and they knew that thoughts—wild thoughts, mundane thoughts, musings sacred or profane—can occasionally provoke mirth. Talking to yourself in your head is an ordinary activity, and regular folk recognize it when they see it. Not only that, but they also recognize its private qualities. Your thoughts are your own, and whatever happens there takes place in a realm to which other people are not admitted.
    I never fail to be amazed by this quality of consciousness. Not only is our experience compelling and vivid for ourselves, it is so *only* for ourselves. In the second or two following my outburst, I realized that I was trying to send out social signals to excuse my behavior. You don't laugh out loud in front of a nearly full train compartment without feeling at least some faint embarrassment. I didn't want to pretend that it hadn't happened, perhaps by trying to cover it up with a coughing fit, but I was still concerned to put out certain messages: that I was not mad, that I was quickly back in control; indeed, that it was already over, the moment of hilarity had now passed. I found myself concocting an expression that was something

like a smile, mixing knowingness, complicity, and embarrassment. Another thought arose to accompany it, a voice in my head that said, *They can't think I'm laughing at them, can they?* Laughter is a social signal, but this joke had been a private one. I had broken one of the rules of human interaction, and I needed to make some statement to acknowledge this fact.

I needn't have bothered. The other people in the carriage, unless they were small children, Venusians, or certain kinds of psychiatric patients, would have understood. So strong is our conviction about the privacy of our inner experience that its alternatives—mind-reading, telepathy, and thought invasion—can be sources of humor or horror. Strangers on a train will quickly recognize the ramifications of this feature of thinking; they will, after all, have had similar experiences themselves. I had just had a striking reminder of the privacy of my thoughts at the same time that I was made powerfully conscious of their immediacy *for me*. That's what having a brain gives you: a ringside seat for a show meant for you alone.

And it was a show in which I was both the audience and the performer. Whatever had just happened, I was the author of it. I have given the impression that I don't know where this random sentence came from, and yet I kind of do. It came from me. With my rational psychologist's hat on, I would say that it was one of those sentences that habitually flit into my mind, just another bit of the mental fecundity that keeps the stream of consciousness flowing.

Claire also has sentences that pop into her head. Her mental voices speak quietly and insistently, and they say things like "You're a piece of shit" and "You'll never achieve anything." Claire is suffering from depression. She is having cognitive behavioral therapy to tackle these intrusive, unwanted verbal thoughts: to document them, to examine them scientifically, and thus undermine them to the extent that they will (it is hoped) ultimately go away.

Jay has words that come into his head as well. These are of a different quality to Claire's. Much of the time they actually sound like a person talking to him. They can have an accent, a pitch, a tone of voice. Sometimes they speak in full sentences; sometimes their utterances are more fragmentary. They comment on Jay's actions and instruct him to do things: harmless things, like going to the shop to get some milk. At other times they are much more difficult to define. Jay has told me that he can know that a voice is there even when it is not actually speaking; on these occasions, it is not so much a voice as a presence in his head. What is a voice that doesn't speak? A few years ago Jay was diagnosed with a psychiatric illness, and now he has what is known as a "recovery story." He has come back from something that some people think of as a degenerative brain disease. He still hears the voices, but he now feels differently about them. He lives with them, not in fear of them.

One voice-hearer who has written eloquently about her experience has also forged a new understanding with her voices. In a TED talk that, at the time of writing, has been viewed more than three million times, Eleanor Longden described how her voices became so aggressive that she hatched a plan to drill a hole in her head to let them out. Several years on, Eleanor's relationship with her voices, like Jay's, has changed radically. Although they are occasionally still very troublesome, she now sees them as remnants of a "psychic civil war" resulting from repeated childhood trauma. With appropriate support, it seems that many people can change their relationship to their voices and learn to live quite comfortably with them. The assumption that they are always a sign of severe mental illness is a limiting and damaging one, which is why I prefer the more neutral term "voice-hearing" to the negative connotations of "hallucination."

If the experiences of Jay and Eleanor really are different from my own mental voices, then exactly *how* are they different? My "voices" often have accent and pitch; they are private and only audible to me, and yet they frequently sound like real people. But at some level I recognize the voices in my head as my own, while Jay's seem alien to him. He says he can usually distinguish between his thoughts, which feel as though they are his own creations, and these other experiences, which seem to come from somewhere else. At other times the distinction is much more blurred. Another voice-hearer, Adam, whose primary voice has a very distinctive, authoritarian personality (so much so that Adam has dubbed him "The Captain"), told me that he can nevertheless sometimes get confused about whether he is experiencing his own thoughts or those of his voice. I have heard voice-hearers describe how the onset of their unusual experiences was like tuning in to a soundtrack that had always been there, as though they represented some background noise of consciousness to which, for some reason, the individual suddenly started paying attention.

One reason why voice-hearers attribute their experiences to something outside themselves is that the voices say things the hearer feels she could not possibly have said. One woman told me that her voice says such horrible and disgusting things that she knows they can't be of her making. But it can work the other way around, too. I have seen voice-hearers laugh out loud at something their voice, utterly privately, has just said to them. Another voice-hearer, explaining how she understood that her wise-cracking mental visitor wasn't "her," told me, "It can't be me. I could never come up with anything that funny."

IT MATTERS THAT WE understand these experiences better. My verbal thoughts and a voice-hearer's voices may be utterly different experiences, or they may have important features in common. They may, at some level, even be the same thing. As ever in the science of human experience, things are more complicated than they first seem. It's important that we don't set out with the assumption that one kind of voice reduces to the other; in fact, we should avoid pursuing an agenda on which anything is supposed to reduce to anything. These experiences happen to people, and people differ (I can't assume, for example, that my own mental chatter will be even remotely similar to yours). In this book, I am interested in all of these voices: the kindly ones, the guiding ones, the encouraging and commanding ones, the voices of morality and memory, and the sometimes terrible, sometimes beneficent voices that some people hear when there is no one else around.

What is it like to have these kinds of experiences? Although much of our mental activity goes on below the threshold of awareness, plenty of it is made known to the person it is happening to. When we struggle with a problem, recite a telephone number, or reminisce about a romantic encounter, we have an experience of doing these things. It is unlikely to be a complete or accurate picture of the cognitive mechanisms involved—we are far from reliable witnesses to what our brains do—but it nevertheless makes for a coherent experience. In the expression favored by philosophers, there is "something that it is like" to be conscious inside a working brain. Getting busy with a train of thought, like diving into a swimming pool or grieving for a loved one, is an experience that has particular qualities.

But there is another important thing we can say about our inner experience. Plenty of popular science books have conveyed, often to an admirable degree of clarity, what we know about how consciousness works. They tend to focus, though, on the wonder of perceptual and affective experience: how that white lily can have that characteristic fragrance, how the aftermath of a family row can open up so many bittersweet emotional possibilities. In other words, treatments of mental experience usually focus on the brain's responses to events in the outside world. When we start thinking about thinking, we have to explain how consciousness can put on its own show. We are in charge of our thoughts, or at least we have the powerful impression that we are. Thinking is active; it is something that we *do*. Thought moves itself, creates something where there was previously nothing, without requiring any direction from the outside world. This is part of what makes us distinctively human: the fact that, without any external stimulation, a man in an empty room can make himself laugh or cry.

So how should we go about studying experiences like these? The very ordinariness of thinking may mean, paradoxically, that we don't give much thought to how it works. The laws of mental privacy also keep the experience hidden from view. We can share our thoughts' content—we can tell people what we are thinking *about*—but it is harder to share the quality of a phenomenon that is meant for ourselves alone. If we could listen in to other people's thoughts, would we find that they are like our own? Or do thoughts have a personal style, an emotional atmosphere that is distinctive to the thinker? What if people *had* been able to read my mind on the Tube that day? What would a mental eavesdropper hear if she was able to listen in to your thoughts right now? The philosopher Ludwig Wittgenstein remarked that if a lion were able to speak, we would not be able to understand it. I suspect that something similar might apply to our everyday stream of consciousness. Even if we could somehow make our thoughts heard, it is likely that other people would struggle to make sense of them.

One reason is that thinking makes use of words in a very particular way. Imagine if I asked you, for example, what language you think in. My guess is that you may not be able to answer the question truthfully for *every* thought that you have, but you would acknowledge that the question made sense. Many of us would agree that thinking has a linguistic quality. If you are bilingual, you might even have an option about which language to do your thinking in. Nevertheless, there are varieties of thought whose linguistic properties are not always obvious. When you are thinking, there are things you don't need to communicate to yourself, because you already know them. The language can be stripped right down, because the message is meant for you alone.

Another reason why our thinking might not be intelligible to others is that words are usually not the only thing going on. At that moment on the Tube, I had a song from *High School Musical* in my head, to go with all my other bodily and emotional feelings. Some of these sensations were connected to the thought; others were mental wallpaper. The point is that thinking is a multimedia experience. Language has a big role to play in it, but it is by no means the whole story.

In this book, I want to ask what it is like to have this sort of thing going on in your head. I want to investigate how it feels to be caught up in the flow of impressions, ideas, and internal utterances that make up our stream of consciousness. Not everything that our minds and brains can achieve will qualify as this kind of experience. Many of the really clever things a human being can do, such as catching a cricket ball or navigating across the Pacific by starlight, can be performed without any conscious awareness of how they are done. In one sense, "thinking" just refers to everything that our conscious (as opposed to unconscious) minds do. But that is still too broad a definition. I would not want to include those unglamorous mental computations such as counting a handful of pebbles or rotating a mental image, which mostly rely on highly automated, specially evolved cognitive subsystems. One reason for not including these processes is that their start and end points are clearly defined. Part of the magic of thinking is that it can be pointless, circular, or directed toward an ill-defined target. Sometimes thinking is indeed "goal-directed," as in the case of solving certain types of intellectual problems. But the stream of consciousness can also meander aimlessly. Thinking often does not have an obvious starting point, and it often requires us to arrive at its goal before we really understand what that is.

This, then, is the kind of thinking I am interested in. It is *conscious*, in the sense that we know what we are thinking, but also in that it possesses what philosophers call a "phenomenal" quality: there is "something that it is like" to be doing it. It is *linguistic*, and, as we will see, often more closely tied up with language than it initially appears to be. Imagery is involved, as are many other sensory and emotional elements, but they are only parts of the picture. Thinking (in words or otherwise) is also *private*: what we think is thought in the context of certain firm assumptions about its imperceptibility to others. Thoughts are typically *coherent*: they fit into chains of ideas that, in no matter how haphazard a fashion, are connected to what has come before. Finally, thoughts are *active*. Thinking is something that we do, and we usually recognize it as our own work.

I'm not the first to be interested in the role that words play in our mental processes. Philosophers have argued for centuries about whether language is necessary for thought (while often being a bit vague about what exactly they mean by "thinking"), and animal behavior researchers have conducted ingenious experiments to find out what kinds of thinking animals can do, including whether they can be taught language. All of these findings will be relevant to my inquiry. But my approach is slightly different. I want to begin with a simple fact of the matter: when we think about our own experience, or when we ask other people to report on what goes on for them, we find that our heads are full of words. That doesn't mean that everyone reports such verbal streams of thought: the fact that some of us do not will need explaining. Asking that question in the right way might prove to be very informative about the relationship between language and thinking.

When I first started thinking about this topic as a graduate student in the 1990s, it did not look like a healthy subject of inquiry. Studying something as private and ineffable as our inner voices was, my elders might have warned me, never going to furnish a successful research career. For a start, it would seem to depend on the almost impossible task of introspection (reflecting on one's own thought processes), which had long fallen out of favor as a scientific method. Another problem is that the idea of an "inner voice" is often used, vaguely and metaphorically, to refer to everything from gut feelings to creative instincts, with none of the robust attempts at definition that you need for doing sound research. There were good reasons, though, for pursuing the quarry, and in recent years the scientific picture has changed profoundly. One thing that is emerging from this research is that the words that sound out in our heads play a vital part in our thinking. Psychologists are demonstrating that "inner speech," as they term it, helps us to regulate our behavior, motivate ourselves for action, evaluate those actions, and even become conscious of our own selves. Neuroscientists are showing how mental voices draw on some of the same neural systems that underlie external speech, fitting with important ideas about how they develop. We now know that inner speech comes in different forms and speaks in different tongues, that it has an accent and an emotional tone, and that we correct errors in it in some of the same ways that we fix slip-ups in external speech. Many of us really do think in words, and there are good and bad forms of this kind of thinking. Negative thoughts, perpetuated in inner speech, contribute to the distress caused by certain mental disorders, and they may also be the key to ameliorating them.

Beyond the science lab, questions about inner speech have been a source of fascination for as long as humans have been thinking about their own thoughts. One thing we can say about thinking is that it often appears to us as a kind of conversation between different voices propounding different points of view. But what do these voices sound like? What language do they speak? Does your thinking self speak in fully grammatical sentences, or is it more like listening to something written down in note form? Are your thoughts softly spoken, or do they ever raise their voice? And anyway, who is listening when your thinking selves are speaking? Where are "you" in all of this? Such questions may sound strange, and yet these qualities of thinking must define what it is like to inhabit our own minds.

All of these puzzles might be explicable if we take seriously the idea (so persuasive to our introspection) of thinking as a voice, or voices, in the head. I want to explore this view and test it to its limits. In one way or another, this approach, which I term the "Dialogic Thinking" model, has informed most of my scholarly work in psychology, and it will be a focus throughout this book. It follows from a particular theory of the emergence of thinking in early childhood, and it is supported by psychological and neuroscientific studies of normal and disordered cognition. Yet, no matter how strong the evidence for the model, it is clear that there are many aspects of our inner experience that are not verbal and voice-like, and I will explore whether the hypothesis can be developed and expanded to account for thinking in people who do not have a language to think in, as well as the evidence that much of inner experience is visual and imagery-based.

I am fortunate in having a very wide range of evidence to draw on. Some aspects of the mystery of mental voices have had hundreds, even thousands of years' worth of attention. Philosophers have struggled with thorny problems about how a mind can represent knowledge, constructing principled arguments about, for example, whether thinking could occur in natural language. Psychologists have set their participants reasoning tasks and asked them to speak their thought processes out loud for close analysis. Neuroscientists have tracked inner speech by recording electrical signals from the articulatory muscles of people who are thinking silently, or by stimulating parts of the brain and seeing how language processes are affected. Writers through the centuries have filled their novels and poems with verbal thinking, and their depictions of streams of consciousness, trains of thought, and knight's-moves of the mind provide an unparalleled source of evidence about how our mental voices do their work.

In the chapters that follow, I will draw on all of these sources of evidence. We will hear from young children and the elderly, sportsmen, novelists, practitioners of meditation, visual artists, and people who hear voices. Is it true that young children don't think in words? Do some psychiatric patients' voices really disappear when they open their mouths? Is it possible to think one thing in inner speech at the same time as saying the complete opposite out loud? What was happening in Joan of Arc's mind, brain, and body when she heard a "beautiful, sweet, low voice" exhorting her to lift the siege of Orléans? How is it that inner speech can happen faster than ordinary speech, without seeming at all rushed to the person doing the thinking? Why do some voice-hearers' voices say such funny things? I will look at how literary and other artistic depictions of the phenomena align with the facts thrown up by scientific research, and how such "objective" treatments compare with the evidence from introspection. I will submit myself to functional magnetic resonance imaging (fMRI) and see how my brain weaves thoughts on its enchanted loom. I will try to describe the ephemera of the voices in our heads as well as tracing their weightier trajectories. I will also detail the stories of several individuals who hear voices, trying to capture how the experience feels, how it can be managed, and what it reveals about the nature of the self.

By the end of this book, I hope to have persuaded you of several things. Talking to ourselves is a part of human experience that, although by no means universal, seems to play many different roles in our mental lives. According to one important theory, the words in our heads act as psychological "tools" that help us to do things in our thinking, just as a handyman's tools make tasks possible that would not be tractable otherwise. Our inner speech can plan, direct, encourage, question, cajole, prohibit, and reflect. From cricketers to poets, people talk to themselves in all sorts of ways and for a whole range of very different purposes.

It stands to reason, then, that the experience will come in many forms. Sometimes inner speech seems to be just like language spoken out loud; at other times it is more telegraphic and condensed, an abbreviated version of what we might utter audibly. Researchers have only recently begun to take seriously the idea that inner speech can come in different shapes and sizes, that the distinct forms of inner speech might adapt it to different functions, and that the varieties of the phenomenon will have different foundations in the brain.

The multifarious forms and functions of inner speech make perfect sense when we look at how it emerges in childhood. There are good reasons for thinking that inner speech develops when children's conversations with others "go underground," or become internalized, to form a silent version of those external exchanges. That means that the thinking we do in words will share some of the features of the conversations we have with others, which are in turn shaped by the interactional styles and social norms of our culture. "To think," wrote the Spanish philosopher and novelist Miguel de Unamuno, "is to talk with oneself, and each one of us talks with himself, thanks to our having had to talk with one another." I'll try to persuade you that some of the mysteries of inner speech become more comprehensible when we recognize that it has the properties of a dialogue.

The social origin of inner speech also helps us to understand the familiar polyphony of human consciousness. Recognizing inner speech as a kind of dialogue accounts for how our minds can be shot through with many different voices, just as a work of fiction contains the voices of different characters with different perspectives. I'll argue that this view helps us to understand some important features of human consciousness, including an openness to alternative perspectives that might be one of the hallmarks of creativity. I'll examine this idea with reference to the work of both verbal and visual artists, asking whether one important way of being creative is to hold a conversation with the self.

I also want to persuade you that this view of inner speech helps us to understand the more unusual voices that feature in human experience. The phenomenon of voice-hearing (or auditory verbal hallucinations) is commonly associated with schizophrenia, but it is also reported in many other psychiatric disorders and by a significant minority of mentally healthy individuals. Many psychiatrists and psychologists believe that it results from a disorder of inner speech, in which individuals come to misattribute their own internal utterances as the speech of someone else. One problem with the research to date is that it hasn't taken inner speech seriously enough as a phenomenon. If we start with a more accurate picture of the ordinary voices in our heads, we might end up with a better account of why some people hear voices when no one is around.

We have little chance of achieving a decent scientific understanding of that experience, however, without recognizing that it, too, takes many different forms. From medieval mystics to creators of literary fiction, human beings across the centuries have described experiences of hearing voices. All of these testimonies need to be examined in the context of the lives, times, and cultures in which they emerged. Understanding voice-hearing also requires us to account for the very strong relationship between voice-hearing and early adversity, and the implication that hearing voices relates to memories for terrible events. I'll talk to some voice-hearers who believe that their voices should be understood as messages from their pasts, revealing unresolved emotional conflicts, rather than as the junk pronouncements of a confused brain. Researchers are now beginning to understand voice-hearing as involving a sense of receiving communications from another entity, with deep repercussions for our theories of how we compute social relationships as well as for our understanding of ordinary inner speech.

This view of mental voices is not without its problems, and possibilities for future research are intriguingly poised. One of the challenges facing the mental-voices view is the fact that some individuals do not report inner speech at all. How does thinking work in such cases? How does it get started before there is any language to shape it? How do words get together with mental imagery to create the vivid, multi-sensory vistas of thought? It seems that the voices in our heads can have both positive and negative effects, and the study of their evolution can illuminate the forces that might have brought language and thought together in the emergence of consciousness. The implications are profound for all of us. Could we one day conspire to enhance and control our ways of talking to ourselves so that mental illness becomes consigned to history? Can we evolve ourselves, as a species, out of intrusive thoughts, irrationality, and distractibility? Perhaps, but then creativity might become a thing of the past, too. One thing that is certain is that a better understanding of our mental voices can give us a richer appreciation of how our minds do what they do, and how we can live more productively with the sometimes happy, sometimes fretful—and always flexible and creative—murmurings in our heads.

2

Turning Up the Gas

CLOSE YOUR EYES AND have a thought. It doesn't much matter what you choose to think about: the subject matter can be profound or mundane. Hold the thought; savor it. Replay it in your mind. Now ask yourself a question: What was it like to think that thought? We know what certain kinds of mental activity are like: dreaming, for example, or working out a sum using mental arithmetic. But what kind of activity is thinking? What varieties does it come in? What does it feel like to be doing this ordinary and yet utterly remarkable thing?

I don't expect that you'll have had any difficulty in filling your head for a second or two. (It would have been considerably harder if I had asked you to *empty* it.) Thinking is something we are doing all the time, not just when we have decisions to make or problems to solve. Even when your brain is ostensibly having downtime, your mind is likely to be anything but silent. The evidence from psychological studies confirms what our own introspection suggests: for most of our waking moments, we are borne along on an internal current of ideas and impressions that guides our actions, founds our memories, and forms the central thread of our experience.

Now ask yourself some more questions about the thought you just had. Did it sound like a person speaking? If so, was that person "you"? Did it feel like *anything*, or was it just the by-product of an active brain, with no phenomenal qualities to distinguish it? Would you recognize the thought if it happened again? How do you know that it was your own?

I believe that all of these questions make sense, but that they are also very difficult to answer. We have uniquely direct access to our own thoughts, but *only* to our own. That makes them very hard to study. Specifically, it is very difficult to be sure that you are making reliable judgments about your experiences, because you cannot compare your judgments with anyone else's. In the previous chapter, I described some reasons for believing that many people's inner experience contains a lot of words. But does it really? How do we answer the "really" question—and what does the question even mean when it comes to asking about our internal worlds? How do we go about studying the contents of our heads?

The obvious approach is to try to make use of the direct access we have to our own experience. "Why," asks the philosopher Socrates in Plato's *Theaetetus*, "should we not gently and patiently review our own thoughts, and examine and see what these appearances in us really are?" The seventeenth-century French philosopher René Descartes saw no problem with that idea. Sitting by the fire in his winter dressing gown, he looked into his own thought processes and saw that their existence was the one thing he could not doubt. *Cogito ergo sum*: I think, therefore I am. Reflecting on his own mental states was the "first principle" of Descartes's method. The American philosopher and psychologist William James, writing in 1890, thought that, while the existence of states of consciousness was undeniable, observing them in ourselves was "difficult and fallible." But that kind of observation was still possible; it was not different in principle to any other method of describing the world. With a sufficiently careful approach, a person could be trained to do it better.

What took introspection out of the philosopher's armchair and into the science lab was the work of the German psychologist Wilhelm Wundt. Founder of the first scientific psychological laboratory, established at Leipzig in 1879, Wundt had another claim to fame as the author of the world's first psychology textbook. In his thinking about inner experience, Wundt distinguished between two kinds of introspection. First, there was what he dubbed "self-observation" (*Selbstbeobachtung*): the kind of casual examination of one's own mental processes that anyone with a mind can do—you don't have to be Descartes to sit by the fire and think about your own thoughts. But for Wundt, this kind of examination was seriously flawed: it did not make for good science. Quite different, he said, was the more formal category of "inner perception" (*innere Wahrnehmung*). Where possible, the scientific method requires that the observer try to stay out of the process of observation, and this was what Wundt had in mind for his second approach, which involved a painstaking separation of the observer from the object being observed. In Wundt's technique of inner perception, the researcher really was taking a clinically detached stance toward his or her own thoughts. By itself, according to Wundt, inner perception was not a decent scientific method; it could become so, however, with the thorough training of participants.

And train his participants Wundt did. Critics of introspection have sometimes given the impression that Leipzig introspection involved a rather casual—Cartesian, in fact—armchair reflection on one's own mental processes. But Wundt's introspectors were trained professionals. It was reported that, in order to provide data for published research, a member of Wundt's lab had to have performed no fewer than 10,000 introspective "reactions." In William James's analysis, introspection was the same as any other kind of observation: it could be done well or badly. You had to get good at it. Merely having the experiences wasn't enough to guarantee that you would have any skill at observing or describing them; otherwise, as James remarked, babies would make excellent introspectors.

Wundt's efforts created a new methodology for studying inner experience that ultimately crossed the Atlantic to America. In the hands of Wundt's followers, such as Edward Titchener, the introspective method became narrower and more mechanistic, and its weaknesses—particularly its reliance on unverifiable self-observation— came more sharply into focus. By the middle of the twentieth century, Anglo-American psychology was in thrall to the behaviorist theories of John B. Watson and B. F. Skinner, with their claims that only the measurement of observable behaviors could guarantee a rigorous science of the mind. Introspection seemed consigned to history. One problem, addressed by William James, was that introspections were always at some level *memories* of experience, rather than the experiences themselves—and memory is notoriously fallible. Above all, there was a growing awareness that experience could not be described without being changed by the very act of observation. Trying to reflect on one's own thoughts was, in James's memorable phrase, like "trying to turn up the gas quickly enough to see how the darkness looks."

For many, the final nail in the coffin of introspection came with the cognitive revolution that began in the 1950s and gathered pace in the subsequent two decades. In 1977, Richard Nisbett and Timothy Wilson reviewed evidence on the accuracy of people's reports about their higher cognitive processes. One of the experiments they reviewed was conducted with people who had been having trouble sleeping. Some of the participants were given an "arousal" pill—a placebo that they were told would produce the physical and emotional symptoms of insomnia, but which actually had no physiological effect. Another group was told that their pills (equally physiologically inactive) would relax them. In each case, the pills themselves had no active ingredients; the volunteers' expectations about their effects, however, were very different, because of what the experimenters had told them.

The researchers then observed how the members of each group dealt with their insomnia after taking the pills. As it turned out, participants who had been told their pills would keep them awake got to sleep more quickly than usual, suggesting that they attributed their arousal to the effect of the pills rather than to their own sleeplessness. For the relaxation group, the opposite pattern was observed. People in that group actually took longer to go to sleep, presumably because they were expecting to feel relaxed and ended up feeling anything but—leading them to conclude that they must be even more wound up than usual. When questioned afterward, however, participants had very little insight into the psychological effect of the pills, attributing the change in their sleep patterns instead to extraneous factors, such as their performance in an exam, or problems with a girlfriend. Nisbett and Wilson concluded that it made little sense to ask experimental participants to explain their own cognitive processes. For all the painstaking observation of the introspectionists, we turn out to have surprisingly little insight into how our own minds actually work.

IT IS A MUGGY July day in Berlin, and Lara is wondering whether to have another beer.

"I was putting down the empty bottle, and it was like in my head I was thinking, *Do I want another one?* I'm pretty sure I thought those words. And that's when the beep occurred."

Lara is a young Chinese American from Los Angeles who is in Berlin for a year's study, and she is taking part in an experiment. She has been asked to carry a small device around with her, clipped to her clothing. It's about the size of a smartphone. At random intervals, the device will activate and make a beeping sound through an earpiece. That's her signal to pay attention to whatever was in her experience at the moment just before the beep sounded. She then has to jot down notes, in whatever format suits her best and on a notepad given to her for that purpose, about that moment of experience. She does that until she has made notes on six beeps and six moments of experience, and then she can take the earpiece out and put it away. The following day she comes into the lab and is interviewed in detail about those six moments. The incident with the beer is from the third beep of her first day of sampling. Interviewing her about these flashes of consciousness is Russell Hurlburt, the inventor of the method.

"Those exact words?" Russ asks her.

"I can't really say one hundred percent those were my exact words, because I didn't write it down exactly. . . . And in that moment I remember the sensation of drinking cold beer and how I really enjoyed that, and wondering, *Do I want another one?*"

"So a recalled sensation of drinking a beer?"

"Yeah, and thinking, *Do I want more of that experience?*"

Is it that she wanted more beer, Russ asks, or that she was having a memory of having previously enjoyed a cold one?

"I think it's definitely both, because I was asking myself that question, and I started recalling that in order to answer that question, I guess."

What were the exact words in her experience at that moment? Lara can't recall. In the future, Russ says, she should jot those words down, because the exact words are going to matter. If we're interested in how we talk to ourselves in our heads (along with all the other things we do in there), the actual words are going to matter a lot.

"And are those words in a voice?" Russ continues. "Or are you reading them, or are you seeing them, or? . . ."

"Yeah, they're in a voice and they're in my own voice."

"Okay. And are they in a voice as if you were speaking them, or as if you were hearing them, or? . . ."

"Um, I guess it'll be as if I was speaking them? But speaking them to myself, the way someone would ask a question. The thing is, as I'm answering these questions, I'm just worried that what I'm saying about those moments might change because I'm thinking about them more, you know?"

Russ Hurlburt is one of a number of scientists who are rethinking introspection. A tall man in his late sixties, with gray hair and spectacles, he started out as an engineer working for a company that made nuclear weapons. What he really wanted to do was play the trumpet. This was the time of Vietnam, and Russ received a draft number that put him high on the list for possible conscription, so he volunteered to join the US Army Band in Washington, DC. There, his skills as a trumpet player found a focus that would indirectly have a momentous effect on his career. He ended up in a job that involved playing "Taps," the ceremonial tune played at military funerals. His role was to wait in Arlington Cemetery for a funeral to arrive and for the guns to be sounded, and then play "Taps" over the coffin of the poor Vietnam casualty. He would then discreetly withdraw to his car, which was parked under a tree nearby, and wait—still in full military regalia—for the next funeral, which might not be scheduled for another two hours. That left him with plenty of time on his hands, which he occupied by filling his car with books from the Arlington County Library. He read everything that engineers don't usually get a chance to read: literature, poetry, history, and, in particular, psychology. Within a few months he had devoured the whole of the library's psychology collection.

"What I found was that every book in psychology would start by saying, 'I'm going to tell you something interesting about people,' and then I'd get to the end of the book and say, 'Well, I didn't learn anything that I thought was actually very interesting; I learned the theory but I didn't learn anything about the person.'" What Russ wanted was something that told you about people's everyday experience. "I thought, if you could just randomly sample these things, that would be good. . . . I was in the truck driving across the desert or the plains of some city and I said, 'I know how to build a beeper.' When I got to the University of South Dakota, which is where I went to graduate school, the director said, 'What do you want to do, Russ?' And I said, 'I want to randomly sample thoughts, and I figured out how to do it in the truck on the way out here.'"

The grad school adviser was impressed by Russ's idea but thought the beeper sounded technically unfeasible. So he proposed a deal: if Russ was able to build the beeper, he would waive the requirement that Russ obtain a master's in psychology (he already had one in engineering) and allow him to proceed straight to the PhD program. In the autumn of 1973, Russ built the beeper and won his wager. He began to use his new technology to try to explore his participants' thoughts, at first through short questionnaires and the complex statistical analyses needed for making sense of the resultant mountain of data. Eventually he realized that his method had not said anything more interesting about minds or people than those of the researchers he had previously criticized, and so he began to focus more on the qualitative nature of the reports: his participants' descriptions of their thought processes and what made them distinctive to that individual.

For the past nearly forty years, Russ has been a member of the faculty at the University of Nevada, Las Vegas (UNLV). He has spent his career refining and testing this method of examining inner experience, which he calls Descriptive Experience Sampling (DES). When he first arrived at UNLV, he made himself wear the DES beeper for a whole year while he was figuring out what to do with it. Thanks to its conspicuous earpiece, his colleagues on campus thought he was deaf, although many were too polite to question him about it. To this day, some people on campus still tend to speak up in his presence.

For Lara, today is just the start of the process. She is not going to be good at describing her DES moments on the first day, because no one is good at it on the first day. In fact, Russ argues, people are generally so bad at reporting on their own experience that the first day's reports inevitably have to be thrown away. But Lara will get better. DES is what Russ calls an iterative process: it's about training the respondent and the interviewer to describe "the unique inner experience of the subject with increasingly greater fidelity." You cannot do that without training, and without learning from your mistakes. People are generally better at hiding their experiences, Russ argues, than describing them accurately.

He also proposes that DES gets around many of the problems that have dogged the enterprise of introspection. For a start, Russ has no agenda as an investigator other than to explore the phenomena as they occur, whatever they might be. He does not approach a DES interview armed with a theory. Nor does DES set out its categories of interest in advance, although it does find specific kinds of experience popping up again and again: visual imagery, bodily sensations, inner speech. Hurlburt calls the latter "inner speaking," to emphasize its active nature. But he is not specifically interested in inner speech, at least not in the way that I am—a fact that probably makes me a less-than-ideal practitioner of the method.

Above all, DES is inspired by a philosophical method known as phenomenology. Phenomenology literally means the study of how things appear, and by curious paradox it was also one of the forces of twentieth-century philosophy that helped to sink the boat of intro-

spection. When Russ became dissatisfied with the quantitative results he was obtaining from the beeper, he immersed himself in the
works of Edmund Husserl and Martin Heidegger, teaching himself
German so that he could study their writings more closely. For Russ,
the most important lesson from phenomenology is what is known as
the "bracketing of presuppositions": the researcher's capacity to set
aside their preconceptions about how things will be, and to observe
how they actually are. If you want to find out what's going on in
someone else's head, you don't want to assume you know what's
there before you start. This is particularly important when you are
interested in a specific phenomenon like inner speech. If you start
out by assuming that people talk to themselves all the time, your data
will probably reflect that presupposition back at you.

For all his years of work on it, Russ does not see DES as the perfect method. For one thing, DES reports are always filtered through
memory—a problem that William James foresaw in 1890—and their
moments of consciousness are reconstructed after the event. These
are some of the reasons why Russ is so interested in the details of
Lara's thought about the beer. She has observed that she is uncertain
about exactly what the thought was; it seems that the process of
thinking hard about the experience is letting doubts creep in. This is
normal, Russ says. "We're going to do as good a job as we can," he
reassures her. "We don't expect you to be perfect, because we don't
think that's possible. We want to try to be good at it."

I ask Lara about the words that made up the thought. Was it, *Am
I going to have another BEER?* or *Am I going to have another ONE?* "I
would say *one*," Lara says: "Definitely one." These are the sorts of
details we will be picking over in the weeks to come. Lara resolves to
make more notes at the moment the beep sounds, and to be more
specific about the instants of consciousness she is describing. As a
participant—one of our first for this study—she is intelligent and engaged, eager to give it a go and try to make it work. You couldn't go
into this casually or half-heartedly; it's too much like hard work. For
Lara, the moments she is being asked to describe are so fleeting, so
removed from what she would ordinarily consider to be the focus of

her thoughts, that it's hard to talk about them. "You know how, when you wake up after dreaming about something and then you forget it immediately? It's like that." Russ encourages her to stick with it. It will get easier. It will never be perfect, but it will be as close to perfect as science can currently get.

That evening I go back to my hotel and transcribe the notes from the interview. A thunderstorm is breaking over Dahlem, the leafy suburb that is home to the Max Planck Institute for Human Development, where we are running the study. Outside of my fiction-writing, I have never spent so much time poring over the details of another person's experience. I email the notes to Russ and he responds quickly, pointing out the errors I have made, places where my expectations about what Lara's experience *should* be like have got in the way of my accurate reporting of it. The bracketing of presuppositions is everything. You have to learn how to make these detailed reports on your own experience, and you have to learn how to handle those that others have presented you with, too.

It seems like a lot of work, but then a great deal is at stake. The critics of introspection have not gone away. A behaviorist might say that peering inside the mind is too fallible, too unscientific, and that we should bypass thoughts and feelings altogether in favor of events that we can be "objective" about. An introspectionist would respond that a science of the mind that pays no attention to subjective experience is empty and meaningless, falling far short of what such a science is meant to do.

This problem seems even more acute with the emergence of new techniques for lifting the hood on the brain. The field of cognitive neuroscience, which combines methods from psychology with techniques for studying neural systems (through scanning, electrical stimulation, or the study of brain damage), has in many areas begun to deliver on its promise of a unified account of mind and brain. But we still need to know what's going on inside. Human beings don't experience activation in their visual cortex or amygdala modulation of hippocampal action: they experience visual images and emotional memories. If we are going to have an integrated science of the mind, we need a way of getting at those experiences. We need DES, or something like it.

Besides, it turns out that the critique of introspection attributed to Nisbett and Wilson pretty much misses its target. Recall that their 1977 paper found many examples of people being unable to report reliably on why they had made certain decisions. People may indeed be very bad at reporting on the *causes* of their behavior, but that doesn't mean they can't get good at reporting on their own *experience*. In fact, in reviewing existing studies, Nisbett and Wilson left the door open for future methods that might go about the task of collecting data on inner experience with sufficient care. "The studies do not suffice," they wrote, "to show that people *could never* be accurate about the processes involved." If a method were able to foreground a moment of experience without interfering with it, to ensure that participants paid careful attention to what was going on in their heads at the time, to help them get better at reflecting on that experience, and so on, we might be on to something. For Hurlburt, that's a pretty good description of DES.

The method is not without its critics, however. Cognitive scientists complain that DES is unwieldy and laborious, and that it's impossible to generalize from a single DES participant to anything that could be a meaningful part of psychological theory. Philosophers argue that Hurlburt is too confident in his ability to factor out his own presuppositions about experience, or to avoid shaping, through his questioning, the very processes he is hoping to describe. In response, Russ points out that taking his method seriously means accepting that we are very often mistaken in our judgments about what goes on in our heads. In contrast to the typical psychology researcher, obsessed with establishing the validity of her measures, Russ sees his method as establishing a shared language for exploring the idiosyncrasies of a participant's inner world, rather than squeezing people's varied experiences into preexisting categories. "It's like the scouts and the warriors," he tells me. "The scouts tell you where to go, and then the warriors have to go there. You've got to have both if you're going to win the battle. Right now there are not very many good scouts in psychology."

My own feeling is that DES is a valuable technique that needs to be combined with others that have different strengths and weaknesses. (We are actually in Berlin to conduct the first integration of the DES method with neuroimaging; in a few days' time, Lara will be going into the scanner for just that purpose.) As the following chapters will show, the voices in our heads have been investigated through many different techniques, some as direct as DES, others much more indirect. I also suspect that DES might underestimate the amount of inner speech that is actually going on, partly because it makes the demanding requirement that participants report exactly what words were in their heads, and partly because of cultural presuppositions about what kind of thing inner speech can be.

In the course of my stay in Berlin, I get a chance to lead some interviews myself and find myself trying and occasionally succeeding in bracketing my own presuppositions about the experience of the people I am talking to. When I'm interviewing Russ for this book, I'm aware of being particularly careful about my choice of words. What effect has all this attention to the fine details of human experience had on the creator of DES? Apart from that one-year stint of wearing the beeper pretty much continuously, he has shied away from beeping himself, out of concerns that his own experience might come to color what he would expect to find in others. In other respects, the method he has been developing for the past forty-odd years has touched on most aspects of his life. He has developed a manner of interacting with people that is thoughtful, responsive, careful, and nonjudgmental. Whether he is this way as a result of all his years of doing DES, or whether DES reflects the qualities of its creator, Russ doesn't know. He is an exemplary listener and an extraordinarily careful questioner. "The bracketing of presuppositions runs pretty deep inside me," he tells me. "The method and me are pretty intertwined."

And what effect does DES have on those who participate in it? Paying such close attention to the details of other people's experience is bound to shift your view on the colorful pageant of human mental life. As a trainee DES investigator who has now spent many hours listening to people describe their thoughts and feelings in minute detail, I have gained some of the same pleasure that I get from reading fiction. One of the tasks that novelists and short story writers delight in is that of re-creating a consciousness on the page. When you witness a great writer documenting the minutiae of someone's experience, some of the same attentiveness rubs off.

For those who are reporting on their experience, the effects can be even more profound. DES can give some striking demonstrations of how your preconceptions about your own experience can be overturned. Although she found the process tiring, another of our participants, Ruth, said that taking part in a DES study had made her more aware of the moment, but also more clued up about what kind of mind she had. Looking back at her beeps revealed that she was generally much more joyful than she had realized, and that she took pleasure in simple things—like the behavior of two familiar robins in her garden—to an extent she hadn't previously recognized. Russ himself has had nearly four decades of seeing the effect that his method has on people. "The most common response of people who have gone through this method is, 'I have learned more about myself than I ever learned about myself before, including with my wife and my bartender and my psychoanalyst with whom I have had five years' worth of therapy.' And that in itself is fairly remarkable, since what we will have done is nothing more than to try and get a high-fidelity view of twenty-five milliseconds' worth of their experience." For some people, Russ says, doing DES is "truly life-changing."

At the same time, methods like this present a huge challenge to those who want to study human experience scientifically. What does it mean to say that someone like Ruth can start off with a mistaken idea about her own experience? In the case of inner speech, Russ has seen many cases where people begin DES with a preconception that their heads are full of words (I myself would probably start with the same impression), only to find that their experience isn't actually very verbal at all. How is it possible that I could be "wrong" about what goes on in my own head? An alternative view, that I cannot know *anything* with any certainty about what goes on in my experience, seems equally bizarre—and yet that is what some critics of introspection have concluded. One thing is certain: if we are going to have a science of the voices in our heads, we will need something like DES's careful attention to our everyday, fleeting moments of experience.

3

Inside the Chatterbox

Nick Marshall can read women's minds. Accidentally electrocuted in a freak accident (hairdryer, bathtub) in his Chicago apartment, Nick (played by Mel Gibson) wakes up with an uncanny ability to tune in to the thoughts of the women around him. The movie is *What Women Want*, and the story is about what happens when the laws of mental privacy break down. For an arrogant and chauvinistic advertising executive like Nick, reading women's minds is a handy trick. Not only does it boost his already impressive bedpost tally, but it also allows him to steal his boss's best ideas and pass them off as his own. We are in the world of Hollywood rom-coms, and the story of Nick's moral challenge and gradual humanization is full of gentle reminders about the values that aren't worth risking for the sake of a career. Stealing is wrong, but there is something particularly repugnant about making off with thoughts that the owner cannot even recognize as missing.

Like other depictions of the art of telepathy, *What Women Want* reminds us how much our sanity depends on our minds remaining sealed off from each other. The first time we see Nick using his new powers, he is waking up in his apartment after the accident with the hairdryer. His maid has discovered him lying unconscious on the floor and is having the thought that he might be dead. But instead of

29

her musings remaining private, as they would have done on any other day, Nick hears them as though they were utterances spoken out loud. In this particular fictional world, thinking is a kind of speaking, one that (in normal circumstances) only the thinker can hear. Nick hears the flow of another person's thoughts as a voice with certain qualities, which combines words to create meanings just as spoken language does.

Soundtrack aside, a movie is an intensely visual creation. There would be nothing to stop directors from portraying thoughts as visual images—as mini film clips, for example, unreeling in the space above a character's head. But this is not how it is usually done, either in film or in other media. Peer into the thought bubbles in any comic book or graphic novel and you will see people's thinking processes depicted as linguistic utterances. Thinking is a voice, we are told, the voice of the self. It is a silent monologue that would be comprehensible, to a speaker of our own language, if it were spoken out loud.

In the days that follow, Nick's feelings about his mind-reading develop from horror into acceptance. There is a funny scene when, anxious to gather more evidence to confirm his horrible suspicion about his new powers, Nick listens in to the brain waves of his two airheaded secretaries, only to discover complete radio silence. In another memorable scene, Nick fails to understand what his boss, Darcy, is saying because she is thinking at the same time. Thinking is linguistic, but what we think is not the same as what we say. The voice of Darcy's consciousness is reading from a different script to her social voice. But it is unmistakeably a voice. When Darcy phones Nick in the middle of the night and then is too shy to speak out loud to the colleague she is falling for, Nick has the extraordinary experience of recognizing her from the sound of her thoughts.

Leaving aside the dodgy gender politics, *What Women Want* also gets certain things wrong about inner experience. When we overhear the Latina maid's thoughts in that early scene, she is thinking in English, when it might be more plausible if she were cogitating in her mother tongue. Two deaf women seen conversing with their hands turn out to be thinking in spoken English rather than, as might seem more likely, in their own sign language. Actually, deafness and other conditions where ordinary verbal communication is disrupted pose a tricky challenge to understanding the relationships between speech, language, and thinking, as we'll see later, when we look at the evidence on deaf people's inner voices.

When we move away from the high and low arts and look at how scholars have described the process of thinking, we find further assertions about its close association with silent speaking. "For many of us," wrote the philosopher Ray Jackendoff, "the running commentary hardly ever stops." Other philosophers, such as Ludwig Wittgenstein and Peter Carruthers, have proposed that ordinary language is nothing less than the vehicle of our thoughts. Perhaps the most extreme view about the ubiquity of inner speech comes from a psychologist: "We are a gabby species," wrote Bernard Baars in 1997. "The urge to talk to ourselves is remarkably compelling, as we can easily see by trying to *stop* the inner voice as long as possible. . . . Inner speech is one of the basic facts of human nature." On another occasion, Baars wrote with almost scientific authority on the apparent ubiquity of inner speech: "Human beings talk to themselves every moment of the waking day. . . . Overt speech takes up perhaps a tenth of the waking day; but inner speech goes on all the time."

These views have gained limited empirical support. While some people will report, like Baars, that they are at it constantly, others describe far less active inner voices. In a study of people lying down and doing nothing for a few minutes in magnetic resonance imaging (MRI) scanners (the so-called "resting state" paradigm), researchers found that more than 90 percent of participants experienced some internal language during that period, but that it was a dominant mode of thinking for only 17 percent. Outside the scanner, Russ Hurlburt's DES method shows that some people's beeped moments contain high proportions of inner speech (94 percent, in the case of one DES participant), while others' contain none. Averaging across two studies, Hurlburt and his colleagues found that around 23 percent of beeped moments contained inner speech, a figure that obscures considerable variation among individuals.

As we shall see, there are reasons to be skeptical about all such figures—not least because they are essentially based on introspection, which has been observed to be problematic in various ways. In particular, asking people about how much inner speech they do requires them to cast their minds back over a particular period of time, which means that the foibles of memory come into play. Even DES, with its carefully elicited snapshots of inner experience, is subject to the vagaries of remembering. We also need to bear in mind the huge variations among people in the wordiness of their thoughts. Some people don't use inner speech at all, and any theory about its function needs to account for the fact that some people's craniums don't contain any.

The evidence suggests, though, that inner speech is a significant part of our mental lives. A quarter to a fifth of our waking moments is a lot of waking moments, a lot of self-talk. What is all this language doing in our heads? By asking when and how people dip into this internal stream of chatter, we might be able to start to clarify what we gain from getting wordy with our thoughts.

MICHAEL TALKS TO HIMSELF in his head. His day job involves a lot of waiting around, punctuated by moments of extraordinary concentration. Doing what he does requires an almost preternatural ability to integrate thought and action in voluntary movements that are as quick as any ordinary person's knee-jerk reflexes. Michael is a professional cricketer, and he talks to himself as he is waiting for a ball to be delivered. "I suppose I'm not speaking out loud," he tells me when I meet him after training one day at the county ground. "But in my head I'm saying, Just little movements with my back foot; I'll just move it across a little bit. And then I try and tell myself, Okay, watch the ball, almost to remove all the thinking that goes into it."

It has long been observed that this kind of self-talk is an important feature of sporting performances. In a classic study from 1974, coaching writer W. Timothy Gallwey drew his readers' attention to a scenario that he believed could be observed on any tennis court:

> Most players are talking to themselves on the court all the time. "Get up for the ball." "Keep it to his backhand." "Keep your eyes on the ball." "Bend your knees." The commands are endless. For some, it's like hearing a tape recording of the last lesson playing inside their head. Then, after the shot is made, another thought flashes through the mind and might be expressed as follows: "You clumsy ox, your grandmother could play better!"

Harsh though it might be on both oxen and grandmothers, Gallwey analyzed these common kinds of self-talk in terms of a relationship between two selves, the "teller" and the "doer." You speak and the body listens. Gallwey's observation touches on a distinction that will crop up in any discussion of why we talk to ourselves: a separation between myself as speaker and myself as listener. If we really do talk *to* ourselves, then the language that ensues must have some of the properties of a conversation between different parts of who we are.

This is an idea whose pedigree in Western thought stretches back at least as far as Plato. "I mean the conversation which the soul holds with herself in considering of anything," he wrote in the *Theaetetus*. "I speak of what I scarcely understand; but the soul when thinking appears to me to be just talking   asking questions of herself and answering them, affirming and denying." For William James, writing at the end of the nineteenth century, listening to a verbal thought as it unwinds was a crucial part of our being able to "feel its meaning as it passes." The self speaks, and the self listens, and in doing so comprehends what is being thought. The American philosopher Charles Sanders Peirce, writing at around the same time as James, conceived of thinking as a dialogue between different aspects of the self, including a "critical self" or "Me" that questions the "present self" or "I" about what it is doing. For the philosopher and psychologist George Herbert Mead, thinking involved a conversation between a socially

constructed self and an internalized "other," an abstract internal interlocutor who can adopt different attitudes on what the self is doing.

The self-talker on the tennis court is enacting something that
stands in common between all these different views of thinking. The
thought that calls you a "clumsy ox" comes from a part of the self
that can adopt a critical distance from what is being enacted. When
you talk to yourself, you step out of yourself for a moment and get
some perspective on what you are doing. In sports self-talk, these
utterances can be made out loud as well as silently. Two main kinds
of self-talk are in evidence in Gallwey's reports from the tennis court.
One seems to have a cognitive function: exhortations to the self to
watch the ball and keep it to the opponent's backhand—utterances
that seem to be about using words to regulate one's own actions. The
second function is motivational, typically with players ticking themselves off after a lousy shot. "That was rubbish," we might hear them
tell themselves. "Pull yourself together."

Both kinds of self-talk seem important in sports performance. In
a 2013 interview, Wimbledon champion Andy Murray claimed that
he never talked to himself out loud, on the court or off. That all
changed, though, after he let slip a two-sets lead in a final at Flushing
Meadows against Novak Djokovic, the then world Number One.
Murray took himself off for a toilet break and gave himself a pep talk
in front of the mirror. "I knew I had to change what was going on
inside," he told the London *Times*. "So I started talking. Out loud.
'You are not losing this match,' I said to myself. 'You are NOT losing
this match.' I started out a little tentative, but my voice got louder.
'You are not going to let this one slip. You are NOT going to let this
slip. . . . Give it everything you've got. Leave nothing out there.' At
first, it felt a bit weird, but I felt something change inside. I was surprised by my response. I knew I could win." Murray carried on
talking to himself when he got back on court, broke Djokovic's serve,
and moved into a three-game lead in the fifth set. He went on to win
the US Open, becoming Britain's first male Grand Slam singles
champion in seventy-six years.

So important is self-talk held to be in sports coaching circles that it has been studied quite thoroughly in both its out-loud and silent forms. Psychologists have investigated personal pep talks in sports as diverse as badminton, skiing, and wrestling. But effective use of self-talk is not just about positive psychology and self-directed platitudes. In fact, a recent review of the literature pointed out contradictory findings on the value of saying nice things to yourself. Divers who were pushing for a place on the Canadian Pan Am team, for example, were less likely to qualify if they reported more positive self-talk, such as self-praise. In competitive diving, at least, it seems you can give yourself too much love.

A brighter picture of the value of self-talk comes from experimental studies, where researchers manipulate the conditions under which someone is performing to see what effect that has, rather than simply asking people to report on what they do in their ordinary sporting practice. The pub game of darts isn't often studied in the laboratory, but one study did just that, asking volunteers to wield the darts while using different forms of silent self-talk. Players performed better in a condition in which they spoke positively to themselves (saying, "You can do it" before each throw) than they did in a condition where they did themselves down ("You cannot do it"). Leaving the valence (positive or negative) of the self-talk aside, successful athletes seem to talk to themselves more: that was the case at least in an analysis of gymnasts qualifying for the US Olympic team. Observations of tennis players, in particular, give us some reasons to think that the valence of the self-talk might relate to whether the speaking is silent or out loud. As you'll know from the TV coverage, a lot of that courtside chat is pretty negative. It may be that players like Murray keep their words of encouragement to themselves, and only overtly express the tellings-off and chastisements, to the alarm of ball girls and line officials everywhere. Recall, though, that the sports self-talk research mostly doesn't distinguish between overt (out loud) and covert (silent) speech, meaning that the hypothesis that all the good stuff is kept within has so far been hard to test.

Among that long list of sports in which self-talk has been studied, cricket is a particularly interesting case. A batsman has to be able to react to the pace, trajectory, and bounce of a cricket ball traveling toward him at speeds of up to ninety-five miles an hour. (Something similar applies in baseball, although that case is simplified slightly by the fact that the ball does not pitch on the ground before reaching the batter.) Psychologists have calculated that a batsman facing a fast bowler has no opportunity to react consciously. The ball is traveling so fast that the recipient must cultivate instinctive reactions allowing him to read the ball's line and length early enough to play an appropriate shot. Working out what to do in that split second after the ball is delivered does not involve ordinary thinking; there is no time for such luxuries.

Which makes the maintenance of attention, in those critical couple of seconds around the delivery of the ball, essential to being able to play your shots and avoid losing your wicket. More precisely, batting requires you to be able to *shift* your attention quickly and effectively. A few seconds before a delivery, you will usually see a batter glancing around the ground on all sides. She is not bored, inattentive, or looking to see if something more interesting is going on; she is sizing up the field, checking where the fielders are, and thus working out where she might score her runs and avoid lobbing up a catch. A second or two later she is having to narrow her attention considerably, from the wider context of the field (too late to worry about that now) to that shiny leather-coated lump of cork in the bowler's hand. It is that shift in attention, from the broad to the narrow, that is one of the things that makes batting so difficult. From being aware of everything, you suddenly have to switch to being aware of the one thing that could send you back to the pavilion.

That's where talking to yourself might really help. Many possible functions have been proposed for sports self-talk, but one of the most important might be its power in controlling attention. I'm no sportsman, but I do drive a car, and I often talk to myself at the wheel as a way of focusing my attention in one direction or another. Approaching a roundabout, for example, I might say, "Look to the right," so that I can give way to traffic coming from that direction. I'm probably more likely to do that if I've just returned from a trip overseas, where I will likely have been driving on the other side of the road. I can't prove it scientifically, but those few words seem to help me to keep my attentional focus.

Psyching yourself up for a new delivery might, then, be a thing best done in words. Simply asking cricketers how, when, and why they talk to themselves might not get you very far, however. As Russ Hurlburt has argued, any such questions are likely to elicit off-the-peg generalizations about how individuals *think* their minds work, rather than really sampling their experiences (one reason why Russ is highly skeptical about questionnaire methods). In an attempt to get closer to how batsmen really use self-talk, a recent study adopted an inventive approach. Five professional batsmen from a single English county club took part. For each batsman, a DVD "highlights" package of six critical incidents from a single innings was constructed: walking out to bat, facing the first ball, a poor shot, a change of bowler, premeditating a delivery, and getting out. A week after their innings, each batsman sat down with his DVD and one of the researchers (who was himself an elite cricketer) to watch the highlights, with the player asked to cast his mind back to what he was saying to himself at each point.

The results paint a picture of self-directed speech fulfilling a range of functions. One player reported that, as he walked out to bat, he focused on getting into a batting rhythm and forgetting about what the scoreboard said. Another tried to put himself in the right frame of mind for his innings through a simple statement of confidence: "I have the opportunity to win a cricket match." Before that critical first ball, one participant looked around at the gaps in the field and said to himself, "[There is a] single off my legs." As any cricketer will tell you, getting off the mark quickly and safely strikes a huge blow against those pre-innings nerves.

Things rarely go that smoothly for long, though. Batting is a very unforgiving activity: one mistake and you can be on your way. The batsmen in this study all noted that their self-talk peaked after playing a lousy shot. A common pattern was self-chastisement followed by a spoonful of sugar. One player noted that self-talk was particularly useful when he was going through a bad patch in his innings, while another simply reminded himself to play straight. Exhortations to "relax" and "hang in" were common when things weren't going well. As the game progressed and the required run rate crept up (these were all limited-overs games), players would talk to themselves to help them premeditate where to hit the ball. For one player, simply itemizing the positions of the fielders helped him instinctively to play productive shots. Finally, all of the players used language not only to beat themselves up after they were dismissed, but also to learn lessons for next time.

All in all, the players' reports suggested a varied narrative of self-talk that began before the innings and carried through until after dismissal, and that was particularly prevalent when things were going badly. As far as that challenge of shifting attention was concerned, one participant actually said the word "ball" to himself as he switched from a broad to a narrow focus. If you get a chance to watch a game of cricket on TV for yourself, you might see something like this in action. Observe England's Eoin Morgan, for example, batting in the middle order, and you will clearly see him mouthing to himself, "Watch the ball," before every delivery. Morgan seems to find it useful to put self-directed words to a cognitive use, narrowing his own attention at that critical moment.

Michael's description of his own self-talk bears out the findings from the video study. When he is in form, the chatter in his head reduces in intensity but also becomes more specific and thus more useful. After a bad shot, he will respond to what he has done in words: "I might say 'Come on' to myself or curse myself a little bit, or say to myself 'Watch the ball.' . . . So it's more like an emotional reminder of what I've just done, and telling myself to get back to where I should be." Our meeting comes shortly after he made his highest score in first-class cricket, a big hundred in a four-day county match. I ask him whether his self-talk changes as he approaches such a milestone. "I probably don't talk to myself more, but what I would say becomes slightly different as the rhythm of an innings unfolds, so when I get into the nineties I know that different anxieties or whatever might come into your head." Michael also thought there was a danger of talking to himself too much, reporting, "I try to keep it as simple as possible, so that I'm not overthinking things and I'm not talking to myself too much." I ask whether he ever hears a particular coach's voice in his head, advising him. "Not as clichéd as a movie scene where I can hear something in their exact voice, but there's definitely tips that people have told me. . . . I'm definitely not hearing a specific voice in my head or a specific coach. I'm maybe thinking of a moment or a memory, and then remembering to bring that into the game situation."

Michael's account seems to echo Gallwey's description of the "teller" and the "doer" on the tennis court. That inner coach may be more a composite of different training experiences than it is a specific voice, and in fact, different kinds of internal interlocutors seem to be in evidence in all of these descriptions of self-talk: a tough critic, a reassuring friend, a sage counselor, and so on. Until recently, there had been few scientific attempts to describe the variety of these internal interlocutors. That changed with a study by Małgorzata Puchalska-Wasyl of the John Paul II Catholic University of Lublin in Poland. Focusing on everyday internal conversations rather than on sports performance, she asked students to describe, using a checklist of emotional words, the internal interlocutor they engaged with most frequently. These ratings were then subjected to a statistical analysis that sorted similar descriptions into clusters. Four distinct categories of inner voice emerged: the Faithful Friend (associated with personal strength, close relationships, and positive feelings); the Ambivalent Parent (combining strength, love, and caring criticism); the Proud Rival (who was distant and success-oriented); and the Calm Optimist (a relaxed interlocutor associated with positive, self-sufficient emotions). A weakness of this initial study was that it didn't take into account the full variety of inner voices that participants engaged with—and so it was repeated, with volunteers being asked to describe their two most frequent interlocutors along with two others that represented differing emotions. The first three categories reemerged from the statistical analysis, but this time the Calm Optimist was replaced by a category dubbed the Helpless Child, distinguished by negative emotions and social distance.

Whether we're adopting one of these roles to offer ourselves advice, consolation, or encouragement, it seems to matter how we address the part of the self that is listening. In his pep talk in front of the mirror, Andy Murray really was addressing himself as another person, directing his exhortations to "you" rather than "I" or "me." When people are instructed to refer to themselves by their own names or through the second-person pronoun, they appear to gain a kind of distance from the self that they would not get if they referred to themselves as "me" or "I." This concept was tested experimentally in a series of studies led by Ethan Kross at the University of Michigan, Ann Arbor, investigating the effects of referring to oneself in the first person when preparing for and performing certain tasks. One of the tasks, engineered to generate social anxiety, involved participants being given only a limited time (five minutes) to prepare to make a speech in public—specifically, to try to persuade a panel of "experts" (actually, experimenter stooges) that the participant was qualified for a dream job. Compared to those who were asked to prepare for the task by referring to what "I" should do, volunteers who had not been told to refer to themselves in the first person made a better job of their speech, felt more positive about their performance, and ruminated about it less afterward. Avoiding first-person references seemed to give participants a distance from the self that allowed them to regulate their behavior more effectively and, in particular, to deal with emotions such as social anxiety.

It seems clear that the benefits of certain kinds of self-talk are not limited to sports. One thing that emerges from all of these studies is that jabbering away to yourself can achieve many different things. For an athlete, self-talk can play a role in regulating action and arousal, psyching oneself up, and directing one's attention under challenging performance conditions. For the rest of us, self-directed speech can allow us to obtain different perspectives on ourselves and some critical distance from what we are doing. How is it that fragile—even silent—words can influence their speakers in this way? To understand how the words in our heads can come to have those powers, we need to ask how they got there.

4

Two Cars

"I'M GOING TO MAKE a train track! I'm going to make a train track, Daddy."

Here's a little girl playing with her toys. She is sitting on the carpet in her bedroom, next to a big shopping bag full of blue and purple plastic bits. They are the components of a construction system called Happy Street, which can be assembled and reassembled to make a toy town with shops, an airport, a police station. We have had hours of fun playing at being town planners, building cities in which old ladies speed around in emergency vehicles and the buns in the bakery are always shiny and fresh.

"What am I doing? I'm going to make a train track and put some cars on it."

She has fitted together a few curves of road and an intersection, and now she could do with some traffic.

"I need some cars on it."

She shuffles on her knees to the bag and reaches in. The bag is huge, twice her size. Going into it is like raiding Santa's sack. She retrieves another piece of road and tries to fit it into her growing network, but the little plastic tags are tricky to fit together.

"I make a train track and put some cars on it. *Two* cars."

That last comment suggests that she wants to add to an existing car. But she hasn't actually chosen any yet; she is still building the road. The thought about needing two cars is just that: a thought.

"This piece hard." She tries again to fit the pieces together, and this time the tags align. "There!"

Now she turns back to the bag, raising an index finger at it. Her expression is teacherly, authoritative, as though she were trying to keep a class of difficult children in line.

"One more piece . . ."

In a way, what my daughter Athena is doing is not so far removed from what Michael reported doing at the batting crease. What's different is that she is not a professional athlete, or even an adult. She is two years old. If this is a similar kind of self-talk, she is getting started on it very early.

As with the athlete, Athena's self-talk seems to have different functions. It is self-regulatory, in that she plans out what she is going to do before she does it. She expresses the thought *two cars* before there is a single car on the scene. Just as the batsman plans his innings as he walks out to bat, or draws lessons after a dismissal for his next match, so the toddler thinks things through in words, and those words actually shape and direct her behavior.

Athena's speech also seems to play a role in regulating her emotions. When the going gets tough, she gives herself a pep talk. "This piece hard," she tells herself, when she is trying and failing to join the pieces of track. When she succeeds, she allows herself a little self-congratulation: "There!"

By age two, most typically developing children are experts in language, and they are very often using it in this self-directed way. By looking at how self-talk becomes established early in life, we can find out a great deal about where the voices in our heads come from and what they turn into. In fact, we get some very important clues about what kind of thing inner speech is.

LEV IS ALSO TALKING to himself. "I want to do that drawing, there. . . . I want to draw something, I do. I shall need a big piece of paper to do that."

It is Geneva in the 1920s. Lev is one of the children from the Maison des Petits de l'Institut Rousseau, a preschool facility of the Rousseau Institute, which from 1921 to 1925 is directed by the legendary developmental psychologist Jean Piaget. Piaget is interested in how Lev's monologues, and those of other children like him, seem to use language without a social purpose. In Piaget's words, "Lev is a little fellow who is very much wrapped up in himself." Piaget tells us that, at six years of age, Lev is not yet cognitively able to take into account the perspective of the person with whom he might be trying to communicate.

Piaget sees this kind of speech as evidencing the small child's *egocentrism*: his tendency to be rooted in his own viewpoint. These are attempts to say something to someone else, but they fail because the child cannot adapt his utterances to what the other person thinks, knows, and believes. "In such cases," Piaget wrote, "speech does not communicate the thoughts of the speaker, it serves to accompany, to reinforce, or to supplement his action." The child's words do not shape the activity or serve to encourage or stimulate it; they merely accompany what is going on.

At the same time, in Moscow, another psychologist is observing children talking to themselves. Lev Vygotsky also sees children speaking along with their activities, but unlike Piaget he does not see these utterances as mere accompaniments to behavior. Rather, what the Genevans termed "egocentric speech" is, for Vygotsky, a means for making a certain kind of behavior possible.

For one thing, Vygotsky notes, children talk to themselves more when they face some obstacle to their activity. (One trick involves making sure that the child lacks exactly the crayon or pencil color needed for a particular drawing task.) If private speech has no function, it should not be affected by task difficulty. In fact, Vygotsky's children actually use their private speech to plan out a solution to the problem. One child, finding that a needed blue pencil was missing, said to himself, "Where is the pencil? I need a blue pencil now. Nothing. Instead of that I will color it red and put water on it—that will make it darker and more like blue."

Vygotsky made many other observations suggesting that children's self-talk performs a functional role. One five-year-old was drawing a tram when his pencil broke. "Broken," he said quietly—and then proceeded to put down the pencil, pick up a paintbrush, and paint a broken tram car that was being repaired after an accident. This child was using his language to change the course of his activity. He was thinking out loud.

On the surface, these are very different views of children's self-talk. Piaget and Vygotsky read each other's work and commented on it, and each held the other in high regard. But they had divergent views about children's private speech, as it is now known, and they understood its significance differently.

For one thing, they each told a different story about the child's entry into the social world. Piaget saw the young child as egocentric, too "rooted in his own viewpoint" to be able to engage fully in social interactions. Vygotsky instead believed that children were entangled in social relationships from the first days of their lives. The arrival of language gave them a means of communicating with others, and the dialogues that resulted formed the basis of their later private conversations with themselves, and ultimately of their inner speech.

I have spent much of my career as a psychologist thinking about the significance of Vygotsky's writings on social, private, and inner speech. I think Vygotsky's account is the best one we have of where the voices in our heads come from, why they have the qualities they have, and why talking to ourselves out loud continues to be of value to us even in adulthood. That said, Vygotsky left many gaps in the theory. He had a brief career as a psychologist, cut short by his death from tuberculosis at the age of thirty-seven. There are places where his writings on language and thinking are ambiguous and obscure. But many of his insights have now also been supported by research: by studies that look at what children say to themselves as they are playing and doing tasks, and by investigations of adults' silent inner speech.

BACK IN ATHENA'S BEDROOM, I'm still filming her track-laying with a video camera. I'm not sure that she knows I'm there. At the same time, I suspect that my presence is catalyzing the speech, even if she's not actually talking to me. She would be doing less of it, I guess, if I wasn't there. This is in fact exactly what Vygotsky found: when he put children together with others who spoke a different language, the proportion of private speech relative to social speech dropped away. Similarly, in one observation he set some kids playing in a room next door to where a noisy orchestra was practicing; the proportion of private speech dropped dramatically.

But I am here, and at some level Athena knows it. Private speech has what one early scientific study called a "parasocial" nature: it happens more when there is the illusion of an audience. That makes sense if you understand private speech as an attempt to hijack words that, in other contexts, would control the behavior of others, and use them instead to control the behavior of the self. It's not that Athena is trying to communicate but can't, she is trying only to communicate with herself. The reason these utterances aren't directed at me is not that she lacks the cognitive sophistication necessary to take my perspective into account. They were never intended for me. They might be stimulated by my presence, but they are for her alone.

That transition from social to private speech has just been demonstrated to me quite clearly. At the start of this urban planning episode, she actually used my name: "Daddy." But then she seemed quickly to forget about my presence. When we are analyzing children's private speech—a labor-intensive process that involves hours of viewing and rewinding video recordings—we code utterances as social when, among other things, they clearly mention a person's name. To be classified as private, there cannot be any hint that the utterance is meant for another. This kind of analysis gives us information about how much private and social speech children are using. We can then use that information to test some of Vygotsky's ideas about the form and functions of self-directed talk.

For a start, if Vygotsky was right that children use private speech as a "psychological tool" for regulating their behavior, we ought to see evidence that it makes some kind of difference. Children who use private speech while performing a task should do that task better—at least if the speech is relevant to what they're doing. Psychologists have tested this aspect of Vygotsky's theory by giving children a task to do, analyzing their private speech while they are doing it, and investigating whether their performance correlates with private speech use. At least some studies have supported the idea that children gain a cognitive benefit from using private speech. For example, in one study we gave five- and six-year-old children a task called the Tower of London, which involves moving colored balls around between sticks of differing lengths. The handy thing about the Tower of London, for this purpose, is that the balls can be arranged to make puzzles of varying difficulty. In line with Vygotsky's predictions about the functional value of self-talk, we found that children who used more self-regulatory private speech solved the puzzles more quickly. We also found the predicted relationships between private speech and task difficulty. Children talked less on the easy puzzles (presumably because they were so easy that they didn't need the boost of verbal self-regulation), more on the puzzles of intermediate difficulty, and then less again on the most difficult ones (presumably because those puzzles were so hard that the child couldn't really get started with a solution, and so self-regulatory speech was not effective).

So much for the function of private speech. What about its form? Vygotsky did not believe that the internalization of speech was a simple matter of self-regulatory speech becoming quieter and quieter until it was fully silent or subvocal (as was, for example, the view of his contemporary, the behaviorist John B. Watson). Rather, Vygotsky thought that the speech that is internalized is fundamentally transformed in the process. One particularly important transformation is that the language becomes abbreviated. In guiding their behavior, children do not need to use full sentences. Athena does not say to herself, "I need two cars for my train track." She keeps it brief: "Two cars." In contrast to Piaget, whose theory states that children's language should become more intelligible as it becomes more adapted to the listener, Vygotsky's theory predicts that private speech will gradually become more contracted and abbreviated—

making it less, not more, intelligible to the external listener. These transformations of language are particularly important when it comes to Athena's later inner speech, seen by Vygotsky to develop out of the self-regulatory utterances she says aloud.

At the same time, private speech retains important features of the social speech from which it derives. If private speech is a partially internalized form of social dialogue, you would expect it to show some of the to-and-fro quality of conversation. Specifically, you would expect to see children asking themselves questions and then answering them. That seems to be the case in Athena's conversation with herself about the train track. "What am I doing?" she asks herself. "I'm going to make a train track and put some cars on it." Just as adults' self-talk can often seem to reflect a conversation with the self, this dialogic quality is quite prevalent in children's private speech. Where children might previously have asked the question of a caregiver and waited for a reply, in private speech they often supply the answers themselves.

Researchers have generally found fairly good support for these different aspects of Vygotsky's theory. But there are gaps, as mentioned above, and a couple of respects in which his writings on private speech give slightly the wrong impression. Although Vygotsky maintained that private speech ultimately "goes underground" in later childhood to form inner speech, it's also clear (not least from the self-talk of athletes) that people continue to talk to themselves as adults. Private speech—the out-loud counterpart of inner speech— seems to have a number of additional functions that go beyond self-regulation, such as practice for a second language, the weaving of autobiographical memories, and the creation of fantasy worlds. If children spend a lot of time talking to themselves aloud, it's not just because it helps them to solve problems.

LET'S SUPPOSE FOR NOW that Vygotsky was broadly accurate in his account of private speech. Should we assume that he was also right about the version of it that goes on silently and internally—in other words, what we have been referring to as inner speech? This doesn't necessarily follow: Vygotsky might well have been wrong to claim that inner speech develops out of private speech. As ever, the unobservability of silent self-talk, and its consequent resistance to empirical study, makes this a difficult question to answer.

That's not least because we have to deal with some counterintuitive ideas. If Vygotsky was right, private speech should take time to develop (in fact, the evidence suggests that it peaks between the ages of around three and eight). Inner speech should lag even further behind that. Does that mean that young children don't experience the flow of internal conversation that permeates many adults' waking lives? Much of our thinking seems to be done in words; should we conclude that the young child's thinking is very different?

Tackling this question takes us right to the heart of what is special about Vygotsky's theory. The thinking of young children probably differs from adult thinking in all sorts of ways, but is there something specific about the wordiness of their thoughts? One clue comes from the study of working memory. The function of this cognitive system is to keep information in consciousness just long enough—a matter of seconds—for it to be used in planning our actions or performing other mental operations. The dominant model of working memory, stemming from the work of the English psychologists Alan Baddeley and Graham Hitch, proposes that a key part of this system is the phonological loop, a component of the system that specializes in storing sound-related information. It's no surprise, perhaps, that this is also a system that needs to be functioning in order for internal and external speech to be produced—in other words, it is a crucial bit of equipment for doing verbal thinking. There is another, separate component responsible for manipulating visual and spatial information—but it's the phonological loop that we draw on most for many of the short-term memory tasks we perform daily. When given a bunch of stuff to remember, adults tend to rehearse the information verbally until it's time to recall it. It's an effective strategy, and you'll have used it if you've ever walked around a supermarket muttering to yourself the last few items on your list.

Because this kind of rehearsal depends on words, it's very susceptible to certain features of those words, such as whether they sound alike or not. Similar-sounding words (such as *man, map,* and *mat*) are easier to confuse if you are rehearsing them verbally, and we make reliably more mistakes on recalling lists of such words than we do when we have to rehearse words that sound different from each other, even when those words are presented visually. This has been termed the *phonological similarity effect,* reflecting the fact that we use a phonological (or sound-based) code for keeping the information in memory. If it takes time for children to start using words in their thinking, then it should also take time for children to show this effect.

And that's exactly what the research shows. Children below about six or seven years of age don't show the phonological similarity effect, suggesting that they don't automatically recode information into a verbal code for short-term storage. It's still possible, however, that verbal rehearsal is a special case, and that children start thinking in words before they get around to realizing that words have this handy function in short-term memory. We tested this possibility by looking at children's rehearsal of visually presented material while studying their private speech. My graduate student Abdulrahman Al-Namlah studied schoolchildren between the ages of four and eight from two schools, one in the United Kingdom and one in Saudi Arabia. Children's private speech was assessed on the Tower of London (the balls-on-sticks task), and they were also given a separate short-term memory task to test the strength of their phonological similarity effect. As expected, children younger than six did not show the effect—their recall was not sensitive to the sounds of the words they had to remember—while the older children struggled more with words that sounded similar. Most interestingly, children's susceptibility to the effect related to how much self-regulatory private speech they used on the Tower of London task. Children who seemed to regulate their puzzle-solving through words seemed more likely to use verbal rehearsal for their short-term remembering. These findings suggest that memory is not a special case. Instead, once children get the hang of using words in their thinking, it begins to affect other aspects of their cognition.

Another way of exploring this question is to see whether interfering with children's inner speech messes up their performance. Only if kids were relying on verbal thinking to solve the task, the argument goes, would you expect to see an interference effect. This is what another graduate student of mine, Jane Lidstone, set out to investigate using a method for blocking inner speech known as *articulatory suppression*, which involves repeating an innocuous word (such as *see-saw*) out loud for the duration of the trial. Articulatory suppression is hypothesized to block the phonological loop component of working memory, which is thought to be essential for generating inner speech. Asking participants to practice articulatory suppression while they are performing a separate cognitive task, and assessing whether this suppression affects their performance on the primary task, is a useful way of examining how much people rely on inner speech in certain contexts. If we can't measure inner speech directly, making an educated guess about when it might be happening—and then looking to see what happens when we try to block it—is a useful method of indirectly examining its function.

Jane chose the Tower of London task because it is seen as a classic planning task, and planning (along with other so-called "executive" functions) has been proposed as a particularly important function for self-directed speech. Jane wanted to establish whether children who generally produced more self-regulatory private speech would perform worse on the Tower of London when they were not able to talk themselves through the task. Using standard articulatory suppression, Jane asked kids to repeat a word out loud to themselves as they thought about the puzzle. They were also asked to imagine moving the balls around in their heads, and to tell the experimenter how many moves they thought it would take for them to solve the puzzle. They had to demonstrate their solution by moving the balls around for real. The idea was that this method would encourage the children to plan, instead of simply launching in and moving the balls around haphazardly.

The results supported Vygotsky's theory. In the articulatory suppression condition, children's performance suffered relative to a control condition in which children simply tapped a foot. We interpreted this outcome as evidence that private and inner speech were typically used in planning, and that blocking both kinds of speech had a corresponding effect on planning. What's more, children who used more self-regulatory private speech on the control condition were more susceptible to articulatory suppression. It seems that certain kids are more reliant on verbal thinking than others, and so they are more negatively affected when that opportunity is denied them.

But there is another, more obvious way to find out whether children think in words, and that is to ask them. As we've seen, asking adults to reflect on their own experience is tricky enough, and the problems become more acute when working with children, who may lack the necessary linguistic skills to be able to give a nuanced account of what is going on in their heads. There have nevertheless been some attempts to do DES-style experience sampling with kids. Russ Hurlburt has used his method with a few children, including one nine-year-old boy who reported on a moment of experience that involved an image of a hole in his backyard containing some toys. In the usual DES way, Russ probed the boy gently about how much the image he had pictured and described was like his actual backyard. The boy replied, "Yes, but I don't have all the toys in it yet. If you had beeped me a few minutes later I would have had time to put all of the toys in the hole." Hurlburt concluded that the creation of mental images might be a skill that becomes smoother and quicker with age and practice. His observations suggest that we need to be careful in assuming that children's inner experience is like our own.

Other researchers have tried a different method of determining what children do and don't understand about inner speech. John Flavell, an eminent developmental psychologist from Stanford University, has spent the past couple of decades asking children what they understand about inner experience. One task involves asking a child what he thinks is going on in an experimenter's head when the experimenter is sitting quietly, looking out of a window. Three-year-olds tend to say that the experimenter's mind is empty, while four-year-olds acknowledge that thinking continues even when a person is not busy with anything in particular. Flavell himself interpreted these findings in terms of three-year-olds' lack of awareness about their own stream of consciousness: they are not yet good enough at introspecting to be able to report on the mental hubbub within. An alternative explanation, though, is that young children simply do not yet have a stream of consciousness; or, more specifically, they have not internalized external speech to form inner speech. They do not think in words, so when they are asked to reflect on the inner experience of someone who is not busy with any activity, they conclude that that person's mind must be empty.

In other studies, Flavell has asked children specifically about inner speech. One study involved children between four and seven watching an adult carrying out a task for which you might be expected to need inner speech: for example, setting out to try to remember items that had been left off a shopping list. The child was asked questions like, "Is she just thinking, up in her head, or is she also saying things to herself, up in her head?" The six- and seven-year-olds acknowledged that inner speech was probably going on, but the four-year-olds were much less likely to do so. In a second experiment, children were given a task designed specifically to elicit inner speech, such as thinking silently about how their own name sounded. Forty percent of four-year-olds and 55 percent of five-year-olds admitted to having used inner speech rather than a visual method for getting the answer, figures that were significantly lower than the equivalent scores for adults.

Again, it's not entirely clear from these results whether the children were not yet able to reflect on their own inner experience or simply lacked spontaneous inner speech. The answer is probably going to be a bit of both. But if it's true that children lack inner speech, the implications are far-reaching. No one should conclude from this that children don't think, but they do seem to lack a mode of thinking that dominates the consciousness of many adults. That's just one of several reasons for concluding that a small child's mind is a strange place to be.

Language, then, does not give the child thought; rather, it transforms whatever intellectual capacities are present before language
comes along. Vygotsky, no doubt influenced by the intellectual fer-
vor of the nascent Soviet Union, described this as a "revolution in
development." In Edward St. Aubyn's 2005 novel *Mother's Milk*,
five-year-old Robert is nostalgic for the time before this revolution.
Observing his infant brother, Thomas, in his blissful wordlessness,
he recalls a period before his own head was full of language: "He had
become so caught up in building sentences that he had almost forgotten the barbaric days when thinking was like a splash of colour
landing on a page." Even at the tender age of five, Robert's thinking
has been utterly transformed by words. "Looking back, he could still
see it: living in what would now feel like pauses: when you first open
the curtains and see the whole landscape covered in snow and you
catch your breath and pause before breathing out again. He couldn't
get the whole thing back, but maybe he wouldn't rush down the
slope quite yet, maybe he would sit down and look at the view."

5

A Natural History of Thinking

"I REMEMBER TALKING TO MYSELF, and at that moment it felt like I was having this mini-debate with myself. . . . It's not like I'm speaking at that kind of pace now but it feels like a conversation within the same space of time that you see these images. It's like a . . . *choot!* . . . and you just know you've had that conversation."

Jordan is another of our DES participants. He is an art student from London, in Berlin for a study abroad placement. For the first time, I am leading the interview, conscious that Russ has temporarily entrusted me with a method he has been working on for four decades. Jordan has happy brown eyes, long dark hair, and a beard. He is dressed for the muggy Berlin summer in a black T-shirt and shorts.

This is the third beep of Jordan's second DES sampling day. At the moment of the beep, Jordan was walking along the street and thinking about a black pug he could see in the distance. There was an image of a friend and his girlfriend, and an argument they had had about wanting to get a pug of their own. Jordan had responded that he thought keeping pugs was cruel, because of the way they are specially bred to have short muzzles, which gives them breathing difficulties. This memory triggered an internal conversation about the rights and wrongs of pug-keeping.

"So the dialogue doesn't unfold in the same amount of time as it would take to unfold in real time?"

"No."

"It unfolds in less time or more time?"

"Less. It's a lot faster."

When people report on their inner speech, they often report that it defies the clock in this way. One of Russ's participants, Melanie (the subject of an entire academic book on the DES method), was once describing a beep in which she had been thinking about having just received the gift of a chair from her university, along with an unusual document that allowed her to designate who in her family would eventually inherit it. The moment of consciousness before the beep was about this odd conjunction of receiving a gift and simultaneously having to think about who would one day receive it as a legacy.

Russ was conducting this interview with a noted skeptic about DES and other introspective methods, the philosopher Eric Schwitzgebel. At one point in the interview, Eric pointed out that Melanie seemed to have done an awful lot of thinking (in a voice that she designated as her "inner thought voice") in the time she had available to have the thought. Was it like a regularly paced speaking voice, or a speeded-up voice, or did it seem compressed in some other way?

"It was compressed," Melanie observed. "I wouldn't say it was compressed into an instant—it was a little bit longer. But it was significantly faster than it would normally take to say a sentence like that out loud."

At this point Eric intentionally sped up his normal speaking voice. "So would it be like someone who was a fast talker getting it out really fast like that? Or was it something that seemed a little different from how speech could be paced?"

"I guess I'd have to say it was something a little different because when it was in my head it didn't feel compressed. It didn't feel rushed or jammed into a really small time like it sometimes does when someone speaks quickly."

"Could it be," Schwitzgebel wrote later in his commentary on this episode, "that inner speech is, for most people, temporally compressed, but only a minority of [DES] subjects notice that fact because it does not seem rushed?"

This conclusion makes perfect sense if you think about how inner speech develops. Vygotsky proposed that language is transformed as it is internalized, which would explain why my daughter Athena's private speech had an abbreviated, note-form quality. Vygotsky thought that there were different ways in which this abbreviation could happen. In its simplest form, abbreviation can mean trimming down the syntax (recall that Athena said "Two cars" instead of something like "I need two cars"). But other, more complex transformations are at work, too. Vygotsky described how, in inner speech, a single word can come to take on a special, idiosyncratic meaning to replace its more conventional one, or become fused with another word to form a hybrid with multiple significances, or even come to stand for an entire discourse (an example Vygotsky gives is the way that literary titles, such as the single word *Hamlet*, can come to stand in the reader's mind for an entire work).

So inner speech is more than external speech without the lip movements. Sometimes it is telescoped, like a note-form version of what we might say to ourselves out loud; at other times its condensation is more like a compression of meaning. One of our DES participants, Ruth, described something like this when she reported a thought about some money her daughter owed her: *I need to actually go through all the receipts to total it up.* The inner speech seemed to be in her own natural voice, but it somehow seemed to be happening faster than ordinary speech. "It seems like it's just a normal talking voice," Ruth told us, "but it's kind of compressed."

If inner speech condensation can explain the paradoxical pace of Ruth's verbal thought, it might also explain one scientist's estimate that inner speech flashes through our minds around ten times faster than ordinary speech. Psychologist Rodney Korba, from the College of Wooster in Ohio, asked people to solve problems silently in their heads, while at the same time he measured electrical activity in the articulatory muscles (of the mouth and throat) responsible for producing spoken utterances. Korba asked people to report what they thought they had said to themselves while solving the puzzle, and compared the time they actually spent doing inner speech with how long it would have taken them to speak the thoughts out loud. The participants' internal speech appeared to unfold around ten times faster than the estimated external rate of speech, allowing Korba to calculate a typical inner-speech rate in excess of 4,000 words per minute.

Given the obvious benefits of this quick-fire efficiency, it may be that condensed inner speech is the norm in our self-talk. At other times, however, our inner speech can seem like a full-blown conversation, where both parts of the dialogue unreel in vivid detail, almost as if we were having a debate with ourselves out loud. One of Hurlburt's DES studies reported how a participant, Benjamin, was eating dinner in a restaurant when he noticed an attractive woman. His inner speech went something like this: "Why are you bringing this woman to my attention?" The answer came, in a matter-of-fact tone: "She's pretty." To which the self, unimpressed, replied: "Uh-huh" (in a *that's bullshit* tone of voice).

I think the distinction between these two kinds of inner speech— what I have termed *condensed* and *expanded* inner speech—is an important one, for reasons that will become clear. For Vygotsky, the transition from compressed verbal thought to full-blown speech was like "a hovering cloud which gushes a shower of words." At the very least, his theory should make us suspicious of the idea that the voice in one's head is just one thing. If talking to yourself can have different functions, it is likely that it will take different forms as well. And the process of internalization during childhood will mean that the nature of inner speech will change, even in adulthood, according to how contracted or expanded it is.

To date, we don't know a huge amount about how inner speech varies in these respects. One approach to finding out what an experience is like is simply to ask people to tell you about it. A widely used method for getting participants to report on their beliefs, experiences, thoughts, feelings, and attitudes is to use what psychologists call a *self-report instrument*, a list of descriptions of a particular phenomenon that participants can choose to endorse or not endorse, depending on what fits best with their experience.

That was the method used in the first systematic investigation of the varieties of inner speech. My graduate student Simon McCarthy-Jones and I presented a sample of students with a list of statements about different possible varieties of inner speech and asked them to say how much each item applied to them. For example, one item read, "I think to myself in words using brief phrases and single words rather than full sentences"—in our sights here was the experience of condensed inner speech. The data were then subjected to a statistical technique known as factor analysis, which showed that our self-report items captured four main qualities of inner speech.

We termed these factors *dialogic, condensed, other people,* and *evaluative.* As its name suggests, the first factor relates to how much people feel that their inner speech takes the form of a conversation between different points of view. The second factor captures the quality that inner speech can sometimes have of being compressed or abbreviated. The third relates to a tendency in a minority of people (about a quarter of responses) to say that the voices of other people feature in their inner speech (for example, "I hear other people's voices nagging me in my head"). The last factor relates to the extent to which people report their inner speech as having a role in evaluating or motivating what they are doing. Such people, for example, might endorse the item, "I evaluate my behavior using my inner speech. For example, I say to myself, 'That was good' or 'That was stupid.'"

In another study, we addressed some of the issues around the quality of silent self-talk raised by the University of Michigan research described earlier. Recall that referring to themselves by their own name (in the third person), or with the second-person pronoun ("you"), gave the Michigan participants an advantage in controlling their emotions and regulating their behavior in a stressful task. That said, the Ann Arbor researchers did not actually measure inner speech; they instructed volunteers to use different kinds of inner speech, and then implemented some checks to see that they had obeyed the instructions. Outside the unnatural constraints of an experimental task, how common is it to shift one's perspective like this in inner speech?

A group of us based at Macquarie University in Sydney, Australia, ran a study in which we interviewed ordinary people and patients diagnosed with schizophrenia about their inner speech. We found no difference between the groups in the use of one's own name when addressing oneself (around half of all participants reported this), or in the use of references to oneself in the second person (again, about half of all participants employed this kind of self-talk). These "distancing" forms of inner speech were outweighed by the use of the first person, which was seen as less adaptive in the Michigan study; around three-quarters of participants in both groups said that they tended to refer to themselves as "I" in inner speech. It's quite possible to do both at different times, of course, and it's likely that first-, second-, and third-person forms will all figure in everyday inner experience. In a subsequent survey, we presented around 1,500 people with several statements about internal self-talk, including one that described the use of the second person ("you"). Around half of the participants said that they referred to themselves in this way (somewhere between *often* and *all the time*), suggesting widespread use of what the Michigan researchers viewed as a more psychologically healthy form of inner speech.

The idea that inner speech manifests itself in different ways is also supported by Russ Hurlburt's work with DES. In a 2013 paper, Hurlburt and his colleagues reviewed nearly forty years' worth of DES findings on inner speaking. They describe an experience of fantastic variety. Internal self-talk, like speaking out loud, can convey emotions as varied as curiosity, outrage, interest, and boredom. It can come with a range of bodily concomitants: some folk experience it as emerging from their torso or chest, while others feel it as emanating from the head, sometimes even from particular parts of the cranium (the front, the back, or the side). Inner speech can be addressed to the self, to another individual, or to no one in particular—and (supporting the findings from our questionnaire) it can even happen in another person's voice. One participant was listening to his friend saying, "Let's go to the gym before dinner," and was at the same time re-speaking those words in his own inner speech, but in his friend's voice. In other words, he experienced two overlapping streams of "Let's go to the gym before dinner," separated by about half a second. The first was spoken aloud by his friend; the second was an utterance, with similar vocal characteristics, generated in his own inner speech.

The variety doesn't end there. Observations with DES show that people can talk to themselves at almost the same time as they are speaking out loud, and sometimes they can be thinking things that are different from what their external voice is saying. Echoing the character Darcy from the movie *What Women Want*, one participant was planning a meal with friends and thinking, "Let's go to Burger King," while she awaited her turn in the conversation. What came out of her mouth, however, was "Let's go to KFC." At the moment of the beep, she felt no surprise that she had said something different from what she was thinking; it was only a few seconds later that she noticed (with some shock) the discrepancy.

In other respects, the picture DES paints of inner speech is different from that presented by Vygotsky's theory. As we have seen, Hurlburt's investigations suggest that inner speech is far from the ubiquitous phenomenon that some researchers have proposed it to be, with only around 23 percent of sampled moments evidencing inner speech. What's more, Hurlburt's data suggest that the abbreviation of internal utterances is not as common as Vygotsky's theory would predict, although there are reasons for thinking that DES might underestimate the frequency of both condensed and dialogic forms of inner speech. Hurlburt's work reminds us that it is too strong a claim to say that people are talking to themselves all the time; a few people don't seem to do it at all. The different methods we scientists have for studying inner speech each have their limitations, and fully under-standing the phenomenon will require us to move beyond fallible self-reports and instead focus our attention on the psychological pro-cesses that underlie it. If we want a clearer view of what inner speech is like as an experience, we could do worse than explore how it relates to the other kinds of language that we produce.

ONE THING WE DEFINITELY all do (unless we have some specific dif-ficulty in producing spoken language) is external speech. What is the relation between the voices we hear in our heads and the words we say out loud? Was Vygotsky right to suppose that the transforma-tions that accompany internalization mean that the two forms of speech are fundamentally different? If inner speech really does come from external speech, studying the relationship between the two should be informative in both directions.

First, though, back to the behaviorists. John B. Watson's view was that inner speech is just external speech minus most of the muscular activity that produces sound waves from the tongue, lips, and articu-latory muscles. "Thought processes," he wrote, "are really motor habits in the larynx." Thinking is speaking with the volume turned down. Vygotsky, in contrast, thought that inner speech is trans-formed as it is internalized. It shares some features with external speech, but it is by no means merely a silent version of it.

At one level, Watson's view can be easily refuted. People who can't move their muscles don't suddenly lose the ability to think, as one 1947 anesthesiology study found when it (temporarily) para-lyzed a participant with the nerve poison curare. A more plausible version of the Watsonian view, termed the *motor simulation hypoth-esis*, holds that inner speech is similar in various respects to external speech, because it is essentially planned in the same way; it just doesn't go through the final stage of delivery. When you think a thought, your brain does everything it would do to cause you to say the thought out loud, short of actually commanding your muscles to do so.

This information gives psychologists an interesting hypothesis to work with. If the motor simulation hypothesis is correct, inner speech should resonate with the same qualities of tone, timbre, and accent as our ordinary external speech. For example, if you speak in a Welsh accent, your inner speech should have the same quality. If something profound changes as inner speech "goes underground," the differences might end up outweighing the similarities.

So far, the evidence pulls in both directions. There are some hints that a motor simulation view might be right about the similarities between internal and external speech. One recent study, conducted by Ruth Filik and Emma Barber of the University of Nottingham, asked participants to read limericks silently in their heads. For example:

> *There was a young runner from Bath,*
> *Who stumbled and fell on the path;*
> *She didn't get picked,*
> *As the coach was quite strict,*
> *So he gave the position to Kath.*

Another limerick read:

> *There was an old lady from Bath,*
> *Who waved to her son down the path;*
> *He opened the gates,*
> *And bumped into his mates,*
> *Who were Gerry, and Simon, and Garth.*

Limericks work, in part, because the final line rhymes with the first and second. Disrupt that rhyme and you no longer have a limerick. But whether two words rhyme or not can depend on what accent you say them in. Crucially, some of the participants had northern English accents, with short vowels (pronouncing "Bath" to rhyme with "Kath"), while the others had the long vowels of a southern accent ("Bath" rhyming with "Garth"). By tracking the volunteers' eye movements, the researchers showed that reading was disrupted when the final word of the limerick did not rhyme for that volunteer's accent—when a southerner read "Bath" then "Kath," for instance.

These findings support the idea that inner speech does indeed have an accent—and presumably other qualities of our spoken voice. As Hurlburt's DES studies have shown, inner speech shares many of the properties of external speech. Inner speakings are generally in the person's own voice, with its characteristic rhythm, pacing, tone, and so on. And yet people who stutter often report their inner speech to be completely fluent, suggesting that whatever is impeding their spoken speech isn't there in the internal version.

Another way of testing whether inner speech has the same richness as external speech is by giving participants material that is hard to say, such as tongue-twisters. Tongue-twisters work because they put together phonemes (basic units of sound) that are similar and thus easy to mix up, as any tradeswoman will tell you if she sells seashells by the seashore. We certainly trip over tongue-twisters when we say them out loud, but do we have the same problems when we recite them in inner speech?

That idea was tested in a neat study by Gary Oppenheim and Gary Dell of the University of Illinois at Urbana-Champaign. They started by identifying two kinds of errors that can occur in language: lexical errors and phonemic errors. Lexical errors involve, say, mixing up complete words (think of a classic spoonerism, such as, "The Lord is a shoving leopard"). Phonemic errors, in contrast, involve mixing up individual speech sounds (such as mistaking *reef* for *leaf*). Both kinds of errors happen in overt speech, but do they plague inner speech in the same way? If the motor simulation hypothesis is correct, internal and external speech should be equally likely to show both kinds of errors. If inner speech is less rich than external speech at the level of individual speech sounds—perhaps because of the kinds of condensation and abbreviation processes suggested by Vygotsky—you might expect people to show certain kinds of lexical errors, but not phonemic errors, in inner speech.

The Illinois researchers tested this idea by giving participants four-word tongue-twisters (such as *lean reed reef leech*) to recite either aloud or in inner speech, stopping to report any errors they made (for example, saying *leaf* instead of *reef*). The tongue-twisters had been carefully generated to allow the researchers to manipulate lexical (word) and phonemic (sound) similarity. The data showed that both kinds of errors occurred in overt speech, but only lexical errors happened in inner speech. Oppenheim and Dell concluded that inner speech is impoverished relative to external speech, displaying less richness at the level of individual speech sounds. Whether that was because the inner speech that was produced lacked these features, or because whatever mechanism that "heard" it internally was not sensitive to these qualities, remained an open question.

Another group of researchers, led by Martin Corley from the University of Edinburgh, thought that it might be something to do with the latter. They argued that one reason why phonemic similarity errors might not appear in inner speech is that they are hard for the participant to notice. To test their idea, they repeated the Illinois experiment, but they made it more difficult for participants to detect their errors in the out-loud condition by playing pink noise—a form of white noise—at the same time that participants were reciting the words. The change abolished the difference between the external and inner speech scenarios. In all conditions, recitation in inner speech showed the characteristic phonemic similarity errors (the *reef-leaf* mistake), in stark contrast to Oppenheim and Dell's findings.

The jury is still out on whether inner speech shows the same range of linguistic properties as external speech. One problem is that all of these experiments involved rather artificial scenarios for covert speech generation, unlikely to stimulate the kind of spontaneous inner speech that fills our everyday thoughts. Another concern is that several of the studies in this area require participants to read material from a screen. As the next chapter will show, it may be that the kind of inner speech that results from silent reading is a special case. We need to try to get at the qualities of inner speech in a more naturalistic way, and that means being more careful about how we ask people to generate it in the laboratory.

There's another tack we can take in understanding the relation between inner and outer speech. With new neuroimaging techniques such as functional magnetic resonance imaging, we have an opportunity to look at what is going on in the brain when different forms of language are being produced. If inner speech is just external speech without the articulation, there should be considerable overlap in the brain regions activated. The only differences should be the ones showing up in areas associated with the articulatory process (which you would not expect to see operating in inner speech). But if inner speech changes in nature as it is internalized, you might see very different brain regions bursting into life.

I HAVE A BIG head, it turns out, measured from front to back, so the technicians have to take out a layer of padding. There is more padding packed in around my ears, ensuring that my skull stays absolutely still. The little pink earplugs are rammed so far inside my head that I feel they must be touching in the middle. I have taken off my shoes, but this is no yoga session or meditation class. Today we're piloting a new method for observing inner speech in the MRI scanner. Essentially, I'm going to be a guinea pig for finding out whether our new experiment works, so that we can then run it for real with some other volunteers.

It's a special day for many reasons. It's the first time I've laid eyes on my own brain—the first time anyone has seen it, in fact, which is pretty remarkable given that it's been doing its job uncomplainingly for forty-odd years. It's my first opportunity to go through the process that I have read so much about in journal articles and news reports. Having your brain scanned is something that's impossible to depict through any ordinary means; you can't put a camera in the room and film it, because cameras contain metal, and the magnet that makes the scanner work is powerful enough to suck the spare change out of a sofa. You'll never see anyone's selfies from the time they took part in a neuroimaging experiment. If you want to know what the process is like, you have to go through it yourself.

The first time you do so, a dominant emotion is anxiety. Even after being carefully quizzed about whether I could have something metallic inside me, the doubt remains: I was implanted, enhanced, or patched up without my knowledge, and now that fatal bit of metal is heating up, getting tugged out of place by three Teslas' worth of magnetic field, and will soon come harpooning through my skin. My vision seems blurred: surely my contact lenses can't have metal in them? There's a weird feeling as the technician turns the mirror around and I see the computer files (which the experimenters are manipulating on the PC next door) coming through on the projector. It's as though someone is tinkering with the software of my own brain. I can see my forehead in the mirror, behind the cage that is covering my face. It feels very sci-fi. Where has that guy gone? Why is no one talking to me? Have they found something horrible? Have they all gone to the pub? There are beeps and bangs. It is not at all relaxing. In fact, it's like a nightmare out of *Star Wars*. Hearing all this banging on the casing that imprisons me, I feel as though I've woken up inside R2D2 during some geeky re-creation of the Battle of Endor.

Put your hand to your skull on the left-hand side, where there is a slight indentation just above and in front of the ear. Your fingertips will be touching on the location of a part of the brain, the inferior frontal gyrus, known to be essential for speech production. Damage to this area leads to a particular kind of problem with generating language that is known as Broca's aphasia (after the neuropsychologist, Pierre Paul Broca, who first described it). Most fMRI studies that have looked at inner speech have reported activation in this area when people are rehearsing sentences silently, and Broca's area is at the top of our list of expected activations.

More importantly, our design also allows us to explore differences in activation between two kinds of inner speech. A problem with existing neuroimaging studies is that they have treated inner speech as just one thing and haven't paid enough attention to its varied forms. If Vygotsky was right about how inner speech develops, much of the time it should have a dialogic structure (and as we have seen, that's a view that is backed up by survey participants' reports of their own experience). Which prompts us to ask: What happens when you ask people in the scanner to do something more like ordinary spontaneous inner speech?

Leading the research is Ben Alderson-Day, a postdoctoral researcher on our Hearing the Voice project at Durham University. "We want to look at what happens when people run through dialogues or conversations in their head," he explains, "and how that might differ from simpler forms of inner speech." The task involves two different conditions. In each, I am asked to imagine a scenario that involves some kind of speaking: for example, making a trip back to my old school, or going for a job interview. In one condition, I have to generate an inner monologue (in the school example, I have to imagine making a speech to the current students). In the other condition, the scenario is the same, but this time a dialogue is required of me (instead of performing at speech day, I have to have a conversation with an old teacher). The basic content of the scenarios is the same; the only difference is whether I am generating an internal dialogue or something more like a monologue. Once I've read the instructions for each condition, the writing blanks out and I am left staring at a cross on the screen: the standard "fixation point" in neuroimaging studies.

The study is designed so that we can see whether dialogic inner speech and monologic inner speech activate different areas of the brain. We certainly expect to see activation in Broca's area and another part of the brain known as the superior temporal gyrus, which includes Wernicke's area (see Figure 1). This language system, typically centered in the left hemisphere, is what you usually see being activated when people are producing speech out loud. But we think that our task provides a more naturalistic way of getting people to talk silently to themselves, and thus catalyzes something that is closer to ordinary spontaneous inner speech.

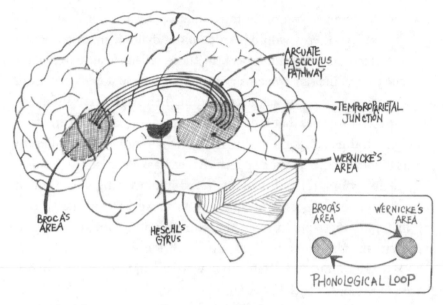

FIGURE 1: The inner speech network of the brain.

Of most interest is the comparison between the two conditions: in particular, the question of whether dialogic inner speech recruits brain regions that aren't drawn on in producing an internal monologue. In a neuroimaging study, you answer that kind of question by contrasting two conditions, essentially subtracting the activations in one condition from the activations in the other. When Ben subtracted the monologic activations from the dialogic ones, he was able to identify those specific neural regions associated with inner dialogue, particularly a set of areas in the superior temporal gyrus on both sides of the brain and in the left inferior and medial frontal gyri.

In terms of brain activations, then, there is something special about dialogic inner speech, and thus further grounds for distinguishing between the two kinds of covert self-talk. The dialogic-monologic comparison also showed activation, specific to dialogic inner speech, in a number of regions collectively known as posterior midline structures, including the precuneus. From previous neuroimaging research, it is known that these areas are particularly associated with thinking about other minds, or so-called "theory of mind" abilities. Studying activation in these areas is, for us, a crucial test of what Vygotsky's theory would predict about dialogic inner speech.

To understand why, think back to those self-critical tennis players. One part of the self, it seems, provides a comment or instruction, and the other part of the self acts upon it. The Vygotskian model of inner speech proposes that it develops from conversations with other people, and thus retains that quality of switching between different points of view. In her private speech, Athena asked herself a question ("What am I doing?") and then answered it by treating it as if it had come from another person ("I'm going to make a train track"). Doing dialogic inner speech must therefore involve some capacity to represent the thoughts, feelings, and attitudes of the people with whom we share our world: in other words, what psychologists call theory of mind, or "social cognition."

Ben was able to test that idea in more detail because we had included a standard theory of mind measure in the experiment. In this task, participants were shown a sequence of three cartoons depicting a simple story, and then had to choose a fourth image to complete the sequence. One condition required them to work out one of the story characters' intentions (such as pointing to see whether a seat was free on a train). Other stories had no theory of mind component, but rather involved reasoning about purely physical events (such as showing a football smashing into some bottles). Comparing activations in the theory-of-mind conditions with the physical reasoning ones gives the researcher a picture of what parts of the brain are involved when reasoning about other people's mental states.

For our purposes, the crucial thing was whether there was any overlap between generating dialogic inner speech and reasoning about other minds. Ben explains: "When we overlapped the areas linked to dialogue and the areas linked to theory of mind, one region was clearly activated in both: a region called the posterior right superior temporal gyrus. This is very close to one of the key areas for theory of mind, the right temporoparietal junction. When we saw that, we had some good evidence to think that dialogue and conversation, even just in inner speech, need to involve other minds in some way."

For the first time, then, we had some evidence of the neural underpinnings of dialogic inner speech. Intriguingly, the dialogic-specific activations correlated with how likely participants were to report dialogic inner speech in our questionnaire about the quality of their inner speech. People who endorsed those items more strongly showed greater dialogic-specific activations. These findings give us a tantalizing glimpse of a link between the subjective experience of inner speech—how you report on it when you are given a questionnaire—and what your brain does when it is generating it.

In a way, it should come as no surprise that talking to yourself has something of the social about it. In the theories of William James, Charles Sanders Peirce, and George Herbert Mead, the self generates a conversation with itself by taking the perspective of another. For Mead, those internal interlocutors are created as we learn more about the social roles that others can play, meaning that the athlete can internalize the role of his coach, for example, and use it to regulate his own behavior. Along with helping us to perform better and manage our emotions, inner dialogue can open up some distinctively creative ways of thinking, in which we can think about what we are doing by taking the critical and constructive perspective of another. The finding that theory-of-mind networks are recruited when the brain talks to itself fits neatly with the idea that, when we internalize dialogue, we internalize other people. Our brains, like our minds, are full of voices.

6

Voices on the Page

THE BISHOP WAS DOING something very strange. The young government official had gone to visit him as usual—visitors were never turned away—in the hope of being granted an audience. Finding the bishop in a rare moment of peace between parishioners, he noticed that the older man was busy with a book, but busy in an unusual way. "When he read," the former teacher of rhetoric wrote later in his *Confessions*, "his eyes would travel across the pages and his mind would explore the sense, but his voice and tongue were silent. . . . It was never otherwise."

Ambrose, Bishop of Milan, was doing something that we probably all take for granted: he was reading silently in his head. St. Augustine's account makes it sound as though this was an unusual occurrence in AD 385. Reading was an activity that you typically did out loud. One history of classical literature states that "a book of poetry or artistic prose was not simply a text in the modern sense but something like a score for public or private performance." Reading took an audience, and the conventional wisdom about reading in that historical period was that the audience was never just the self.

Augustine's account of Ambrose's silent reading is the first explicit account of someone extracting meaning from text without moving his lips. It had a profound influence on Augustine himself, whose later conversion epiphany in the garden in Milan was marked by his engaging in his own bout of silent reading, of a codex of the Epistles: "I snatched it up, opened it and read in silence the passage on which my eyes first lighted." Ambrose's innovation has in turn been seen as a pivotal moment in the development of Western culture. For the first time it was possible for a reader to respond to a text privately, without being overheard. The writer Sara Maitland, commenting on the Ambrose story, claimed that "the practice of silent reading led to individual, or independent thinking." Augustine himself noted possible motives for Ambrose's nifty trick: if he revealed aloud his responses to the text at hand, a nosey parishioner might ask him to expand on his concerns, thus wasting valuable reading time. Or perhaps he was just preserving his voice, which Augustine had noticed was "easily weakened." From whatever prosaic considerations, there grew a method of processing text that would have profound influences on both Christian scholarship and the individual's relationship with God.

There has been plenty of debate about whether Ambrose of Milan really invented silent reading. Several scholars have detailed apparent examples of covert reading in the classical era—Theseus seems to read a letter silently in Euripides's *Hippolytus*, for example. Others have pointed out the logical error in assuming that just because folk tended not to read silently, it meant they couldn't. The scholar A. K. Gavrilov suggested that Augustine wasn't amazed by Ambrose's actions so much as upset by them: the bishop was carrying on reading to himself when he should have been giving his undivided attention to the young man. Indeed, an inability to read silently would not fit with what we know about classical culture. "If the ancients did not read to themselves," Gavrilov wrote, "that would not show their love for the spoken word and for the euphonies of speech, but a severe psychic handicap." Defending the Ambrose story, Maitland pointed out that a document of AD 349 exhorted women to keep quiet in church by reading "quietly, so although the lips speak no other ears must hear what they say." If silent reading had been a thing at that time, Maitland argued, it would have been a much simpler solution to the noisy-woman problem.

Whatever its history, silent reading happens. Most children learn to read out loud and then gradually subvocalize until they are reading completely silently. Reading in your head is faster than reading aloud: instead of having to translate the visual into a phonological (or sound-based) code and then extract its meaning, the vocal stage is cut out, and the reader can go straight from the visual to the semantic. There is simply less for the brain to do.

But silent reading has a phenomenology as well. I remember as a child being asked by a teacher whether, when I read a novel, I could hear the characters' voices sounding out in my head. I'm pretty sure I answered in the positive, and I know that when I asked my own ten year old son Isaac the same question, the answer was a rapid, unequivocal yes. Silent reading is not a silent experience. Indeed, one critic of the Ambrose story noted that paying attention to the nuances of rhythm and intonation in a text requires the ability to jump backward and forward, taking in more than just the chunk of text currently being processed. This point might have been even more important when the writing was in *scriptio continua*: thestyleofwritingwithoutwordbreaksthatwasuniversalbeforeAugustinestime. A good reading performance, in any era, requires a combination of silent and vocal processing of text.

Silent reading, then, stimulates inner speech, or something like it. Writing in 1908, the American psychologist E. B. Huey noted that "although there is an occasional reader in whom the inner speech is not very noticeable, and although it is a foreshortened and incomplete speech in most of us, yet it is perfectly certain that the inner hearing or pronouncing, or both, of what is read, is a constituent part of the reading of by far the most of people. . . . And while this inner speech is but an abbreviated and reduced form of the speech of everyday life, a shadow copy as it were, it nevertheless retains the essential characteristics of the original."

Psychologists have investigated whether the phonological representations that result from silent reading have the sound of inner voices, or whether they are more abstract. Working at Arizona State University, Marianne Abramson and Stephen Goldinger asked participants to read a variety of words and non-words that varied according to the lengths of their vowels, and thus the length of time they took to pronounce. For example, *ward* is a "long" true word while *wake* is a short one; *labe* is a long non-word while *tate* is a non-word that can be read quickly. The task was simply to decide whether the word was a true one or not. As predicted, participants took longer to make that judgment for the longer words, suggesting that, in making their decision, they were sounding out the words in their heads as they read. The previously considered effects of accent on limerick reading, and of tongue-twisters, would also presumably not emerge unless covert reading involved some kind of silent performance of the language for oneself.

Reading-related inner speech often shows visible signs, too. No one would be surprised to see a child learning to read by sounding words out silently with her lips. Even skilled readers move their tongues when reading, particularly when the text is difficult. At first glance, such findings seem to support a behaviorist view of inner speech, in which it develops through a gradual stripping-away of the physical actions of speaking. That doesn't mean that John B. Watson was right about inner speech more generally, though, as reading may be a special case. This caveat is probably worth bearing in mind in any discussion of the phenomenology of silent reading. Psychologists have focused on this kind of reading because it is an easy task to control: you can manipulate what the participant reads, the instructions they are given, and so on. But the inner speech that results may not look the same as ordinary spontaneous inner speech. Nor do these findings imply that an absence of lip movements means an absence of inner speech. As Huey noted a century ago, "In my own case, the lips are seldom moved, but I can never escape the inner pronunciation that forms a part of all my reading."

This view is supported by efforts to sample people's experience when reading. Findings from Hurlburt's DES method concur with Huey's view that at least some people speak the words to themselves while reading, alongside the other things that enter their experience, such as visual imagery. Other people, according to DES, seem able to process text without either images or inner speech. Studies of brain damage are also relevant here. In the case of one experimental participant who suddenly became mute as a result of a stroke, inner speech wasn't necessary for reading at all. The patient could neither speak to himself nor make basic phonological judgments, but he performed well on a standard reading test. It was noted, however, that he read slowly, word by word—and that after each word he stared straight ahead for several seconds, eventually nodding to himself as though to indicate that he had got the word's meaning.

As we learned from the limerick experiment, the inner speech that is stimulated when you read can sometimes be in your own voice, with the characteristics of your own accent. When you are familiar with the author, however, it can be his or her voice that you hear in inner speech. I can think of at least one writer friend who gives me a strong and very pleasant feeling of hearing her speaking out loud when I read her books. There is some scientific support for this personal observation. At Emory University, psychologists Jessica Alexander and Lynne Nygaard familiarized participants with the voices of two speakers, one of whom spoke slowly, while the other spoke faster. The volunteers were then asked to silently read some passages of text that they were told had been written by one of the two speakers. It turned out that the participants read the fast-talker's text more quickly than they read the slow speaker's text, suggesting that this aspect of the speaker's delivery had been assimilated into their own inner speech (they were reading silently, remember, not simply parroting the speaker's speech out loud). The effect was particularly pronounced when the text was more difficult.

It seems, then, that there is truth in the idea that readers get to know a favorite writer's "voice." A writer can quite literally speak to a reader through the pages of her book. As the writer and psychoanalyst Adam Phillips has pointed out, there is something odd about "the experience of a relationship in silence" that characterizes the reader's pact with a writer. What kind of relationship is it in which no one speaks? The answer is that writers *do* speak through their written words, and in reading, readers listen.

Often, though, a writer is not concerned to put her own voice into a reader's head so much as the voices of others. The voices that a novelist is arguably most interested in are the voices of her characters. They can include the voice of the individual telling the story—the narrator—or the words that protagonists say to each other out loud. They can even be a character's private thought processes or inner speech. That's one of the things that makes reading fiction such a remarkable experience: it fills our heads with voices.

"THE NAME'S BOND. James Bond."

Sound familiar? You won't have struggled to process those five words for meaning, of course. But I can also confidently predict that your experience of reading them will have had a particular quality to it. In my case, I can't read those sentences without also hearing Sean Connery's voice in my head (readers of a different generation might find themselves channeling Pierce Brosnan or Daniel Craig). I have watched many Bond movies, of course, and so perhaps it's no surprise that reading 007's catchphrase triggers the sound of the actor's voice saying the famous words. But this kind of sensory activation of characters' voices also seems to be an important part of the experience of reading fiction.

Many readers say that, when reading a novel, they hear the voices of the protagonists sounding out in their heads. When, with the help of the British newspaper *The Guardian*, my colleagues and I asked a sample of over 1,500 people whether they heard the voices of fictional characters in their heads when they were reading, around 80 percent admitted to hearing them. One in seven said that those voices were as vivid as hearing an actual person speaking. Some readers said they actively sought to establish a voice for a protagonist: "It's usually early on in a story my mind seeks out a voice for a character I feel shouts out to have one. Sometimes, I will read dialogue out loud to establish it." For others, failing to hear the voices meant that the book was never going to work for them: "I always hear the voices of characters in books, and if I can't, it's usually because I'm not that into the book." Other readers reported experiences that were much less voicey: "I generally just hear my own internal voice. . . . I don't see characters clearly either. Generally I think I assign a few vague traits to them, and draw backgrounds from memory."

These findings of varied responses to reading are confirmed by those of the psychologist Ruvanee Vilhauer of Felician University, New Jersey. She went on to the Q&A website "Yahoo! Answers" and searched for references to people hearing voices when reading. A hundred and sixty questions and answers were thrown up by her search, which were then subjected to what social scientists call a content analysis, involving a systematic process of identifying themes that emerge in a collection of texts. As in our study, around 80 percent of the readers' posts referred to hearing voices, which often had speech-like qualities such as identity, gender, pitch, loudness, and emotional tone. The voices heard were sometimes identified with the reader's impression of how the character in question might have spoken, and sometimes with the respondent's own inner speech. For some readers, the voice they heard was a particular version of their own internal speech: a special "inner reading" voice. "[Y]es! i hear my own vocie!" wrote one fast-typing Yahoo! user, "but the vocie in my head doesnt sound like my vocie when i speak :o [sic]." A small proportion reported their inner-reading voices as being uncontrollable and even irritating: "I get very distracted from what I'm reading because I can't get the voice to go away—it annoys me so. This has really become a problem recently because it's almost as if I've developed a phobia for reading, because I can't stand to hear that clear voice in my head when I read!" Sometimes the experience was quite unpleasant: "Like when I'm trying to read I hear a voice reading it out loud in my head or when I just think I can hear what I'm thinking about. I also can have conversations with this voice. . . . Every so often this voice also just pops up with horrible things."

Hearing the voices of fictional characters seems, then, to apply to adult readers just as much as to my ten-year-old son. Novelists use two main methods for depicting what characters say in their stories. They can present exactly what the character said, usually marking it with quotation marks—what is known as *direct speech*. Or they can report the utterance at second hand, in so-called *reported* (or *indirect*) speech. It's the difference between writing the words *Mary said, "The game was interesting,"* and *Mary said that the game was interesting.*

Psychologists have shown that direct speech is generally perceived as more vivid than reported speech. At Stanford University, Elizabeth Wade and Herbert Clark asked participants to report a conversation that some other people had had, and to either make the account entertaining or simply make it informative. When participants were trying to entertain rather than simply convey information, they were more likely to choose direct speech as their medium.

At the University of Glasgow, researchers have asked what goes on in the brain when people read the two kinds of speech. Bo Yao and colleagues began with the hypothesis that, when we read reported speech, we only process the meaning; when we read direct speech, we go so far as to sound the speaker's words out in our heads. In line with their predictions, they found differences in brain activations in participants listening to direct versus reported speech. Specifically, listening to direct speech led to greater activation in areas of the right auditory cortex (housed in the temporal lobe), which is known to be particularly important for processing voices. This wouldn't be expected if both kinds of speech led to processing the depicted speech at the same level. The findings provide a neural basis for the observation that direct speech is experienced more vividly than reported speech, because it activates areas of the brain that represent the qualities of voices.

In a second study, the Glasgow researchers replicated these activation differences when participants listened to direct or indirect speech. To ensure that any differences were not caused simply by direct speech sounding more interesting or exciting when read out loud, they ensured that both kinds of texts were delivered in a monotonous reading voice. Compared with the reported speech, the direct quotes activated almost exactly the same areas of the brain as were busy in the earlier study, suggesting that the brain was filling in the rich, voice-like information when it wasn't actually there in the stimulus. This finding supported previous evidence from the same group that people read direct speech more quickly when they think the quote is from a fast speaker compared to a slower one, but that that effect doesn't hold for indirect speech. When we read direct speech, we really do seem to sound out the words in a voice-like manner, even if our lips are still.

Other studies have shown support for the idea that our familiarity with particular voices affects how those voices are experienced in our heads in silent reading. A group of researchers led by Christopher Kurby from Washington University presented participants with scripts from a 1950s radio show, *The Bickersons*, involving conversations between John and Blanche Bickerson, the married couple at the center of the show. Participants first listened to recordings of the scripts being reperformed by actors, and then read either the same scripts or different ones involving the same characters. At random intervals, the procedure was interrupted by an auditory word-recognition task involving the presentation of a word in one of the characters' voices. (The task simply involved the volunteers making a judgment about whether this was an actual word or not.) The rationale was that, if Blanche's voice, for example, was already activated for the reader, and then the word-recognition probe was presented in Blanche's voice, the reaction should be quicker than if the voices didn't match.

That's exactly what the researchers found. Participants made the word judgments more quickly when the test word was presented in the voice they had just been listening to. But that effect was only found when the participant was reading a script he or she had previously heard performed out loud, not a new script describing the voice of the same character. How much experience with hearing the voice was necessary for readers to summon up their own mental version of it, and transfer it to a chunk of dialogue they had not actually heard read aloud? In a follow-up experiment, the researchers found evidence that the effect did occur with unfamiliar scripts, but only if the participant had had extended experience with the voices. They concluded that, with repeated exposure, the characters' voices became entrenched in memory representations of what that voice sounded like, which were then activated when the participant silently read that character's speech.

This leaves us with a puzzle, though. If it's true that reading fictional dialogue activates characters' voices in our inner speech, that must also be the case when we have never heard the voice speak for real. I can conjure up a vivid mental image of April Wheeler trying to persuade her husband Frank to pack up and move to Europe, in Richard Yates's classic *Revolutionary Road*, even though she is a fictional character and I have never watched the movie based on the book. At some level the voice I hear must be of my own making; I must be creating it and ventriloquizing it in my own inner speech. As we'll see, asking what makes that act of creation possible tells us something about how writers conjure up the voices that populate their pages.

One approach, adopted by psychologists Danielle Gunraj and Celia Klin from Binghamton University in New York State, is to give readers information about a voice they have never heard, without actually letting them hear it. When the main character was described as speaking quickly, participants read that character's speech more quickly. This outcome echoes the earlier findings that speaking rate translates into reading rate. The important difference in the Binghamton study, though, was that the participants never actually heard the character talking fast; they were only told, in a description of the voice in the text itself, about the speedy speaking style. Although this effect held for reading aloud, it only worked for silent reading when readers were instructed to take the perspective of the character and to read the text in such a way that they could hear the character's voice in their head. The implication is that the creation of an auditory image of a speaker's voice is not automatic; it requires some active work on the part of the reader. In reading fiction, the researchers argued, an emotional engagement with a character may be enough to ensure the effect, which would explain why we are sometimes disappointed, on seeing the movie of a treasured book, that they have got the voice of a particular character "all wrong."

But novelists don't just concern themselves with depicting the words their characters say out loud. They tell us what their characters are thinking as well. The mode of writing that literary scholars call *free indirect style* works by mixing representations of internal thought with standard narrative discourse. In Gustave Flaubert's *Madame Bovary*, for example, the thoughts of the protagonist are thoroughly integrated with the narrative voice:

> "I've a lover, a lover," she said to herself again and again, revelling in the thought as if she had attained a second puberty. At last she would know the delights of love, the feverish joys of which she had despaired. She was entering a marvellous world where all was passion, ecstasy, delirium.

Here, the heroine gives us some direct speech, but she follows it up with thought. Crucially, the author does not mark the frame of the thought sequence with the usual markers ("she thought," etc.). It is as though he allows readers to assume that they are still in Madame Bovary's head, in a sense, and he can depict her thoughts without clunky devices to distinguish between the character's perspective and the narrator's.

To date, there have been no experimental investigations of whether this kind of depiction of a character's inner speech leads to the voice taking on life in the mind of the reader in the way that direct speech does. But there's no doubt that mixing characters' inner speech with a regular authorial voice is one of the ways that novelists make their prose come alive. Writers can also have a lot of fun with the fact that people often say things that are the opposite of what they're thinking (recall the DES participant who thought "Burger King" while saying "KFC"). Fictional characters can go about their internal lives safe in the knowledge that their thoughts will not be overheard by the characters with whom they are conversing. Eavesdropping on those contradictory messages is one of the pleasures of reading fiction.

There are fictional worlds, though, in which the privacy of inner speech can be threatened. In a fantasy context, writers can get drama out of the fact that listening in to people's thoughts can be catastrophic for human relationships—just as it was for Nick Marshall when he acquired the ability to listen in to his workmates' inner lives in the film *What Women Want*. In his 2008 *Chaos Walking* trilogy, the novelist Patrick Ness imagines a world in which thoughts are audible. Streams of consciousness merge into a perceptible, multimedia collective consciousness known as The Noise. "It's crash and clatter and it usually adds up to one big mash of sound and thought and picture and half the time it's impossible to make any sense of it," the first-person adolescent narrator, Todd, tells us. What a person thinks in this storyworld can be overheard: "The Noise is a man unfiltered, and without a filter, a man is just chaos walking." Todd learns this, to his cost, when he discovers a girl living wild in a swamp and finds that she is different—and strangely silent. He fears that he might infect her with the germ that has caused his society's thoughts to become audible; his problem is that he can't keep these fears to himself, and thus can't stop her from learning of his infection.

Sometimes the tension between the inner and the outer can be exploited in more subtle ways. Aamer Hussein is a Pakistani writer who is often preoccupied in his fiction with the differences between internal and external speech. In his haunting short novel *Another Gulmohar Tree*, he tells of an Urdu speaker, Usman, who struggles to convert his innermost thoughts into a form that his English wife can understand: "She found herself wondering, as she had often done before, whether he translated his hesitant, measured phrases from his own language; they sounded as if he'd written them out before he said them."

Inner speech in Urdu is called *khud-kalami*, or "self-talking." Because the language is so steeped in ancient cultural traditions, thinking to yourself in Urdu is very different from thinking in English. It is more poetic and close to the literary. Differences in the grammatical structures of the two languages also mean that there is less of a divide between inner and outer speech in Urdu than there is in English. For a bilingual fiction writer like Hussein, switching from one language to the other leads to a different relationship with the inner voice: "When I started writing in English I found that my stories were very interior; they were very often about people thinking quietly, so that dialogue or any kind of external activity happened as a memory, as a thought, as an intrusion. . . . In Urdu it is very easy to work in that inner mode." Hussein explains to me that Urdu contains linguistic devices that mark the shift from a narrator to inner speech in ways that are not possible in English, allowing the author to fuse interior monologues with external actions in ways that don't require modernist trickery.

Another way to fuse thought and speech is to play around with the punctuation, such as quotation marks, that usually distinguishes them on the page. In the early twentieth century, James Joyce replaced what he disparagingly referred to as "perverted commas" with a line break and a horizontal dash. In the present era, American writer Cormac McCarthy has done away with quotation marks and left the reader to work out what's out-loud speech, what's private thought, and what's authorial narrative:

> They slipped out of their backpacks and left them on the terrace and kicked their way through the trash on the porch and pushed into the kitchen. The boy held on to his hand. All much as he'd remembered it. . . . This is where we used to have Christmas when I was a boy. He turned and looked out at the waste of the yard. A tangle of dead lilac. The shape of a hedge.

Experiments with inner and outer voices came to a head in the work of modernist writers like Joyce and Virginia Woolf. Joyce's use of free indirect style in his 1922 masterpiece *Ulysses* fuses traditional narration with seemingly direct access to the thoughts of its protagonist, Leopold Bloom, seen here heading out to the shops from the house he shares with his wife, Molly:

No. She didn't want anything. He heard then a warm heavy sigh, softer, as she turned over and the loose brass quoits of the bedstead jingled. Must get those settled really. Pity. All the way from Gibraltar. Forgotten any little Spanish she knew. Wonder what her father gave for it. Old style. Ah yes! of course. Bought it at the governor's auction. Got a short knock. Hard as nails at a bargain, old Tweedy. Yes, sir. At Plevna that was. I rose from the ranks, sir, and I'm proud of it. Still he had brains enough to make that corner in stamps. Now that was farseeing.

Joyce's text here moves imperceptibly from traditional third-person narrative to a vivid depiction of Bloom's private thoughts. But inner speech is not presented as it was in Flaubert, as an internal version of external speech. It is transformed. It is telegraphic and condensed, like a child's private speech. It contains emotional expressions and instructions to the self. It is dialogic, with Bloom questioning and then answering himself about the provenance of the marital bed. It even incorporates the voice of his father-in-law, old Tweedy, quoting him ironically about his progression to the rank of major in the army. In Joyce's writings, the boundary between internal and external becomes permeable. The world is taken into the mind, and thoughts extend back out into the world.

The great modernist writers had a well-documented fascination with individual psychology and the artistic challenge of how to depict it on the page. But writers were alert to the conversational quality of inner speech long before the era of Woolf and Joyce. In Geoffrey Chaucer's fourteenth-century poem *The Book of the Duchess*, the narrator has a dream-vision of the mysterious Man in Black, who seems to be lamenting the death of his beloved in a fraught internal conversation: "He spak noght / But argued with his owne thoght, / And in hys wyt disputed faste / Why and how hys lyf myght laste." Robinson Crusoe, the protagonist of the first novel in English, first published in 1719, found it helpful to converse with the voices of his inner speech; they made his solitary life "better than sociable." A century after Daniel Defoe's novel appeared, novelist Charlotte

Brontë imagined the character Jane Eyre, who is frequently found debating with herself:

> What do I want? A new place, in a new house, amongst new faces, under new circumstances. . . . How do people do to get a new place? They apply to friends, I suppose. . . . I then ordered my brain to find a response, and quickly. It worked and worked faster. I felt the pulses throb in my head and temples; but for nearly an hour it worked in chaos.

WRITERS FILL OUR HEADS with voices in many ways. They give us fictional characters speaking out loud, and they play on our ability to reconstruct those voices in our own minds, sometimes even without hearing them speak. Writers also eavesdrop on the words their characters do not say out loud. They give us minds in dialogue, imaginary creatures engrossed in internal conversations. Fictional depictions of inner speech, particularly in the hands of the modernist masters who tried so hard to re-create it on the page, give us an incomparably fertile description of the transformations that happen to words as they make their way into our thoughts, as well as of the qualities of inner speech that betray its origins in ordinary human conversation.

In one sense, those represented voices are a writer's predominant building materials. In an interview, the novelist David Mitchell described his occupation as a kind of "controlled personality disorder. . . . [T]o make it work you have to concentrate on the voices in your head *and* get them talking to each other." The literary scholar Patricia Waugh has written on how novelists harness the power of their readers' inner voices to create characters whose thoughts and feelings touch and are touched by those of the people reading about them. The voices we encounter in a novel can express our desires, threaten our safety, challenge our morals, and speak of what cannot be said. They take us into a place of expanded possibilities where we can try on other identities. Through their expert control of fictional voices, novelists lead us into a controlled dissolution of the self, and then bring us safely back to who we are.

That's quite an achievement for what is quintessentially—perhaps thanks to Ambrose of Milan—a solitary, silent process. When it goes well, reading a novel is arguably as intimate an engagement with another mind (or minds) as you can get. For most readers, it is a pleasurable, affirming, soul-nourishing experience. But voices can get out of hand. For some individuals, fictional voices can make audible what we would rather remained silent. In Patricia Waugh's words, voices on the page transport the self "beyond its safely policed boundaries," showing us "the precarious harmony that is the polyphony of consciousness." They remind us that we are not one, but many.

7

Chorus of Me

You sit alone, with no capacity for movement, in a dimly lit place whose dimensions you cannot verify. You know that your eyes are open because of the tears that stream from them endlessly. You are seated with your hands on your knees and no support for your spine, and you are speaking. Without ceasing. It's pretty much all you can do. The voice that you hear sounds alien, and yet it can only be you who is producing it. Sometimes there is more than one voice. Singular or plural, it seems to be able to impose its will on you, giving you no choice but to listen. And yet it is your mouth that is uttering it. You are listening to yourself, but what you are listening to is not "you."

The Irish writer Samuel Beckett had a fascination with the ways in which individuals—in some of his texts we can barely call them humans—construct themselves through language. In his 1953 novel *The Unnamable*, the creation of a desolate monologue is the only way in which the eponymous narrator can establish his own existence. Often seen as a metaphor for human isolation, this typical Beckettian creature is compelled to communicate when communication is impossible: "Ah if I could only find a voice of my own, in all this babble, it would be the end of their troubles, and of mine."

Beckett also had a fascination with inner speech. In a letter to his friend Georges Duthuit, written around the time he composed *The*

Unnamable, Beckett observed, "You are right, to want the brain to function is the height of crassness, or is sinister, like the loves of an old man. The brain has better things to do, stopping and listening to itself, for instance." The Unnamable himself voices a regret that he has not done enough of this kind of thing. "I have never spoken enough to me, never listened enough to me, never replied enough to me, never had pity enough on me."

Beckett's writings illustrate a paradox about human experience. We spin narratives about ourselves to make sense of who we are, and those narratives make us simultaneously the author, the narrator, and the protagonist of the story. We *are* the cacophony of our mental voices. We listen to them as well as utter them; they construct us through their incessant chatter. But there is nothing mad or pathological about these voices in the head. The narratologist Marco Bernini argued that the Unnamable's voices correspond to the natural sounds of inner speech, which have been presented by the author (Beckett) in an unfamiliar, "detuned" form, as a kind of fictional experiment into how these mental utterings cohere into a self.

That technique works because we more ordinary humans bring our own inner speech to the task of running this fictional simulation. As we saw in the previous chapter, literary texts have a power to elicit inner speech and get us sounding out its voices. We do this, too, when we read the Unnamable's multivoiced inner speech. We use our own inward chatter, as readers, to "activate its content," running Beckett's cognitive simulation in our own minds.

The Unnamable's populated consciousness makes perfect sense from a Vygotskian point of view. Inner speech develops through the internalization of dialogues with others, and it retains its social nature throughout. The conversations I had with others, when I was developing as a human being, equipped me with the cognitive structures that allow me now to have a conversation with myself, or to orchestrate a dialogue between the different voices that make up who I am. As we've seen, this idea finds support from studies that have asked people what their inner speech is like. Respondents often acknowledge that their internal chatter has a dialogic structure, and the presence of other voices emerges as a factor in surveys of the nature of the stream of consciousness. For many of us, inner speech is shot through with other voices.

This multivoiced quality of experience is the essence of what I call *dialogic thinking*. It's not a term that Vygotsky used, but I believe that the idea is there in his writings. A solitary mind is actually a chorus. We can go so far as to say that minds are riddled with different voices because they are never really solitary. They emerge in the context of social relationships, and they are shaped by the dynamics of those relationships. Other people's words get into our heads. This is more than the currently fashionable formulation that we have "social brains"—that we are wired up to engage with others from the first days of life (although that is also true). It's saying that our thinking *is* social. Our minds contain multitudes, just as a work of fiction contains the voices of different characters with distinct perspectives. Thinking is a dialogue, and human cognition retains many of the powers of a conversation among different points of view.

The concept of "dialogue" here has some special features. The Russian literary scholar Mikhail Bakhtin noted that a voice always represents a particular perspective on the world: it comes from a person with a point of view, and it thus reflects particular understandings, emotions, and values. Dialogue, for Bakhtin, is the process through which these varied points of view come into contact. For a couple of examples, think of the perspectives of "coach" and "pupil" that comment on and respond to each other in our imaginary tennis player's inner speech, or the different perspectives of Faithful Friend and Proud Rival that people describe among their internal interlocutors. When you internalize dialogue, as you do when you develop inner speech, you internalize a structure that allows you to represent other perspectives. Those perspectives, in dialogic interplay, give your thinking some very special characteristics.

I have spent much of my own career as a psychologist trying to work out the implications of this view of thinking and to develop a scientific model that could make sense of it as a basic blueprint of human cognition. Not all cognition, by any means; there are plenty of things that the conscious mind does, like mental arithmetic and starlight navigation, that don't require the ability to coordinate different perspectives. But at least some mental tasks seem to require the flexible articulation of different points of view. The idea is there in the writings of Plato, William James, Charles Sanders Peirce, George Herbert Mead, and Mikhail Bakhtin, as well as in Vygotsky, but it had never been spelled out in the terms of modern cognitive psychology. The Dialogic Thinking model was intended to fill that gap.

At its heart, the theory is an attempt to get some greater specificity about this fuzzy concept we term "thinking." The Dialogic Thinking model proposes that there is a group of mental functions—operations that our minds can perform—that depend on an interplay between different perspectives on reality. They involve taking a point of view, and then taking another one, and enacting a dialogue between them. For these kinds of thinking (and possibly *only* these kinds), language is crucial, because language is particularly powerful at representing different perspectives and bringing them into contact with each other. Crucially, the development of dialogic thinking requires experience of social interactions, patterned by language, to make them work.

That all sounds very abstract, so let's look at a concrete example: the scene in which my daughter was building a train track while I listened to her talking to herself. What's significant about this sequence of private speech is that Athena represents different perspectives to herself and brings them into dialogic relation with each other. She stages a conversation between different points of view. "What am I doing? I'm going to make a train track and put some cars on it." It's a rudimentary conversation (she is only two years old, after all), but a conversation nonetheless. The perspectives she brings to the dialogue are represented in words, and they are coordinated flexibly: one perspective "answers" another perspective, just as if it had come from another person. "I make a train track and put some cars on it. *Two* cars." And those perspectives are about the same thing—her emerging toy town plan—just as in any good dialogue: both sides take the same object as their focus. If you're having a conversation with someone and you are talking about entirely different things, then you're not really having a conversation.

Athena can do this because, before she started talking to herself, she had real dialogues with actual people. Internalizing those dialogues, and enacting them purely for herself, provided her with a cognitive mechanism that now allows her to work with different perspectives and make them question, answer, and comment on each other. Her thinking has what I call an "open slot," in which she can park a perspective and then generate a dialogic response to it. Athena can now put anything she likes into her open slot: her own voice, the words of a playmate or parent, or the voice of an imaginary entity. Because she has grown up among dialogues, and has participated in them from her earliest days, she can fill her mind with other voices.

This is what I mean by dialogic thinking. It involves ordinary language, or some other communication system, such as sign language. For most of us, it is more or less inner speech, in all the varied forms that takes. It is also social—that is, structured by our interactions with other members of our species, particularly during infancy and childhood. And it gives our cognition some very special properties. For one thing, Athena's out-loud thinking about the train track is open-ended, meaning that it is not geared toward the attainment of some specific goal—as would be the case with other, non-dialogic forms of thinking, such as mental arithmetic. It is self-regulating. No one is telling Athena what to think. She is directing the flow of thought herself, just as in a dialogue between two people, which needs no external director telling it where to go (one reason why conversations can end up in very different places from where they started). Athena's dialogue with herself is endlessly creative. Because it doesn't know where it is going before it sets out, it can come up with ideas it has never had before. In internal dialogue, we follow the train of thought wherever it might lead us.

ONE GLOOMY JULY DAY in 1882, walking through the meadows behind Schenkweg (the street on which he lived in The Hague), Vincent van Gogh saw a dead pollard willow. Noting the scaly, snake-like texture of its bark, he thought it would make a good subject for a painting. Five days later he wrote to his beloved brother Theo about it:

> I have attacked that old giant of a pollard willow, and I think it is the best of the water colours. A gloomy landscape—that dead tree near a stagnant pool covered with reeds, in the distance a car shed of the Rhine Railway Company, where the tracks cross each other; dingy black buildings, then green meadows, a cinder path, and a sky with scudding clouds, grey with a single bright white border, and a depth of blue where the clouds are momentarily rent apart. In short, I wanted to make it the way the signal man in his smock and with his little red flag must see and feel it when he thinks, "It is gloomy weather today."

In evidence here is a theme in Vincent's letters. Still in his late twenties, he had only recently made the momentous decision to become an artist. After a row with his parents at the end of the previous year, he had moved out of the family home in the country town of Etten and set up a small studio in The Hague. Although he was still convalescing from a hospital stay (involving a gruesome treatment for gonorrhea) and a fair amount of relationship turmoil, Vincent was working on his new vocation with "great pleasure." Along with requests for financial support, he would send Theo sketches and descriptions of the pieces he was working on. In his account of the pollard willow sketch, he is commenting on a piece that has already been made. Although the willow is mentioned in an earlier letter, it is described there as an interesting object rather than as a plan for a composition. It is not until Vincent can describe the piece he has made (and enclose a sketch for the eventual finished piece) that we get a sense of his intentions for it.

A month later, Vincent sent his brother a sketch of an autumnal scene painted in the countryside close to his house:

> In the woods, yesterday toward evening, I was busy painting a rather sloping ground covered with dry, mouldered beech leaves. This

ground was light and dark reddish-brown, emphasised by the weaker and stronger shadows of trees casting half-obliterated stripes across it. . . . The problem . . . was to get the depth of colour, the enormous force and solidity of that ground . . . to keep that light and at the same time the glow and depth of that rich colour.

The sketch does not survive, although there are several oil paint-ings and studies of similar woodland scenes from the same period. What is different in this letter is that Vincent seems to be grappling with the problems of composition (achieving the necessary depth of color, the management of the light) at the same time as he is making the work. Like a child thinking out loud about a sequence of play, it is almost as if Vincent is commenting aloud on his ongoing creative process.

In June the following year, Vincent found his attention drawn to a refuse dump:

This morning I was already out-of-doors at four o'clock. I intend to attack the dustmen, or rather the attack has already begun. . . . I have caught the sheepfold-like effect of the interior in contrast with the open air and the light under the gloomy sheds: and a group of women emptying their dustbins is beginning to develop and take shape. But, the moving back and forth of the wheelbarrows, and the dustmen with the dung forks, that rummaging under the sheds, must still be expressed without losing the effect of light and brown of the whole: on the contrary, it must be strengthened by it.

The letters of Vincent van Gogh are an extraordinary literary cre-ation. They document his work as an artist during its most sensitive and tumultuous periods. In these letters from the early 1880s, you get an impression of someone arguing with himself about what each composition needs. Indeed, it's reasonable to wonder whether this commentary on the creative process is as much for Vincent's benefit as it is for his brother's. The artist is using his letters—a kind of hand-written private speech—to set out plans, to choose among alternative sketches and approaches, and to pin down what is still needed from the composition.

A letter from the following week gives an even clearer sense of an artist planning out a picture at least partly in words:

> Just while making these studies, the plan for an even larger drawing is beginning to take root, namely one of potato digging. . . . I should want the landscape to be a level ground with a little row of dunes on the horizon. The figures about a foot high, a broad composition, 1 by 2. . . . Right in front . . . kneeling figures of women gathering the potatoes. . . . On the second plane, a row of diggers, men and women. . . . I have the grounds pretty well in my mind, and will choose a fine potato field at my ease.

The sketches of this scene that emerged in Vincent's subsequent letters were not based on any actual observations of potato-digging. It was June, the wrong time of year, and Vincent knew that he would have to wait another month or two to witness any potatoes being lifted. He would choose a field at his leisure, when the time came. He was imagining the scene rather than documenting it, but his letters show that that act of imagination was at least in part a verbal one.

There is a stronger claim that could be made about van Gogh's letters and their fascinating juxtaposition with what we have inherited of his sketches, drawings, and paintings. Van Gogh in this period was developing rapidly as an artist. He was still a couple of years away from producing the first of what are now regarded as his major works (another tuber-related piece, *The Potato Eaters* from 1885, is generally considered to be his first mature painting). The progression described here—from the pollard willow to the woodland scene to the refuse dump to the potato diggers—represents a shift in his strategy away from using his letters to describe works that had already been made toward using this form of out-loud thinking to plan what a work *should* look like. There is no question that van Gogh's visual imagination played the greater part: What else would you expect from a painter? But creating beautiful visual artworks was not, at least in Vincent's case, an exclusively visual process.

It is also no accident that these letters formed part of a dialogue. Ostensibly they are for his brother Theo: they don't just describe developing artworks, but also Vincent's often troubled emotions, his stormy relationship with his father and several painfully unrequited loves. In collections of the van Gogh letters, Theo's responses are sparse inclusions, and it is often hard to decode from Vincent's missives what communications from Theo he is responding to. If it was a dialogue, it seems a little one-sided. Judging from the documents that survive, Vincent wrote about six hundred letters to Theo over the course of his life, but only about forty of Theo's possible replies still exist. Correspondence with other family members shows that Theo was an assiduous letter-writer, and he undoubtedly wrote more to Vincent than the surviving documents suggest. But even if Theo's responses were prolific, there still is a strong sense of Vincent thinking out loud and not necessarily expecting a reply. Like a child's private speech, the words are for the self as much as—perhaps even more than—for the other.

The writer Joshua Wolf Shenk has analyzed the relationship between Vincent and Theo as a creative partnership: an example of one of many such productive couplings which give the lie to the "myth of the lone genius," scribbling or sketching away in his garret. Rather than seeing Theo merely as a supporter and sounding board for Vincent's creative expressions, Shenk describes him as a "hidden partner" in a productive relationship. "Though his brother Theo never picked up a brush, it's fair to identify him—as Vincent did—as the co-creator of the drawings and paintings that are among the most significant in history. The van Gogh brothers . . . had supremely distinct roles, styles, even identities. But from their separate domains, each contributed to a joint project of honest, daring art."

Shenk's analysis emphasizes the dialogic nature of the creative process that resulted in the artworks attributed to Vincent van Gogh, although in Shenk's reading it is a real, external dialogue: an exchange of letters between two brothers. We don't know whether the letters quoted above are recording thought processes that had already happened, or whether Vincent was working out the ideas as he was setting them down. It was probably a bit of both. But I think there must also be a sense in which this dialogue carried on in Vincent's head at times when (as was usually the case, except for a short period later in his life when they lived together in Paris) Theo wasn't around. It is impossible to know, and it certainly cannot be divined from the letters, but it seems plausible that Vincent carried on this conversation in his own thoughts as a fully internalized version of the letter exchange.

Some kind of internalized creative dialogue must surely be a major part of any such partnership—how otherwise would anything get done? John Lennon was not limited to being a musical genius only when Paul McCartney was in the room, and vice versa. Creative partnerships (of which the history of various art forms is littered with examples) may come to have their power at least in part because the artist re-creates an internalized version of the actual dialogue that would have taken place over cups of tea and cigarette breaks.

I would go further and say that, once established, the inner dialogue develops to a point where it no longer needs the other contributor. Leaving aside the requests for cash, I doubt that Vincent would have stopped writing in this way even if Theo had been dead for several years. (He might presumably have put all of the commentaries into his journal, and thus saved himself some postage.) As Shenk noted, Vincent certainly struggled to find the right distance from his brother: his early letters were full of longing to be near him, but when they were together they often fought. Like a child's private speech, the letters are "parasocial": open to the possibility of a response, even if one is neither expected nor needed.

There's another sense in which van Gogh's letters illustrate Vygotskian views about the use of language in self-regulation. Vygotsky argued that, if it has a genuine self-regulatory function, the speech that accompanies action should, over the course of development, shift its position in time relative to the behavior. From an early stage in which children's self-directed speech merely accompanies and describes ongoing actions ("I'm building a train track"), it develops into speech with a clear planning role, appearing *before* the behavior in question ("I'm *going to* build a train track"). Although this developmental progression has been hard to document empirically in children's private speech, some trace of it seems to be there in Vincent's letters. "*I am painting* a woodland scene" becomes "*I am going to paint* some potato diggers."

Linguistic, dialogic, shifting between externalized and internalized forms: dialogic thinking seems to be a useful tool for creativity. An oft-abused buzzword that can be an emblem of some very woolly thinking, the idea of creativity—which we can define as the production of the "new, beautiful, and useful"—is one of the most elusive and mysterious of human abilities. Creativity is not necessarily about the arts. Scientific research—the kind that shifts paradigms, but also the sort that finds an ingenious solution to a local problem—requires dollops of the stuff. It involves going from what is known to what is unknown; from what is old to what is new. It is a kind of thinking, but one in which you don't know where you are going until you get there.

That open-ended quality of the creative process has been one of the obstacles to understanding it scientifically. Psychologists like to work with tightly specified paradigms with definite boundaries: such control over events is arguably essential to the experimental method. How on earth do you get a scientific grasp on a process that has no clearly defined end point?

It doesn't stop psychologists from trying. Many lab hours have been spent with versions of the "candle" problem, in which participants have to work out how to suspend a lighted candle using only a small range of props (book of matches, box of thumbtacks, corkboard) so that the wax doesn't drip onto the table below. The candle problem is usually seen as a test of people's ability to "think outside the box," by employing objects for uses other than those for which they were intended. (Spoiler alert: in this classic problem in the psychology of creativity, you simply retrocon the tack box as a candleholder and fix it with the thumbtacks to the corkboard.) On one description, the task requires you to be open to an alternative perspective (use the box as a candleholder, rather than as a receptacle for the thumbtacks). If you approach this task by thinking in words, you might find it useful to ask yourself questions and then answer them: "Why not use the box for something else?" "Like what?" "I don't know—stop thinking of it as a container for the tacks. Try another use for it." Many other creative moments might be similarly characterized in terms of an openness to another way of looking at things, a willingness to hold a particular perspective in mind and respond to it with another one. As we've seen, that's a pretty good definition of the ability to engage in mental dialogue.

Thinking about creativity as a form of dialogic thinking helps us to understand that flexibility. Dialogue is creative. You may have some idea of what you are going to say, but you sure as hell don't know what your interlocutor is going to say, at least until your own utterance is out there. And once it is out there, you may not actually need your interlocutor. All you need to do is respond to that initial utterance as if it had come from another person, and you're on your way to having a conversation with yourself.

Is there any evidence that thinkers use dialogic inner speech to solve these creative problems? This is where the science gets tricky. As we have seen throughout this book, it's very difficult to get a window onto people's thought processes. Vincent van Gogh himself seemed skeptical of the idea that we wear our minds on our sleeves: "Do our inner thoughts ever show outwardly? There may be a great fire in our soul, yet no one ever comes to warm himself at it, and the passers-by see only a wisp of smoke coming through the chimney, and go along their way." You can gather so-called "thought protocols" from people who have done a creative task, essentially asking them after the fact what their thought processes were and how they went about solving the problem. But these can only ever be rather belated reconstructions of what went on. With further developments in experience sampling, it might be possible to probe people as they are pondering and thus capture the flavor of the thought process at the crucial moment. But any such methodology would risk destroying the very process it was meant to be investigating. As the famous story of Samuel Taylor Coleridge and the visitor from Porlock illustrates, creative processes (in this case, the composition of Coleridge's unfinished masterpiece "Kubla Khan") are notoriously sensitive to distraction. Documenting the arrival of creative insight as it happens will never be an easy matter.

Instead of trying to capture creativity as it occurs, another approach is to look at differences between individuals in how much they engage with dialogic inner and private speech. Again, the relevant studies have yet to be done. One bit of evidence suggests that children who use more self-regulatory private speech score higher on standard measures of creativity than their peers who use less of it, but no studies have yet tried to relate creativity to inner-speech measures, or, indeed, to specific subtypes of inner speech.

As van Gogh's example shows, creative people leave other, more durable evidence of their thought processes. I know that when I am working on a creative problem I am constantly asking myself questions and then answering them. My fiction notebooks are full of snippets of private dialogue. Many other writers have discovered the benefit of conducting a conversation with themselves on the page. The psychologist Vera John-Steiner analyzed the notebooks of a variety of original thinkers, finding evidence of cryptic, condensed utterances to the self, which often showed many of the features of abbreviated thought to accompany inner speech. For example, she quoted a passage from Virginia Woolf's notebooks:

> Suppose I make a break after H.'s death (madness). A separate paragraph quoting what R. himself said. Then a break. Then begin definitely with the first meeting. That is the first impression: a man of the world, not professor or Bohemian . . .
>
> Give the pre-war atmosphere. Ott. Duncan. France.
>
> Letter to Bridges about beauty and sensuality. His exactingness. Logic.

Woolf's first "Suppose I . . ." is a question addressed to the self: following the question, still in her handwriting, are possible answers. They show all the qualities of compression and abbreviation that we see in James Joyce's fictional depictions of inner speech. As we'll see later, Woolf was not averse to talking to herself out loud as she worked on a problem in her fiction; here we see that her dialogic inner speech found another external expression, in this case on the crowded pages of her notebook.

Perhaps there's a way of understanding writers' notebooks as a condensed version of the kind of expanded creative dialogue that is in evidence in van Gogh's letters to his brother. In whichever form we do it, there are good psychological reasons why conducting dialogues on the page might benefit the creative process. If I'm doing my thinking in writing, as opposed to silently in my head, it will have the benefit of reducing my processing costs, particularly the demand on working memory. For one thing, if I've written my question down, I don't have to divert mental resources toward holding it in memory while I think of how to answer it. The notebook page becomes an external version of the "open slot" in which we park a perspective while generating a response to it. Giving our thoughts a material, external form helps to cut down the amount of work we need to do to process them. Something similar happens when we think out loud in private speech. Rather than having to hold a perspective silently in my head, I can voice it out loud and know that it will resonate for a while in my auditory memory. Speaking our thoughts aloud, like writing them down, appears to be a handy way of cutting down the resource costs of doing it all in inner speech.

That issue of processing cost may be the secret to understanding the power of dialogic thinking. Creativity involves bringing bits of information to bear on a problem that may not be obviously relevant (thinking about a tack box as a candleholder, for example). As soon as you express one perspective in words, you drastically constrain the range of possible dialogic responses to it. Conversations have to be about the same thing, or they are not really conversations. The philosopher Daniel Dennett illustrates this point by asking, "Have you ever danced with a movie star?" To answer this question, you don't have to run through a list of every single person you have ever danced with, and check to see whether any of them are Hollywood A-listers. You simply have to put the idea out there, in a question aimed at yourself, and then answer it, through what Dennett describes as "relatively effortless and automatic" reasoning processes.

It may be that something about the linguistic act of posing a question to yourself can make your intentions about what you are planning usefully clear. The linguistic structure of Woolf's self-questioning "Suppose I . . ." might have nudged her into being more determined about what she really wanted from the work she was thinking through, possibly more than she would have been if she had simply declared the thought as a statement ("I shall . . ."). This idea was tested in a study by the psychologist Ibrahim Senay and his colleagues at the University of Illinois at Urbana Champaign. They gave participants a task involving solving anagrams, but asked them to prepare for it in silence, either by asking themselves questions about what they were about to do, or simply by making statements about it. When they were instructed to question themselves silently, the volunteers solved more anagrams than when they merely declared their plans to themselves in inner speech. The researchers concluded that quizzing yourself in self-talk can push you beyond what you might otherwise achieve if your inner speech is full of bald statements of intention.

Writing novels and solving anagrams are of course tasks that involve manipulating language. The striking thing about van Gogh's example is that he was using language to create works in a visual medium. But words can do that. Some have argued that language has a special ability to integrate streams of information that would ordinarily be processed by separate cognitive systems. For example, data about geometry (how objects are laid out relative to each other) are thought to be processed by a cognitive "module" that is entirely different from the system that processes, say, color. In which case, how are we ever able to integrate the two kinds of information? As an illustration, think about how you might use data about color to help you to navigate around an environment, such as in processing an instruction like "Turn left at the red house." If two completely different modules are involved, how do we get them talking to each other?

One answer is that we use verbal thinking. At least one study has shown that, if you block their inner speech, participants lose the ability to achieve this kind of integration. Preventing people from using self-directed speech has also been shown to affect people's more basic perceptual abilities. When volunteers were asked to search for a particular object among an array, such as a selection of items on a supermarket shelf, they did better if they spoke the items' names aloud as they were doing so, at least if the items were reasonably familiar. Something similar seems to apply to the ability to sort objects into categories according to color, for example, while ignoring other properties of the object, such as shape. It doesn't follow from this observation that the language you speak can actually change the categories through which you perceive the world, as versions of the controversial "linguistic relativity hypothesis" propose. Rather, it suggests that directing language at yourself can make it easier to operate with the categories you already possess.

All of this points to a role for inner speech in processing kinds of information that would seem to have nothing to do with language. We've seen that self-directed speech has a role in planning behavior and in controlling it when it is in progress. What's at stake here is whether we can go a step further, and say that inner speech can tie together aspects of our cognition that might otherwise remain separate. That's a view that some researchers, like the philosopher Peter Carruthers of the University of Maryland, have arrived at. Carruthers has proposed that inner speech is a kind of *lingua franca* in the brain, able to integrate the outputs of systems that would otherwise remain relatively autonomous. If that view is correct, it might explain how van Gogh's words could get some traction on the visual images he must have been manipulating as he planned his compositions. The pictures spoke the language of his inner speech.

IT's TIME TO TAKE stock of what we've learned so far about the voices in our heads. It seems that inner speech is nowhere near the ubiquitous phenomenon that some have proposed it to be, but it does feature significantly in many people's experience, and it seems to play several different roles in our thinking. It can help us to plan what we are about to do and to regulate a course of action once it has started; it can give us a boost in keeping information in mind about what we are supposed to be doing, and in psyching ourselves up for action in the first place. For many of us, it provides a central thread to our conscious experience and is integral to the sense that we have a coherent, enduring self. But inner speech also contains multitudes. Many of its varied qualities seem to betray its origins in out-loud conversations with others, as well as reflecting predictable similarities with external speech. When we need to, we can save on processing resources by going back to our childhood mode of talking to ourselves aloud, and even conduct a conversation with ourselves on the pages of a notebook.

It's that dialogic quality of inner speech that is the most obvious sign of its social origins. Self-talk gives us a perspective on ourselves that might be a key ingredient for thinking in a flexible, open-ended manner. We can give voice to a point of view on what we are doing, and we can respond to that point of view in the give-and-take of a dialogue. That *dialogicality* helps to explain why inner speech takes the different forms that it does, from condensed and telegraphic at one moment, to a full-blown internal conversation at the next. Most of all, it starts to make sense of the multiplicity of who we are. The polyphonic nature of our inner speech makes it possible for writers to "play" their multivoiced compositions in our minds, allowing us to explore the boundaries of the self safely. And the uses of inner speech are not restricted to tasks that involve language. Inner speech may have a special role to play in tying together the outputs of our minds that might otherwise remain separate, contributing to the distinctive multimedia quality of our stream of consciousness.

We are also getting closer to understanding how inner speech might work in the brain. Earlier we saw evidence of an underlying structure—a pattern of interaction among distinct neural networks— that might underlie the ability to engage in internal dialogue. When

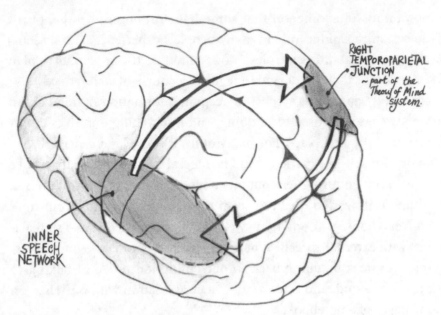

FIGURE 2: Interaction between the inner speech network and the social cognition system of the right hemisphere.

my colleagues and I scanned people's brains while they were doing dialogic inner speech, we found activation in the left inferior frontal gyrus, a region typically implicated in inner speech. But we also found right hemisphere activation close to a region known as the temporoparietal junction (TPJ) (see Figure 2). As discussed previously, that's an area that is typically associated with thinking about other people's minds, and it wasn't activated when people were thinking monologically.

These are early days for this research, but the interaction between the inner-speech and theory-of-mind networks may turn out to be the neural basis of dialogic thinking. The social cognition system provides the structure necessary for representing an alternative perspective: the "open slot" of inner dialogue. A perspective is generated—an opening gambit for the dialogue—and placed in the open slot. Another perspective is then articulated in the inner-speech system to "answer" that perspective. The new perspective then moves to the open slot while a continuing perspective is being articulated, and so on. Two established networks are harnessed for the purpose of responding to the mind's responses in an interaction that is neatly cost-effective in terms of processing resources. Instead of speaking endlessly without expectation of an answer, the brain's work blooms into dialogue.

8

Not I

"HE'S DIFFERENT."

The speaker is a woman with an educated English accent. A doctor type. She sounds familiar, but he also knows that he only heard her voice once, in a phone conversation he had seven or so years ago. He hears her voice distinctly, as if there were someone standing there in the room. Knowing the speaker, but not yet finished with the process of inferring her identity. In fact, it takes a second or two for him to work out whether this whole thing really happened. The voice came from outside, from the street outside the Wetherspoons pub he was sitting in, which puts her physical location at least fifteen feet away. What kind of voice can speak at you through a plate-glass window, with no loss of volume?

"And the *he* is you?"

He is always "he." They speak about him in the third person, like you might talk about someone making a fool of himself on the street. Knowing of course that the object of their attention can hear them. That's the point.

"That's me, yeah."

"And what did *different* mean, do you know?"

"Maybe different to what I make out to people, or to what people know about me? That's what I think the voice meant."

When the beep happened, Jay was sitting at a table in the pub, engrossed in the screenplay he is writing. He tells us that he had been concentrating on writing in order to block out the sound of the voices he had been hearing that morning. Paradoxically, background noise makes them louder, as though they are fighting to gain attention above the hubbub.

"It almost sounds like *you're* trying to work out what was meant by that . . ."

"Yeah, it's almost like I have to interpret what the voices say, you know, in a kind of metaphorical way?"

Ben is leading the interviewing. It's a summer's day, the windows are open, and we can hear the sounds of happy students on Durham's Palace Green.

"So right in the moment of *he's different*, you don't necessarily know what the voice is talking about?"

"Yeah, that's right. I don't know at that point when the beep goes off."

Ben asks Jay how he knew that this was his usual voice. He hears three main voices, he tells us; they are familiar and instantly recognizable. This particular voice is always the same.

"It sounds like it's older than me . . . you know, with a kind of middle-class accent. Kind of an intelligent voice. . . . It's always a reflective tone, like it's having a conversation. It never shouts or anything."

Russ asks about this paradoxical quality of the voice, whose volume is apparently increased by the background noise going on around. Is it as though the speaker herself is raising her voice, in order to improve her chances of getting heard, or is it like the volume being turned up on an amplifier, with no change to the voice's acoustic qualities? Russ illustrates his point by getting up from his chair, going out of the room, and closing the door while continuing to speak to us. We can still hear his laid-back midwestern accent, but his voice is of course muffled and diminished. He wants to illustrate how the acoustic qualities of his voice are changed by the barrier of the wooden door.

"The quality of the voice is not changed," Jay says as Russ returns. "It's not shouting, but it sounds loud, because around me there's a lot of noise."

The fact that Jay can hear the voice clearly, from fifteen feet away through a plate-glass window, is one of the ways he has learned to tell that it is one of his voices he is hearing, and not the sound of an actual person. There's no question that the voices are "real"—they are a meaningful aspect of his experience—it's just that they don't have any physical substance to them. On a cognitive level, he has no problem recognizing that.

"The fact that it's physically outside of Wetherspoons, I can't see it, yet it sounds loud. . . . Part of me senses there's a presence of a voice there, but I know there's nobody there as well."

Through cognitive behavioral therapy (usually known by its abbreviation CBT), Jay has been learning these ways of applying rationality to his own experiences. CBT has taught him to "deconstruct" his voices, to understand the psychological and emotional processes that lead him to experience them. The beep has caught him in the moment of making those attributions: bringing what he has learned about his experience to the business of interpreting that odd perception. CBT has helped him to realize that the belief that naturally follows the perception—that there is someone out there on the street outside Wetherspoons, talking to him—is actually a delusion. Recognizing the ungroundedness of such beliefs is a big part of the therapeutic process. Usually when Jay hears one of his voices, he now recognizes its way of speaking, infers that he is having another of his anomalous experiences, and concludes that he shouldn't trust it as a true perception.

But that's a process that takes time. Not much time, but enough to pull apart the links of his reasoning and allow the temporal precision of DES to bite. In the moment of consciousness that we are investigating—the moment before the beep sounds in his ear—he has not yet rationalized his experience. It's almost embarrassing for Jay to admit it, but, at the exact moment the beep went off, it did sound to him as though there were someone there.

"And someone there in a visual way?" Russ asks. "Do you see this person?"

Jay tells us that he has never seen the voice—nor has he had any other visual hallucinations. I ask him whether the experience feels like it could be a memory. Jay's response surprises me: "Yeah, it is a memory. . . . I'd spoken to this person on the phone who was a doctor, and the voice sounds like the person I spoke to on the phone. The voice has never changed."

So this person who is inhabiting his mind has taken the auditory form of an anonymous doctor he spoke to seven years ago. A woman who was not significant in his life, but whose voice has been appropriated by someone—or something—that is. Jay links the content of the voice—that enigmatic utterance, "He's different"—to how he was perceived by his family as a child. His mother and grandmother had a critical attitude toward him and made him out to be a certain way, and the voice was contradicting this: "He's not who all you people make him out to be. He's different." Jay doesn't find it unusual that his mental interlocutors should come to his defense like this. "The voices, to me, aren't always negative. I can find them quite useful, actually."

Ben asks Jay about his earlier comment about feeling the voice's presence. What is that like?

"It feels like they are people. I do understand that these voices are not the voices of anybody actually, you know, they *are* voices. And probably the voices are composites of different people I've known through my life, although they might sound like a particular person. But it does actually physically feel to me that there is someone standing there."

"And what's that physical feeling like?"

"Well, just as I'm sitting in this room and I'm talking to you, one understands that there are three other people in the room. You know, other people. The sense of knowing that there is somebody there? I don't know how to put that in better words, but that's what the experience of hearing a voice is like."

Ben relates it to his own personal "awareness" that I am sitting in the room alongside him, even if he turns his back on me and thus can't see or hear me. "It's not like there is anything in my experience of Charles," he says, "other than maybe the knowledge that he is there."

"Mm, and that's what it's like when you hear a voice. . . . It's an experiential thing. You feel uncomfortable. But then I have to step back from it and deconstruct it, and realize it is just a voice. It's an active process, deconstructing it."

One of the many fascinating things that emerges from talking to Jay is that the feeling of presence seems to dissociate from the experience of hearing the voice. Sometimes there's a voice without the corresponding feeling of presence; at other times there's a presence but no voice. Today, for example, Jay could hear the doctor voice out on the street, and could also feel that she was there, the way you know someone is standing behind you in a room when your eyes are closed. But there is another voice there as well, on the street outside Wetherspoons. At the moment of the beep, he was sensing the presence of both voices, but only one of them was speaking.

"And are they in the same place?"

"Yeah, they're both standing outside on the street, next to each other."

They're usually together like that, Jay tells us, sometimes along with his third main voice. That's a different female voice, nagging, aggressive, and smothering. She only appears when Jay is upset. Jay calls her the Witch. But he hasn't heard her today.

On another occasion in our DES sampling, Jay told us about hearing the Witch's voice but not feeling her presence. Jay was on his way to Durham when the train went through a tunnel and the carriage was plunged into darkness. He heard the Witch saying, "But I tried to make him feel important." Angry that his jealous, negative voice was claiming credit for trying to help him, Jay was shouting back, "Oh fuck off, you didn't!" No words were passing his lips: the yell was an internal one. The voice was coming from in front of him in the train compartment, about fifteen feet away. As with the Wetherspoons voice, it was experienced as loud—loud enough to be heard over the noises of the train—but it was not shouting. Although Jay heard the unpleasant female voice on this occasion, he didn't sense that she was present. His two other voices, in contrast, were present, but they were not saying anything.

What is a voice that does not speak?

Jay's experiences have changed over the years. He heard his first voice when he was fifteen, after a spell of treatment at an anorexia clinic. It was the voice of his doctor, calling his name and encouraging him to eat. It was a one-off. He heard nothing more until he was nineteen, following the death of his grandmother, with whom he had a very close relationship. After that, there was nothing until he was twenty-four and he heard the female doctor voice for the first time; the other two voices arrived around the same time. He left his job as a bartender and went back to working as a dance instructor. The voices continued. They were baffling and disorienting, particularly when he was trying to teach a class. Jay began to drink heavily in the evenings in an attempt to suppress the voices and get some sleep. In the end they were keeping him awake continually. He remembers trying to prepare for a class on the top floor of a classroom building, standing at the front of the room and looking over at the window, and hearing the voices shouting up from the street. He has memories of sitting alone at his kitchen table, drinking, and hearing the same voices shouting up at him. Believing that there were people there, making these noises, and that they had followed him home.

After a week in which he stayed home from work, hiding from the voices, Jay admitted himself to the hospital and got a diagnosis of schizoaffective disorder. He was told he could be on long-term benefits. "They were just interested in giving me a label. And actually the label was very disabling, because then I saw myself as somebody who had an intractable psychiatric problem. . . . At that time, because I was surrounded by people with mental health problems, I started to believe that I had a terrible mental illness. I saw myself as being a schizophrenic at that point."

In the years since, Jay's diagnosis has changed. He has found a different psychiatrist and a private therapist who have helped him enormously. He still doesn't usually tell people that he hears voices—the other instructors at the dance school, for example. But he has developed his understanding of why he has these experiences and what they say about him, and he has learned to cope with them so well that he was recently discharged from psychiatric care. The voices never speak directly to him, but they converse with each other. They are always experienced as coming from outside his head, usually from the next room. They are not sensed in any other ways: there is no tactile element, or smell, or visual hallucination. Sometimes they can attach to other perceptual experiences. Hearing footsteps on the wooden floor in the flat above him, for example, he will sense that they are somehow connected to his voices, even though he knows rationally that they are the sound of real people, his neighbors, who have nothing to do with him.

Some days Jay doesn't hear his voices at all. If he had to put a number on it, he would say he probably hears them three or four days a week. They can last for a few minutes or for several hours. He is most likely to hear them when he is tired, or when he is drifting awake in the morning. They are usually triggered by something, sometimes even his own thoughts. The idea that he is going to hear a voice can be a self-fulfilling prophecy. Yesterday, for example, he had taken his DES beeper out when he was writing at the library, and he had the thought that he was now bound to hear a voice. He did. "It's almost like I can bring it on like that," he says. "I can make them happen." He has also gained, through CBT, some control over how he interacts with his voices. He talks to them silently, in his head, but never out loud. He sets aside half an hour or so each day, in the evening, when he will interact with them and engage them in conversation. That's one reason why hearing the voice of the Witch on the train was an uncommon experience. Usually, if he hears a voice outside the time he sets aside for talking to them, he can ignore it. But the Witch's utterance on this occasion was so irritating that Jay felt compelled to respond.

In the end, only a minority of Jay's DES beeps involve voices. For the rest of the time, his inner experience looks like anyone else's: there is quite a lot of ordinary inner speech, some sensory awareness, and so on. At one beep, for example, he was considering including a particular item in his screenplay, and he was silently asking himself, "Do I include this or not include it?" At the end of the sequence of sampling days, we asked Jay how he felt about the process. He told us that he had been encouraged over the years to think deeply about his voices, but never his ordinary inner experience. He had been worried that the beeper might catch the voices saying something that he wouldn't feel comfortable sharing with us, but that hasn't happened. "I have recorded absolutely accurately what I have heard, and I've felt comfortable with doing that." The voices haven't commented on his participation in the experiment, either. They're more worried about the screenplay he is writing. That's where he will name names. That's where he will set out how all this came about.

In any case, his voices need not have worried. Asking Jay to engage in experience sampling with us hasn't been a single-minded quest to catch those visitors to his consciousness (although we would of course have been interested in them had they chosen to speak up). Rather, we believe that as researchers we cannot fully understand an atypical experience like voice-hearing without understanding the typical experiences that provide its context. When someone reports hearing a voice, that person is (implicitly or explicitly) making a comparison. He or she is saying, "Here's this unusual thing in my experience, and it's different from what's typically there." But one cannot understand unusual things without knowing something about usual ones. Which is why we are asking Jay in such depth about every aspect of his experience, whether quotidian or bizarre. There is language in all of it, words sounding out in the head. What is the relationship between the ordinary voices of his consciousness—the utterances of his inner speech—and his three mysterious visitors? Asking that question turns out to tell us a great deal about the many different voices in our heads.

9

DIFFERENT VOICES

WHAT DO YOU THINK when you think of someone who hears voices? In Nathan Filer's prize-winning 2013 novel *The Shock of the Fall*, the diagnosis that the protagonist, Matt, has been landed with is so terrible that it cannot even be named: "I have an illness, a disease with the shape and sound of a snake." Everyone knows what schizophrenia is. For many, the sound of its sibilant label triggers fear and prejudice. Analyzing data from the 2006 US General Social Survey, a group of researchers found that nearly two-thirds of respondents said they would be unwilling to work with a person with the diagnosis, while 60 percent expected that someone with schizophrenia would be violent toward others. Looking back at the data from ten years earlier, the authors reported little change in attitudes. Although the 2006 respondents were more likely than their 1996 counterparts to attribute schizophrenia to a neurobiological cause, that shift in understanding seemed to have gone with an increase rather than a decrease in negative attitudes.

One problem is that "schizophrenia" is a highly misunderstood term, and one that functions differently in many different discourses. In the popular imagination it is often taken to refer to a split personality, of the kind that turned Dr. Jekyll into Mr. Hyde (and back again). There are various reasons for this misunderstanding, including the fact that the term does indeed literally mean "split mind," even when those who minted the word were trying to get at something more like "disconnection" or "shattering." The Swiss psychiatrist Eugen Bleuler coined the term in 1908 in an attempt to update the earlier concept of *dementia praecox*, which was characterized by delusions (persistent false beliefs) and hallucinations (compelling perceptual experiences in the absence of any external stimulus). By the middle of the twentieth century, with the publication of Kurt Schneider's analysis of the cardinal (or "first-rank") features of schizophrenia in his textbook *Clinical Psychopathology*, the disorder had become a cornerstone of Western psychiatry. Clinicians worked together to finesse its definition, and the quest to understand it scientifically became psychiatry's preeminent goal. "To know schizophrenia," wrote Roy Grinker, "is to know psychiatry." In Thomas Szasz's memorable phrase, schizophrenia became psychiatry's "sacred symbol."

For many reasons the monolith has crumbled in recent years, mostly owing to concerns over the construct's scientific validity. Nowadays, schizophrenia is more accurately seen as referring to a syndrome, or cluster of related conditions. For a long time characterized as a progressive brain disease (with the implication that there was a single biological process underlying it), schizophrenia is now viewed as a complex, varied disorder from which some individuals can make a full recovery. Experts now see the disorder as representing one end of a spectrum, or continuum, of symptoms and anomalous experiences. Finding a genetic basis for it has been a particularly thankless task, with one recent study reporting evidence that schizophrenia is actually a cluster of eight genetically distinct disorders. In the psychiatrist's "bible," the *Diagnostic and Statistical Manual of Mental Disorders* (*DSM*), the spectrum is divided into numerous subtypes, such as schizoaffective disorder and delusional disorder. What all have in common are "abnormalities" in one or more of five domains, including delusions, hallucinations, thought disorder, odd motor behaviors, and negative symptoms. The term "schizophrenia," along with its definition in the manual, continues to be highly controversial, and many advocate that it be replaced with the more neutral term "psychosis," although some have argued that replacing one vaguely specified cluster of disorders with another is hardly a sign of progress.

In plain terms, hearing voices when there is no one present is a psychotic experience, because it involves a break with reality. Other things we do also involve such a disconnect: dreaming or imagining, for example. But someone who is imagining is aware that what they are doing is a creative act: in psychiatric parlance, they have "insight" into what is happening to them. Dreaming, on the other hand, is not psychosis because it happens in the absence of full consciousness (with the possible exception of celebrated cases of "lucid dreaming," you can't really have insight if you are asleep). Technically speaking, a hallucination is born when an individual experiences a break with reality but lacks awareness of the fact that the experience was "unreal."

In reality, of course, things are much more complex. When a child hears the voice of her imaginary friend talking to her, she can be totally absorbed in the pretense; that insubstantial playmate is real for her. When someone is fully immersed in a movie or a book, something similar can happen. When Jay hears the voice of the Doctor, or when Adam, another voice-hearer, hears the authoritative voice he calls the Captain speaking to him, they are aware that what they are experiencing is one of their regular hallucinated voices. And yet the experience is still real for them. On some occasions, Jay will momentarily respond as though there is someone there actually speaking to him; the process of rationalizing it as a hallucination takes a little bit of cognitive work. Jay has insight into his experiences, but it does depend a bit on when you ask him about an experience, and where he is in the ongoing process of making meaning out of it. The *DSM*'s definition of a hallucination as "a perception-like experience with the clarity and impact of a true perception" is only useful up to a point.

As we shall see, the presence of insight is just one of the many ways in which voice-hearing experiences can vary. If auditory verbal hallucinations are a hallmark of schizophrenia, they are a many-colored one. But hearing voices is by no means restricted to schizophrenia. Voice-hearing is associated with a whole host of other psychiatric diagnoses, including epilepsy, substance abuse, posttraumatic stress disorder, Parkinson's disease, and eating disorders. Jay has had several different diagnoses over the years, his most recent being borderline personality disorder. The idea of hearing voices as "the sacred symbol of the sacred symbol"—the archetypal symptom of schizophrenia— seems problematic. Around three-quarters of people with a diagnosis of a schizophrenia spectrum disorder experience auditory verbal hallucinations, but so do a similar proportion of individuals with dissociative identity disorder (a condition in which people can express multiple personalities), around half of those diagnosed with posttraumatic stress disorder, and a smaller proportion of those with bipolar disorder. Voice-hearing can be highly distressing and debilitating, but it does not equate to schizophrenia.

In fact, voice-hearing does not even equate to madness. There is a certain history to the idea that hearing voices in the absence of any speaker can be a part of normal experience. A hundred and twenty years ago, the Society for Psychical Research in London set out to explore unusual experiences like voice-hearing in a sample of 17,000 members of the general public. "Have you ever," they asked, "when awake, had the impression of seeing or hearing or of being touched by anything which, so far as you could discover, was not due to any external cause?" Around 3 percent of respondents reported having heard voices. In the surveys that have been conducted since, population rates of voice-hearing experiences have ranged from 0.6 percent to 84 percent, depending on exactly what questions were asked. A reasonable estimate is that between 5 and 15 percent of ordinary people have had occasional or one-off voice-hearing experiences, with about 1 percent having experiences that are more complex and extended, without seeking psychiatric care.

Despite the fact that many of us appear to hear voices, the general perception of voice-hearing remains pretty negative. "But only crazy, dangerous people hear voices!" Victoria Patton is sometimes told. "You don't have to work with any of them, do you?" Victoria is communications officer for our Hearing the Voice project at Durham, and she has taken the lead in our outreach activities designed to reduce the stigma that is so often associated with this experience. "Unfortunately, that view is extremely widespread," Victoria told me. "We are trying to change this by raising public awareness of voice-hearing and getting people to understand that not all people who hear voices are mentally ill." There is still much to be done. When voice-hearing is mentioned in the media, it is almost universally in a context of loss of control, violence, and injury to self and others. When psychologist Ruvanee Vilhauer looked at a sample of nearly two hundred newspaper articles published during a one-year period in 2012–2013, she found that only a small percentage of them contained any suggestion that voice-hearing can be part of normal experience. Perhaps unsurprisingly, most media reports connected voice-hearing to mental illness, usually schizophrenia, with a minority recognizing that voice-hearing can occur in other disorders, too. More than half of the articles linked it to criminal behavior, mostly involving violent crimes. Just under half of the reports linked hearing voices to violence toward others, and just under a fifth made a connection to suicide or suicidality.

As the experience of people like Adam shows, misleading media representations don't just worsen the problem of stigma; they also negatively affect voice-hearers' own understandings of their experiences and themselves. Studies have shown that such self-perceptions can have pervasive influences, including lowering self-esteem, leading individuals to avoid treatment or to fail to adhere to it, and increasing the risk of hospitalization. "When you say you're a voice-hearer," Adam said in a radio interview, "people instantly think: *Ooh, possibly dangerous*. I'm not that person at all. Yes, just because somebody says horrible things within my head, it doesn't mean that I am that person."

ADAM WAS SPEAKING TO the broadcaster Sian Williams on BBC Radio 4's *Saturday Live* program. The interview had come about as a result of a film we had made with Adam about his experiences, which had been shown at a festival at the Barbican Centre in London. I traveled with Adam to Broadcasting House, also in London, for the interview, and watched him through the window of the control booth as he told a live radio audience what it is like to live with voices in your head.

It was an exceptionally sensitive and informative interview, conducted by someone with a deep understanding of the complexities of mental illness. At one point the conversation turned to the relationship between Adam's voices and his ordinary thoughts. "It's a cross between thoughts and speech," he said. "It becomes so confusing when you have it for so long. You're talking to yourself, but you're getting a response. You're talking to yourself, but you're getting asked questions. Which can be very difficult, because, say, if you think of something, you aren't sure if it's you who's thinking it. . . . I have another person living inside my head. . . . It isn't me, but it is me."

Are Adam's voices the strange result of some distortion of his ordinary internal conversation? Is he hearing utterances in his own inner speech that, for some reason, are perceived as coming from that "other person" living in his head? If so, what is it about the processing of inner speech that might have gone awry? Who, or what, do you hear when you hear a voice?

When I was first mulling over the ideas of Lev Vygotsky and Mikhail Bakhtin as a graduate student in 1990, it occurred to me that they might offer a new way of thinking about hallucinated voices. If children develop inner speech by internalizing external dialogue, there might be a phase—when internalization is not yet complete—in which their heads are full of bits of dialogue that have not yet been fully assimilated: voices, in other words. Coupled with the young child's relatively weak grasp of the distinction between fantasy and reality, this could result in experiences of hearing utterances that are not recognized as coming from the self. In turn, some developmental problem with this process could lead later to the full-blown experience of hearing voices.

When I turned back to this question after a decade or so of researching children's self-directed speech, I saw that people were indeed taking seriously the idea that voice-hearing might have something to do with verbal thought—and had been doing so for some time. In sixteenth-century Spain, St. John of the Cross presented an explanation for how divine voices could arise as a result of misattributed inner speech. Building on his predecessor St. Thomas Aquinas's view of thinking as "the interior word," St. John noted how novices at meditation could have the experience of a divine voice when, in fact, "it is for the most part they who are saying these things to themselves."

From its origins in European theology, this view later became established in the medical literature. In his 1886 book *Natural Causes and Supernatural Seemings*, the British psychiatrist Henry Maudsley wrote of "a vividly conceived idea which is so intense . . . that it is projected outwards into what seems an actual perception . . . in the case of hearing, an idea so intense as to become a voice." A century later, in the late 1970s, Irwin Feinberg proposed that auditory verbal hallucinations might arise as a result of a disorder to the brain systems that usually monitor which actions are self-produced. Like all good ideas, Feinberg's notion is at its heart a simple one. An individual generates an utterance in inner speech—the kind of ordinary internal conversation that has been our focus so far—but for some reason fails to recognize it as his own work. There are words in the head, but they don't feel like the words of the self. The individual experiences them as an utterance from without: a heard voice.

When I started my own investigation into the nature of inner speech in adults, psychiatry was an unfamiliar discipline to me. I had trained as a development psychologist and focused my research on babies and young children. In the United Kingdom, the United States, and many other countries, psychiatry is a branch of medicine, a specialty that people enter once they have finished training as a medical doctor. Psychologists like me can also study abnormal mental processes, and some specialize in clinical psychology in order to work with patients, but this was not an option I had personally pursued. Here were people in the psychiatry world talking about inner speech as the raw material of auditory verbal hallucinations. I had been studying the development of inner speech in childhood as possibly being a result of the internalization of private speech. Were we talking about the same thing?

Yes and no. The inner-speech theory of voice-hearing really became established in the 1990s with the work of Chris Frith and Richard Bentall, who, working independently, developed Feinberg's ideas in slightly different directions. In one research group, Frith and his colleagues at University College London were developing a theory that the symptoms of schizophrenia stemmed from a problem in monitoring one's own actions. In an early study from their group, patients with the diagnosis did not do as well as a control group in a task that involved correcting the errors they made when moving a joystick. The idea was that, if you had a problem in monitoring your own behavior, you might fail to recognize some of the actions that you yourself produced as being your own work. And that could include inner speech: the words you produced, for yourself, in your own head.

In Liverpool, a team that Bentall led was investigating whether auditory verbal hallucinations could be understood in terms of a problem in monitoring the source of information. A similar idea had proved very powerful in the study of memory, where it was used as a basis for explaining why people sometimes confused memories of what actually happened with the products of imagining what *might* have happened. The theory proposes that, in working out whether an internal representation is a memory or not, we go through a forensic process of drawing together lots of different varieties of information (about how vivid the representation is, how easily it comes to mind, and so on) and ultimately decide whether the event really happened or not.

Bentall applied this approach to voice-hearing by asking people to detect a signal embedded in a masking stimulus, such as a bit of speech played against a background of white noise. In a number of studies using such "signal-detection" tasks, psychiatric patients who hear voices have proved more likely to judge that speech is present even when it is not. If you have a bias toward judging internal experiences as coming from out there in the world, you may be more likely to say that an element of inner speech had an external origin (in other words, to say that it had been produced by another individual) than to say that it had an internal one (that is, to correctly identify it as a self-generated bit of inner speech).

A particularly strong demonstration of this bias came from a study by Louise Johns and Philip McGuire at the Institute of Psychiatry in London. They worked with three samples of people: schizophrenia patients with hallucinations, schizophrenia patients without hallucinations, and people with no psychiatric illness. Participants were asked to read single adjectives aloud into a microphone at the same time as listening to some speech through headphones. On some trials a participant would hear his or her own voice, which had been distorted by having its pitch dropped by a few semitones; on other occasions the same participant would hear the voice of someone else (either distorted or unmodified). The participants who had experienced hallucinations were more likely than the participants from either of the other two groups to attribute their own distorted speech to another person. This finding supported the idea that such individuals have a specific difficulty keeping track of the sources of their own internal experiences. A person who shows a bias toward saying "That came from outside," rather than "That came from within," is arguably more likely to misattribute a bit of his or her own inner speech to an external voice.

Another line of evidence for the inner-speech theory comes from the study of the physiological changes that take place during the voice-hearing experience. In the late 1940s, the American psychiatrist Louis Gould showed, using a technique known as electromyography, that the onset of schizophrenia patients' hallucinations coincided with an increase in tiny movements in the muscles associated with vocalization, particularly in the lips and chin. In one extraordinary case study from 1981, Paul Green and Martin Preston recorded the faint whispers produced by a middle-aged male patient as he was hallucinating, which came from a female voice he knew as

"Miss Jones." Amplifying the signals electronically and playing them back to him, Green and Preston were able to orchestrate a dialogue, at normal speaking volume, between the patient and his hallucinated voice. Peter Bick and Marcel Kinsbourne later showed that asking hallucinating patients simply to open their mouths when the voices were occurring made the voices stop. The authors argued that mouth-opening prevented the faint subvocalization movements that accompany inner speech, thus blocking the raw material of the hallucination.

Each of these inner-speech accounts of voice-hearing faces serious problems. For one thing, all rely on a rather limited conception of inner speech. Like the neuroimaging studies we encountered earlier, they have tended to treat inner speech as a monolithic thing, something like silent rote repetition, that doesn't admit of varied forms. What struck me most, coming to this research from the outside, was that attempts to understand voice-hearing in terms of inner-speech processes had suffered from a lack of any particularly deep thinking about what kind of thing inner speech is, how it develops, and what functions it serves. When we start taking inner speech more seriously as an internal conversation with the self, its relation to voice-hearing begins to make much more sense.

THERE IS A COMPELLING plausibility to the idea that voice-hearers like Adam or Jay are experiencing a distorted fragment of inner dialogue that somehow doesn't sound as if it is coming from the self. To see how this might work, take, as an example, an ordinary bit of internal conversation. The thinker is the celebrated physicist Richard Feynman, who is describing how he conducts arguments with himself in solving scientific problems: "The integral will be larger than this sum of the terms, so that would make the pressure higher, you see?" "No, you're crazy." "No, I'm not! No, I'm not!" Imagine one-half of this dialogue being for some reason experienced as not coming from the self—perhaps the phrase "No, you're crazy." It's easy to see how those words might present themselves to the thinker as the utterance of a hallucinated voice.

Now consider an example from the clinical literature. A patient approaches a vending machine in a hospital. "Should I get a Coke or a cup of water?" he thinks. As if in response, a voice resounds in his head: "You should get the water." The clinicians Aaron Beck and Neil Rector interpreted this moment as the transformation of one side of an internal dialogue into a hallucination. The self speaks to the self, but one-half of the exchange seems anything but self-derived. In other examples from Beck and Rector's clinical work, the more permissive voice in the internal conversation takes on the alien quality of a heard voice. The same patient was sitting in the group room of the hospital when he had the thought "I shouldn't eat another snack." Immediately he heard a voice saying, "You should eat the snack."

Other examples from Beck and Rector describe the emergence of more critical voices. A patient was rushing to get ready for college when she thought, "I'm going to be late and my friends will be disappointed." She then heard a voice saying, "You think too much. . . . [Y]ou are too rigid." If this was a distorted internal dialogue, she was perhaps hearing something like the voice of a Faithful Friend. Another patient was trying to solve a math problem when he thought, "I'll never get it." "But you're a genius," the voice in his head said.

Thinking about voice-hearing in terms of inner speech has proved useful, but paying attention to its dialogic quality breaks it open in fascinating ways. In my first article on this topic, I proposed that one reason why inner-speech theories had not made further progress in explaining voice-hearing was that they had not taken inner speech seriously enough as a phenomenon. Instead of struggling to explain what all these alien utterances are doing in a patient's head, a Vygotskian account shows us how our heads are already full of other voices. If we take dialogicality seriously, we can use the inner speech model to explain how those inner voices might be perceived as coming from another person, complete with the person-specific properties—such as timbre, tone, and accent—that make the other voice sound different from the hearer's own voice. When you talk to people who hear voices, you frequently hear them describing this "alien yet self" quality. They recognize that the experience is ultimately coming from their own brains, but they say that it nevertheless *feels* strange and foreign. Vygotsky's ideas also force us to think about how inner speech can take different forms: at one moment it might be tightly condensed and note-like, while at another it is expanded into a full-blown internal conversation. Both of these qualities of inner speech—dialogicality and condensation—had been ignored by standard inner-speech models of voice-hearing.

I proposed that the key to understanding voice-hearing was not to do away with the inner speech model, but to furnish it with a richer conception of internal self-talk as a dialogue between different internalized voices. Central to the model was the idea that, in our ordinary inner speech, we can move flexibly between expanded and condensed forms. Usually that movement is experienced as a seamless transition between note-form inner speech and full inner dialogue. In people who hear voices, something unusual might happen where condensed inner speech is "re-expanded" to form a fully articulated inner dialogue. A conversation with the self that would ordinarily be stripped down and compressed suddenly blooms into diverse voices.

Testing these ideas scientifically requires us to rethink what we understand by "typical" inner experience in both voice-hearers and non-voice-hearers. For one thing, we need to ask about the ordinary inner experience of people who experience auditory verbal hallucinations. A couple of studies have looked at varieties of inner speech in typical undergraduate samples, linking them to participants' proneness to hear voices. In the study I conducted with Simon McCarthy-Jones, we found four main themes in the inner speech reported by two samples of undergraduates (recall that we named these *dialogic, condensed, other people,* and *evaluative*). In the same study we gave participants a standard self-report questionnaire on their proneness to auditory hallucinations. Combining the data from the inner-speech questionnaire with the figures on hallucination proneness, we found that people's likelihood of reporting auditory hallucinations was predicted by the amount of dialogicality in their inner speech: those who more strongly endorsed the dialogic items were more likely to report auditory hallucination-like experiences. At least in healthy undergraduates, a more conversational, back-and-forth style of self-talk seems to go with a greater likelihood of hearing voices sounding out in the head.

How does the picture look when you ask voice-hearing psychiatric patients about their inner speech? We were able to begin to address this question in the study conducted at Macquarie University with schizophrenia patients. In the interviews, we asked patients not only about their voices, but also about their internal self-talk. Although there were no significant differences, on the whole, between the quality of the patients' inner speech compared to non-patient controls, the patients were slightly less likely to report having dialogic inner speech. A limitation of this study is that the interview that we gave patients about their voices was not as detailed as the questionnaire that we developed subsequently. Recently, Paolo de Sousa at the University of Liverpool administered our instrument to a sample of patients with schizophrenia, finding that patients did not rate the dialogicality of their inner speech any differently from control participants—thereby supporting the findings of the Macquarie University study that there wasn't much of a difference between patients and non-patients in this respect. However, the schizophrenia patients did score higher on the condensation subscale of our questionnaire: they were more likely to report their inner speech as having a compressed, note-form quality. This finding implies that less of their inner speech would have had an expanded quality, fitting with the idea that such inner speech is attributed differently in such individuals, sometimes, perhaps, as voices.

Much more needs to be done in finding out about regular inner speech in patient and non-patient samples. It's possible that the varied qualities of inner speech relate to voice-hearing differently in those who are ill compared to those who do not seek help for voices. Another problem concerns why voice-hearers report any ordinary inner speech at all. If auditory verbal hallucinations are misattributed inner speech, then why isn't *all* inner speech perceived as an external voice? You certainly wouldn't expect internal conversation to look so normal in patients who hear voices. Jay, for example, reported plenty of ordinary-looking inner speech in his DES interviews, such as saying to himself, "I hope I'm going to get all these forms signed," when mulling over a particular workload challenge.

There are reasons, however, to suspect that inner speech in patients who hear voices might have particularly developed acoustic properties. A study by Frank Larøi at the University of Liège showed that about 40 percent of a sample of voice-hearing schizophrenia patients rated their thoughts as having some sound-like properties, such as pitch or accent. In comparison, the figure for healthy controls was more like 20 percent. One patient described an inner dialogue that became more pronounced just before his voices started. He sensed "thoughts, like a voice, talking to you in your head. . . . [I]t is normal to have an internal dialogue, only mine is more pronounced."

All of this points to the need for closer attention to phenomenology. We have to ask the "What is it like?" questions across the different diagnoses in which voice-hearing occurs, and then extend that inquiry further to include voice-hearing in people who do not seek psychiatric help. As we'll see, the results of such inquiries show that voice-hearing is a diverse experience, and understanding it requires that we pay attention to that diversity, rather than lumping together experiences that might be very different. We need to give the same attention to those "What is it like?" questions when we think about ordinary inner experience: not just because it is interesting and important in its own right, but because it helps us to understand the typical inner experiences against which unusual experiences, such as voice-hearing, are understood.

If voices derive from inner speech, then it makes sense to ask whether the two things show some similarities. Asking the "What is it like?" questions is not easy, especially when the experiences are so often associated with confusion and distress. But the right approach can reveal a rich phenomenology. From the earliest days of psychiatry, heard voices have been described in limitlessly varied ways. Voices abuse, threaten, and command, but they also encourage and support. They speak in single words and complex sentences; they whisper, shout, mumble, and intone. One fact in our favor is that the experience has happened to some of the most remarkable writers and thinkers in history. If we want to know what hearing voices is like, we can do worse than look into the past.

10

THE VOICE OF A DOVE

THE YOUNG WARRIOR WAS FURIOUS. The king of the Mycenaeans had gone too far. All of his stubbornness over the release of the captured Chryseïs had been amply punished by the plague sent by Apollo. The Greek army was on its knees. Achilles had made the mistake of suggesting to the assembly that this might be the time to return home and give up the siege of Troy. The angry king had finally agreed to return the woman, but only in exchange for the young warrior's own trophy, the beautiful Briseïs. Just as Achilles was wondering whether to strike Agamemnon dead there and then, the gray-eyed goddess Athena came down from heaven, caught him by his yellow hair, and urged restraint. His anger checked, Achilles pushed his sword back into its scabbard. "Obey the gods," he replied to the vision, "and they will hear you well."

Now fast-forward a few years (and most likely a few decades of literary history, given what we know about the dates of composition of the texts). Another Greek warrior, Odysseus, has found his way home from the Trojan campaign after a convoluted ten-year journey, only to find his wife, Penelope, besieged by unruly suitors. Furious at the liberties they have been taking in his house, Odysseus hatches a plan to deal with them. "There he stood and kept the firelight high / and looked the suitors over, while his mind / roamed far ahead to what must be accomplished." As in many other places in the *Odyssey*, the hero is faced with a tricky problem, and he is seen thinking things through just like a regular modern guy.

When the going gets tough, the Achilles of the *Iliad* hears the voices of the gods. Odysseus, in the later poem, thinks things through for himself. This apparent disparity between the two classic texts of Greek antiquity formed the basis of an extraordinary 1976 book by the Princeton psychologist Julian Jaynes, which still features regularly in many conversations about voice-hearing. The book was *The Origin of Consciousness in the Breakdown of the Bicameral Mind*, and it proposed that about a thousand years before the Christian era— that is, around the time of the composition of the *Iliad*—human brains were effectively split in two. The term "bicameral" means "two-chambered," and in this case it refers to a schism between the two cerebral hemispheres, which are joined not only by a structure known as the corpus callosum, but also by other structures, including a smaller, more tenuous bridge of nerve fibers called the anterior commissure. Ordinary speech was produced in the left hemisphere, consistent with current neuroscientific evidence that, for most right-handed people, language processes are concentrated on the left of the brain. But the right side of the brain has the same language-making structures as its counterpart on the other side, housed in the inferior frontal and superior temporal gyri. Jaynes argued that it was this side of the brain that "spoke" in times of cognitive challenge, such as when an individual (like Achilles) was faced with a choice for which a habitual response would not suffice. The signal was passed from these right hemisphere areas to the anterior commissure, and was thus transmitted to the left hemisphere, Jaynes said, where it resonated as language. But because the people of that time lacked self-awareness, those messages weren't experienced as the "language of man." They were perceived as the voices of the gods.

By the time the *Odyssey* was composed (thought to be around the eighth century BC), sociopolitical changes, along with the invention of writing, had led to the two chambers of the brain becoming more integrated. The voices of the gods became the utterances of inner speech. Odysseus makes decisions for himself, and he thinks them through in his own language. The gods still appear to him—there is a memorable scene where he uses his new mental powers to play games with the fiery Athena—but they do not have a hotline into his brain in the way they did during the Trojan campaign. The two Homeric texts, in Jaynes's words, represent "a gigantic vault in mentality." The implications of his analysis are still resonating, but they can be summed up simply: Before around 1200 BC, ordinary people did not talk to themselves in inner speech. They experienced a continual auditory verbal hallucination, which for cultural reasons was attributed to supernatural beings. Hearing voices was a basic condition of human existence.

Jaynes's neuroscientific analysis makes many contemporary scientists wince. The idea of the two hemispheres having different "personalities" is far too simplistic, and it does not do justice to the immensely complicated literature on brain lateralization. While it's true that "split-brain" patients, who have had the corpus callosum surgically removed, can appear to have two hemispheres functioning relatively independently, it is inconceivable that such a gross structural change could have happened in the human brain within the past three millennia.

Jaynes's literary analysis has its weak spots, too. Some scenes in the *Iliad*, such as Hector's decision to take on Achilles, seem to be classic cases of conscious, and even verbally mediated, volition. "But he spoke in dismay to his own great heart," the *Iliad* tells us. "Such were his thoughts as he waited." Indeed, in the same section at the opening of the poem in which Athena appears to Achilles—which Jaynes holds up as a prime example of the lack of consciousness and introspection among the characters in the *Iliad*—the warrior is described as being "torn in thought" and "pondering" his actions "in his mind and his heart." Within a few lines of the hallucination of Athena, Achilles is doing something very much like ordinary thought.

For all its flaws, Jaynes's analysis makes us think hard about how we should make sense of accounts of inner speech and voice-hearing that come to us from the distant past. If Jaynes is wrong about those massive structural brain changes occurring in our relatively recent history, we need to ask why the authors of the *Iliad* chose to depict ordinary inner speech in that way. In that sense, Jaynes's book prompts us to consider whether the ancient Greeks might have thought about their inner experience in ways quite different from how we think about our inner experience today. They did, after all, have quite different views on cosmology and metaphysics, the existence and potency of supernatural entities, and the relations of the individual to society. Why should they have settled on modern-sounding views of inner speech as the outputs of "a voice in the head"?

It's equally important that we situate accounts of voice-hearing in their historical context. Rather than asking whether the *Iliad* "proves" that the ancients heard voices, we should ask how more firmly grounded accounts of voice-hearing might have been portrayed. If voice-hearing really is a pervasive aspect of human experience, we should find testimonies of it appearing through the ages.

There are dangers, though, in trying to work with historical accounts of private, subjective experiences like voice-hearing. Mass literacy is an invention of the modern world, and many of the people whose experiences we might be most interested in would have been unable to read or write. Their testimonies are therefore usually filtered through the belief system and sensibility of someone who could do those things: usually a holy man, such as a monk or a priest. These accounts were often highly distorted and fictionalized. We are naturally also limited to artifacts that have survived and can now be interpreted, which, as we go further and further back in time, are represented in dwindling numbers.

Take the example of one of the most famous voice-hearers of antiquity, the philosopher Socrates. Socrates himself left no writings, so we rely on the testimony of his pupils and followers, who offer us sometimes contradictory views of the great philosopher's experience. Socrates's pupil Plato, for example, observed that the voice that his master had heard from childhood was always negative and critical, never positive; while Xenophon, another pupil of Socrates, depicted the philosopher's voice as guiding and constructive. One modern scholar makes sense of this discrepancy by proposing that Socrates would have been more likely to hear his "sign," or voice, when the going got tough: in the parlance of modern psychology, under conditions of stress and cognitive challenge.

Few doubt that Socrates was anything other than a shaper of modern thought, and remarks that he was a closet schizophrenic tend to be made ironically, to illustrate our culture's kneejerk association of voice-hearing with that disorder. For other historical figures who experienced similar things, a retrospective "diagnosis" has often not been far away. The prophet Ezekiel, for example, has been saddled with the label "schizophrenic" by some scholars who have interpreted his apparent episodes of thought insertion, thought broadcast, and voice-hearing (one estimate has him hearing the voice of God ninety-three times) without any reference to the spiritual beliefs that underpinned the prophet's experience, and without any attempt to understand the background of beliefs and assumptions against which those experiences were described and recorded. As the theologian and psychiatrist Chris Cook has noted, such retrospective diagnoses inevitably impose one framework of understanding—that of modern biomedical psychiatry—upon another, without paying enough attention to the context in which those experiences took place.

It is even more important that we act as conscientious visitors to the past when we are dealing with an experience as politically charged as voice-hearing, with all its resonances about ordinary mortals receiving direct communications from spiritual forces. Socrates's voice got him into big trouble: it was cited at his trial as evidence that he was guilty of the charge of impiety. Another historical voice-hearer, Joan of Arc, reported voices that spoke to her in French (not Latin, the official language of the Roman Catholic Church), and that apparently prevented her from disclosing certain "revelations about the king." Admitting to such experiences was a risky business. Hearing the voice of God could be a sign of divine communication, but not when He spoke to a lowly peasant girl. Joan's fate at the hands of her inquisitors is well known.

Although it demands caution, a historical approach to studying the voices in our heads might present them in an entirely new light. As long as we are careful to recognize the ways in which historical testimonies have been filtered through the experiences of others, and try to understand the reasons why they were written down in the first place, taking the long view can show us how attitudes toward the experience—from those of voice-hearers themselves to those of the people around them—have changed, and how they relate to the wider understandings of the society. If we tread carefully, we can catch those processes of meaning-making in action.

FORGIVE THESE MEN THAT DO ME PAIN. Christ asks the audience to behold his wounds. My head, my hands, my feet. Her Lord, or His image, had hung above her from the cross mounted on the wagon. She had wept at the scene, as she did at any reminder of Christ's Passion. Standing beside her, John had yelled at the soldiers. He showed his love for their Lord with a man's anger, at something precious being stolen away.

When the stone fell upon her in church she had thought that her back was broken. The pain was incredible. She feared she would be dead soon. She knew that others, the many in the congregation who doubted her, wanted to see her punished by God. But this wasn't God's vengeance. It was a test of her ability to endure suffering. The friar had had the stone weighed, along with the piece of the beam that fell with it. Master Aleyn said that it was a miracle that Margery had survived. Miraculous, too, how the Lord had taken away her suffering. She had cried out once—"Jesus, mercy"—and her pain had disappeared.

Her only pain now was this hunger and thirst. She had not eaten since York yesterday. She walked behind her husband on the hot, empty road. He had something on his mind.

"If a man were to ride here with a sword in his hand, and threaten to strike off my head if I did not make love to you now, what would you say?"

"I would say that I have kept myself free of it for two months, and I cannot understand why you're bringing it up now."

"I want to know what you'd say. You boast that you cannot tell a lie."

"You want the truth? I'd rather see you struck dead than lay a hand on me."

She weighed the beer bottle in her hand. It was a scorching June day and they had been walking all morning. She was so hot under her shirt. The hair it was woven from scratched and inflamed her flesh. It pleased God, though, that she wore it. She longed to drink from the bottle she was carrying, but it was His will that she would not touch it.

"You're not much of a wife," the man said.

"I'm taking a vow," she replied. "As soon as I can find a bishop to swear it to. How far is Bridlington?"

They stopped to rest at a cross by the roadside. Her husband sat down under it and called her to him.

"I'll leave your body alone," he said, "on three conditions. We go back to sharing a bed, without the sex. You sort out the problem about the money. And you give up all this fasting nonsense. In weather like this, you must at least drink."

He had a cake tucked against his chest inside his clothes. He was hiding it out of respect for her vow. He knew she was famished. He wanted to keep the temptation out of her way.

"No," she replied. "I've sworn an oath. I will not eat or drink on Fridays."

"I'm going to take what I want, then."

He stood up and started unfastening his clothes. She begged him first to let her pray. She went into a field and knelt by a cross and wept. She had prayed for three years to be left alone in celibacy, and now she had her chance to cement the deal. But the fasting was a promise she had made. She couldn't keep both vows. She prayed at the foot of the cross. Guide her, Jesus, and tell her what she should do.

And Christ spoke to her. She heard His voice as though there were someone standing next to her in the field, speaking from a short distance into her ear. It was sweet and gentle, the voice of a kindly man, but loud enough that, if anyone else had spoken to her at that moment, she would not have been able to follow them. The voice gave her a plan. She should ask her husband to keep his side of the bargain. John would swear to celibacy, and Margery would give up her fast. She should go to her husband now, eat the cake, and drink with him from the bottle of beer.

The year is 1413. Margery Kempe is traveling from York with John, her husband of twenty years. They have been to see the Corpus Christi plays, a cycle depicting Christ's Passion with a vividness that haunts her to her core. She has borne John fourteen children. The daughter of a former mayor, she has failed in business twice, once as a brewer and once as a mill-owner. More and more these days, she finds herself on the road. In the weeks to come she will visit the bishops of Lincoln and Canterbury to speak of her revelations. She will make pilgrimages from her home in Lynn in Norfolk—she hopes soon to head off to Jerusalem—and seek audiences with the highest clerics in the land. She wants the world to know about these revelations of Christ, the voice from nowhere, the visions of the Virgin and her child. Margery's reputation precedes her. People hear of her gift of tears, her tendency to burst out in loud crying whenever she sees a reminder of Christ's Passion. But this is a suspicious world. There are heretics everywhere. Her dressing all in white raises hackles: Who does she think she is? She is chased as a Lollard and threatened with burning. With the teachings of Augustine in mind, the holy men quiz her about whether she hears Our Lord speaking in her mind or with her bodily ears. These are important distinctions. You can be burned for less.

Anyway, it is Christ that she hears. She converses with Him on a daily basis. She hears the voices of the Holy Father and His saints, and perceives their presence with her ghostly eye. One kind of sound she hears is like a pair of bellows blowing in her ear: it is the susurrus of the Holy Spirit. When He chooses, our Lord changes that sound into the voice of a dove, and then into a robin redbreast, tweeting merrily in her right ear. Sometimes the Father of Heaven converses with her soul as plainly and certainly as one friend speaks to another through bodily speech. No wisdom on earth can explain where this voice comes from or where it goes. She has received such sounds in her inner hearing for the past twenty-five years.

She cannot read for herself, but she knows the writings of St. Bridget of Sweden, whose visions of the Holy Ghost inspired her to found a new order, and of Mary of Oignies, who was so overcome by the confession of her sins that she cried out like a woman in labor. A woman's frailty prepares her for receiving these signs from God. But how is Margery to know that these are true communications from heaven? The devil is a master of deception. He could be implanting these voices in her mind. What does the true voice of our Lord sound like?

The voice commands her to go to Norwich to visit an anchoress who has wisdom in these matters. The woman lives in a cell attached to the Church of St. Julian, not far from the hubbub of the quayside. Margery can hear the shouts of the stevedores from the jetties along the Wensum, the clatter of carts ferrying woolsacks to the barges at Conisford. After Lynn, Norwich is a vast metropolis—the second-biggest city in England, and a major port. It seems an odd, frantic place in which to hide away from the world. But anchorites are expected to offer spiritual guidance, and Margery enters the parlor adjoining the cell knowing that her request for advice will be heard. She speaks to the anchoress through a small window. The inhabitant of the cell is in her seventies; her face is wizened and pale within its white cowl. Her eyes have the serenity of someone who has already passed from this life. A maidservant, Alice, brings Margery some beer. The anchorite's cell is tiny, with a cot and an altar, a bucket and some beads. On the other side, a narrow window looks through into the church, where the occupant can see the altar and the tabernacle containing the sacrament. The cell has no door. There is no way in and no way out. The anchoress entered through a small portal, which, after some prayers, was then sealed up. Who knows how many years ago that happened? It was her earthly death, and she was congratulated on it. When it is time for her spirit to be with her Lord again, she will die here in her anchor-hold without ever seeing the sky again. As someone who seeks crowds and attention, who craves to tell princes and archbishops of what she has seen, Margery cannot imagine that the universe could be shrunk down like this. She would die of this solitude.

The women talk for hours. Other visitors come by, and Margery waits, eventually leaves, and returns the next morning. The visit lasts for several days. Margery later describes her revelations in detail, in the hope that any deception will be apparent. The fiend will show his hand in the smallest details. The anchoress reassures her that the voice Margery hears is a true voice if it does not speak against the will of God or the benefit of Christians. The Holy Ghost never urges a thing against charity; to do so would be to confound God's own goodness. "God and the devil are always at odds," Julian tells her. "They shall never dwell together in one place, and the devil has no power in a man's soul."

Another sign that Margery's voice is true is that God has blessed her with a gift of tears. The devil abhors weeping. To see her crying in public causes him a torment greater than the pains of hell. Above all, Margery must have faith. She has to believe in the goodness of the voice. The more people mock her for her experiences, the more God will love her, just as He loved St. Bridget before her. But the Lord of Heaven never showed Bridget the things that have been shown to this creature of Lynn. Christ Himself has guaranteed this fact to her. Whatever Bridget witnessed with her ghostly eye, it was nothing compared to what Margery has seen with hers.

MARGERY KEMPE CHOSE WELL in seeking counsel from the Norwich anchoress. Like the younger woman's voices and visions, which began after the birth of her first child, Dame Julian's revelations also had their origins in bodily distress. On May 8, 1373—forty or so years before her meeting with Margery—she had been bedridden in the aftermath of an illness in which she had first regretted and then accepted what she understood as her impending death. She was thirty and a half years old, about the age that Geoffrey Chaucer was at the time. In the early morning, the parish priest arrived bearing a crucifix, and invited Julian to look at the face of Christ and draw comfort from her Savior. In contrast to the rest of the room, which was dimmed by her failing sight, the crucifix retained an "ordinary, household light"— and in it she saw red blood trickling down from under the crown of thorns, "freshly, plentifully and vividly." As the vision of the dying Christ grew more and more grotesque—in one image covered in dried blood; in another, dark blue and close to death—Julian heard these words form in her soul. There was no voice or opening of lips, just a simple explanation: "By this is the Fiend overcome."

The visions continued throughout that day, with the last of the fifteen occurring well into the afternoon. A final, sixteenth vision occurred the following night. Julian completed her book years after she had experienced the revelations, and the account demonstrates the extraordinary care with which she had tried to reconstruct them and sift them for meaning. She wrote that each of the revelations was in three parts, with every "shewing" containing aspects of visual imagery, of words formed in her understanding, and of spiritual or "ghostly" sight the latter being the hardest thing for a "poor and unlettered creature" to portray in words. The voice that she had heard had encouraged her and vouched for its own authenticity: "Know well now that what you saw today was no delirium; accept and believe it, and you shall not be overcome." The word that Julian used for "delirium" was *raveing*; some translations put it as "hallucination."

Not much is known about Julian's life. Her writings concern themselves with uncovering the meaning of her revelations far more than with describing her material surroundings. It is likely that she was from a reasonably well-to-do family and that she was a mother, possibly a widow. Sometime after the "shewings" of May 8, 1373, Julian resolved to write them down and devote herself to meditation, in the hope of recapturing some of their grace. It is not clear whether she was at this time living in Norwich; her literary name likely comes from the church of St. Julian in Norwich where she later settled as an anchorite, occupying a cell attached to the church in the solitude needed for meditation. It was here that Margery went to meet her. Although very different in age and background, they would have had much in common. As women in a patriarchal society, both were capable of hiding their intellectual gifts. Julian referred to herself as "a woman, ignorant, weak and frail," while Margery's epithet for herself as "this creature" suggested an even deeper humility. As long as devout women trod cautiously, the later Middle Ages afforded them an uneasy role as visionaries, following in the tradition (established most strongly on the Continent) of Hildegard of Bingen, Catherine of Siena, and others. Sublimation of traditional female roles is evident in both of their books: Margery writes of forging an almost erotic relationship with Christ, while Julian turned the strictures of her society to her advantage, creating a homely meditation on faith that values female roles and domestic imagery. In one of the most memorable scenes of Julian's book, she describes a vision of a tiny thing, the size of a hazelnut, lying in the palm of her own hand. "What can this be?" she asks herself in her near-death state. And the answer comes, "It is all that is made."

The two women who met in Norwich are now considered among the outstanding literary figures of the English Middle Ages. No one before Margery, man or woman, had ever set down their life in writing in English, making *The Book of Margery Kempe* the first autobiography in the language. Margery dictated her narrative to an amanuensis; Julian wrote hers with her own hand, making it the first book in English known to have been written by a woman. Both heard voices and wrote about their experiences, although it seems unlikely that Margery knew of Julian's writings, despite her reputation as an expert in these matters. The older woman was not just a highly original theologian; she attended to the details of her experience with a naturalist's care. Julian's assiduous efforts to discern the truth or falsity of her voices and visions is evident in the fact that she wrote two versions of her *Revelations of Divine Love*, separated in time by about twenty years, suggesting that she was constantly reading and rereading her memories of the "shewings" in ways that left her perpetually unsatisfied.

That was not least because of the problem of discernment. For those on the receiving end of revelations of the divine, being sure that they were authentic was the most fundamental worry of all. It was the reason Margery sought out Julian in the first place: to ask her advice on whether her voices were true signs of holiness. In the fifth century, St. Augustine had distinguished among three types of visions: corporeal (perceived with the external senses); imaginative (perceived as an inner vision or voice); and spiritual or intellectual (received directly by the soul without the perception of any sensory qualities). For Margery, as for others who had these experiences, the distinction was a serious one. What was the difference, in terms of its spiritual truth or falsity, between hearing God speaking to her "in her mind" and hearing Him with "her bodily ears"?

Discernment was a big issue in the Middle Ages. For the churchmen, judgments about what was or was not God's true word were often judgments about the morality of the person involved. As women were defined as having a weak character and a particular susceptibility to temptation by the devil, their experiences often fell afoul of the priests' criteria. Margery herself was constantly being cross-examined by officers of the Holy Church to assess her devoutness and spiritual purity. In this respect, she faced the same dangers as Joan of Arc would a few years later. In the discussion of her voice-hearing experiences at her trial in 1429, Joan's voices were seen to be of the lowliest kind, because they were perceived through external hearing. In Joan's first experience, at the age of thirteen, she had been in her father's garden on a summer's day. She had heard a voice coming from her right, from the direction of a nearby church. The voice was described as "beautiful, sweet and low," and it was usually accompanied by a light. It protected her, and it called her Jeanne the Maid, daughter of God. She heard it most days. In Augustine's scheme, the external nature of the voice (contrasted with the "ghostly" voice that sometimes spoke directly to her contemporary Margery's soul) made Joan's experiences suspicious. Women like Margery and Julian were not expected to know about these theological distinctions, but they were clearly very well informed. It was dangerous not to be.

It is no more meaningful to attempt to diagnose the two English mystics (nor others, like Joan, from the tradition to which they belong) than it is to call Socrates a schizophrenic. Needless to say, retrospective differential diagnoses keep bubbling up in the literature. If Joan wasn't schizophrenic, she had "idiopathic partial epilepsy with auditory features." Margery's compulsive weeping and roaring, combined with her voice-hearing, might also have been signs of temporal lobe epilepsy. The white spots that flew around her vision (and were interpreted by her as sightings of angels) could have been symptoms of migraine. But in other respects Margery's positive, compassionate voices resist a reduction to medical symptoms. They certainly don't fit with the idea of her having epileptic seizures. The medieval literary scholar Corinne Saunders points out that Margery's experiences were strange then, in the early fifteenth century, and they seem even stranger now, when we are so distant from the interpretive framework in which Margery received them. That doesn't make them signs of madness or neurological disease any more than similar experiences in the modern era should be automatically pathologized. When Margery's book was first published in the 1930s, after the rediscovery of the manuscript in the library of an old Catholic family in Lancashire, the reviewers of the time (no doubt influenced by then fashionable psychoanalysis) were quick to judge her outpourings as "hysterical." We see the past through the lens of the present, and that is never more true than when we are dealing with experiences that deviate from the ordinary.

If we can avoid the reductionist dishing-out of diagnoses, comparisons with modern voice-hearing experiences can be illuminating. One striking feature of medieval accounts of voice-hearing is that they are rarely limited to one modality. Julian didn't just hear the voice of God: she saw Christ and felt His presence in her "gostly understonding." As we will see, historical accounts of voice-hearing experiences hold important lessons for us on how we should avoid prioritizing voice-hearing at the expense of experiences in other sensory modalities. But we also need to keep in mind why these testimonies were made. The voices and visions that got Joan into such trouble might owe their multisensory nature to the context in which they were reported. If you are hearing the voice of a doctor you once spoke to, there's no reason to think that you might see her face, too. If Christ or the Virgin are appearing to you, you are arguably more likely to get a hit on all your senses. Even if you don't, you might be more eager to make out that you did, if your life depends on validating that vision.

In trying to understand what Julian wrote, it's important to remember that she tells us at the outset that she actively sought— indeed, prayed for—these revelations of Christ. The voice of God did not come unbidden, and so it is perhaps not surprising that the communications were, for the most part, clearly received. On other occasions, her voices sound more like the complex, ambiguous experiences of many people who hear voices today. Visited by a vision of the devil at the end of her sequence of revelations, Julian feels the fiend's heat and is overwhelmed by his vile stench. But her hearing is stimulated, too, by something which seems to have a human cause: "Also I heard a bodily jangeling as it had be of two bodies, and both, to my thynkyng, janglyd at one time as if they had holden a parlement with a gret bysynes. And al was soft muttering, as I understode nowte what they seid. And al this was to stirre me to dispeir."

Above all, the experiences of the medieval mystics need to be understood in the context of their faith—in their characteristics as experiences, but also in the painstaking efforts of people like Julian and Margery to understand what was happening to them. As always when trying to interpret historical writings, we must ask why the texts were set down and for whom they were written. Julian was writing for all Christians, but she was also writing for herself, in an attempt to make sense of the events of that miraculous day. Twenty years later, in the second version of her *Revelations*, she is still worrying away at the meaning of what she saw and heard. Joan's testimony, by contrast, was set down by her inquisitors for a very different purpose: as a record of her condemnation. Taking such different texts at face value is unlikely to get us any closer to the truth of what those experiences were like for the women who received them.

The lively and characterful voices that fill the pages of Margery's book should also be understood in terms of the reasons she recorded them. In contrast to Julian's assiduous sifting of her showings, Margery's book is a frank, earthy account of an ongoing conversation with God. Her modern editor, Barry Windeatt, emphasizes the inner dialogue that runs through her book: "It is time to read Margery Kempe's inner voices as a projection of her own spiritual understanding of divine interaction with her, and hence as an insight into her own mentality." Whether she is talking to God about her social ostracization or consoling Mary after the death of Christ, Margery is not recording the external entities that spoke with her so much as debating with herself what those experiences might mean, under all the limitations of her own capacity to understand the answer to that question. We eavesdrop on "a praying mind talking to itself." The theme recurs of minds full of voices in dialogue. In Margery's case, it was an inner conversation with a very special substance: the relationship between a woman and her God.

11

A Brain Listening to Itself

WHETHER OR NOT YOU believe that God really spoke to Margery Kempe, there is a sense in which hearing a voice is an event that unfolds in one person's mind. Just as with ordinary inner dialogue, the same brain is producing the utterance that speaks and the utterance that answers. What is different in the case of Margery is that one of the voices in the inner dialogue is perceived as having an external or even a supernatural cause. The voice *feels* as though it is coming from somewhere else. Somewhere in Margery's experience, that supernatural utterance takes bodily shape. Sacred or profane, voice-hearing is, in its simplest form, about language resonating in the brain.

Women like Margery and Julian would not have known much about the workings of the organ between their ears. Anatomy in that era was the preserve of educated men. Although Aristotle had centered the rational aspects of human cognition in the heart, the first stirrings of a scientific psychology—building on the work of the Greek anatomist Galen, and emerging as an organized field of inquiry toward the end of the thirteenth century—had transplanted cognitive functions to the brain. Thinking was a process that had two aspects: the activities of the rational soul, or what we would now call "mind," were mirrored by physiological processes unfolding in the cerebral organ, particularly the transformation of the "vital spirit" (part of a three-part system of spirits deriving from Arabic philosophy) into the "animal spirit" (which controlled sensation, movement, imagination, cognition, and memory).

What was understood about the anatomy of the brain in that period was largely due to the Persian polymath Ibn-Sīnā (or Avicenna), whose works were translated into Latin (and thus made accessible to the Western intellectual elite) in the twelfth century. His *Kitab Al-Najat* (*The Book of Deliverance*) built on Galen's ideas about the brain being divided into five cells corresponding to five partitions of the ventricles of the brain. Here were housed the "inner senses," which were responsible for integrating data from the external senses and constructing thoughts from their component concepts, or "forms." The construction of these *phantasmata*, as they were known, was crucial for explaining why someone like Margery Kempe could hear a voice in the absence of any speaker, and how such experiences depended, in turn, on how the brain integrated thoughts and emotions.

In the forward part of the paired front ventricles, sensory information was processed in the *sensus communis* (also known as "common sense") and then transmitted into the temporary memory system of the *imaginatio*, in the rear half of the front ventricle. Those impressions were then passed on for creative recombination in the front part of the middle ventricle, the *imaginativa* (later termed "phantasy"), which connected to the *estimativa* (in the posterior part of the same ventricle), whose role lay in the making of memory-based and affective judgments. Finally, in the rear ventricle of the brain, *memorialis* was the storehouse of memory. For information to enter the rear ventricle, it had to pass through the wormlike structure known as the *vermis*, which was seen as a valve that could switch between thinking and remembering. One medieval writer even proposed that physical movements of the head could open and close this crucial valve, accounting for observations that people typically tilt their heads back when actively recollecting.

Hearing a voice or seeing a vision could then be explained in terms of the dynamic interplay between two of these components:

the *imaginativa* (or active imagination) and the more rational *estimativa*. In certain circumstances, the creative power of the *imaginativa* could sway and deceive the rational processes of the *estimativa*. If there was an imbalance in the four bodily humors (black bile, yellow bile, blood, and phlegm), that delicate balance could be affected. An excess of yellow bile, for example, could overstimulate the image-production systems of the front ventricle, resulting in perceptions that were not founded in reality.

Medieval science thus offered an account of anomalous perceptions based in physiological processes. It is not the case that all such experiences were automatically seen as resulting from supernatural agency, either demonic or divine. St. Thomas Aquinas, for example, writing in the middle of the thirteenth century, thought that such experiences could be triggered by spontaneous physical changes, or "local movement of animal spirits and humours." Although few in Western societies would have been aware of the science, and many would have rushed to theological interpretations, the era of Joan, Julian, and Margery was seeing the beginnings of an understanding of how voice-hearing experiences might arise in the brain.

THE IDEA OF A "hallucination" is a modern concept. Although the term had been in common usage for some time—Julian of Norwich used the Middle English equivalent, *raveing*—it wasn't until 1817 that the concept took shape as a psychiatric symptom. The French psychiatrist Jean-Étienne Esquirol defined it as "the intimate conviction of actually perceiving a sensation for which there is no external object." Hearing voices, seeing visions, and experiencing other anomalous perceptions were brought together under a single label and distinguished from persistent false beliefs (delusions) and mistaken perceptions (illusions).

Esquirol's distinction is largely still intact today. The key features of a hallucination are generally agreed to be its occurrence in the absence of any actual stimulus, its perceptual force (it seems as real to the experiencer as any corresponding genuine perception), and its resistance to voluntary control. You can choose to imagine a pink elephant or the voice of a workmate; when you hallucinate, you have no such control. In the words of the late Oliver Sacks, "you are passive and helpless in the face of hallucinations: they happen to you, autonomously—they appear and disappear when they please, not when you please."

What these experiences do have in common is that something is happening when it shouldn't be. In psychiatric parlance, hallucinations count as a "positive symptom": they represent an excess of something rather than its lack. Experiencing a hallucination could thus be explained in terms of an ordinary mechanism of perception becoming derailed by some other anomalous event. The seventeenth-century introspectionist and philosopher René Descartes proposed a mechanistic explanation of hallucination using the analogy of a bell-pull, by which servants could be summoned from other floors of a house. A ringing of the bell in, say, the kitchen might be caused by the mistress calling for service from upstairs, but it might also be caused by someone pulling the wire in an intervening room. To those in the kitchen, a false, anomalous signal of this kind would be indistinguishable from a genuine summons. Descartes believed that mechanistic chains of events in the brain and body underlay our perceptions, and thus that an analogous glitch in the transmission of a signal could result in a hallucination.

Stimulate the machine, then, in the absence of any actual external stimulus, and you might create anomalous perceptions of voice-hearing. That was what happened in a series of studies by the Canadian neurosurgeon Wilder Penfield, who was conducting brain surgery on patients with epilepsy, looking for a way of disrupting the seizures that were causing their problems. Partly because the brain has no pain receptors, and partly as an important safety check, patients must remain conscious during such a procedure. Penfield was using an electrode to stimulate the surface of the brain in order to determine where to operate. When he began his studies, he knew that the brains of epilepsy patients with auditory hallucinations tended to show anomalous activation in the superior temporal gyrus, a key part of the inner speech network. Sure enough, when Penfield stimulated that part of the brain, patients often reported hearing a voice, particularly when the stimulation was in the nondominant hemisphere (the right, in the case of a right-handed person).

Could random activations of the auditory system be the cause of at least some voice-hearing experiences? In the case of a genuine perception of sound, signals transmitted along the auditory nerves enter the brain in an area known as the primary auditory cortex (a small region in the superior temporal gyrus) before being processed in higher cortical centers such as Wernicke's area, further back in the superior temporal lobe. Consistent with the bell-pull analogy, random activation in this system could lead to the perception of an auditory signal in the absence of any stimulus. Such a theory would struggle, though, to explain why such an anomalous perception would so often lead to the experience of a human voice (and in many cases, one that is familiar to the experiencer), rather than any other sound.

It seems likely that other neural regions would have to get involved. In the inner speech model of voice-hearing, voices are hallucinated when an individual generates an element of inner speech but for some reason does not recognize it as his or her own work. If that theory is true, we would expect to see much more than random neural noise in the auditory system; we would expect to see a brain talking to itself, and somehow failing to recognize the signal as being generated by its own efforts. By that logic, the nerve firings you would expect to see when a person is hearing a voice should be similar to those observed when people are doing inner speech. Based on what we already know about how inner speech works in the brain, that should mean seeing activations in the inner speech network, including regions like Broca's area and the superior temporal gyrus.

The earliest brain-imaging studies of the inner speech network were designed with that question in mind. Philip McGuire and his colleagues at the Institute of Psychiatry in London conducted a series of studies in the 1990s using a method known as positron emission tomography (PET). PET works by tracking the uptake of a harmless radioactive molecule when it is injected into a person. One of Mc-Guire's studies reported increased activation in Broca's area when schizophrenia patients were hallucinating compared to when they were not, suggesting that the brain's mechanisms for generating speech were also activated when these patients were hearing voices.

With the advent of functional magnetic resonance imaging (fMRI), researchers had a more powerful tool to investigate inner speech and hallucinations as they occurred. This type of imaging differs from PET by detecting blood flow in the brain, which in turn offers clues about neural activations. It also provides much better spatial resolution, allowing researchers to tell with greater accuracy exactly where in the brain activations are occurring. A drawback of fMRI is that it has much worse *temporal* resolution—in other words, it is not as good as other scanning methods at telling researchers exactly *when* an activation occurred.

The temporal resolution can in some cases be just about good enough to show how hallucinations unfold in the brain. Working in McGuire's Institute of Psychiatry group, Sukhwinder Shergill and colleagues scanned the brains of two schizophrenia patients who were having frequent hallucinations. They showed that Broca's area became activated in these patients a few seconds before the onset of the hallucination. The same group had previously shown that Broca's area was at work during inner speech in healthy participants. The findings appeared to confirm the link between inner speech and auditory verbal hallucinations in schizophrenia.

There are numerous problems with interpreting these studies. One issue relates to the difficulty of capturing hallucinations as they occur in the scanner. In Shergill's study, six participants had to be excluded from the analysis, three because they did not hallucinate at all during the scanning session, and three because their voice-hearing experiences were too close together. Even if you can find a participant who will hallucinate on demand (recall that part of the definition of hallucinations is that they *cannot* be summoned like this), another problem arises: how to get participants to indicate when a hallucination is occurring. Typically one has the subject press a button to indicate the onset of a voice. But that method is flawed because it requires the participant to initiate an action when the hallucination has already begun; the decision to press the button and the act of actually pressing the button may distort the imaging result.

If we can't catch the fleeting experience of hearing a voice during a scanning session, we can look instead to see whether there are any reliable differences in brain activations when voice-hearers are not hearing voices compared to non-voice-hearing controls. Shergill's group conducted a study of this sort—in other words, the researchers didn't try to catch people hearing voices in the scanner; instead, they looked for more enduring differences between the groups. Of particular interest were activations during an "inner-speech" condition, when participants had to complete a phrase silently in their heads after hearing the target word ("swimming") on an audio recording. In three further conditions, participants were asked to create different forms of auditory verbal imagery, by covertly uttering the same phrase in their own voice, or by imagining the phrase being spoken by the voice on the recording and addressing them either in the second or third person.

No differences were found between the patient and control groups on the inner-speech condition. Instead, differences between the groups only emerged when the researchers compared activations in the imagery conditions. When imagining others speaking to them, patients who heard voices showed less neural traffic than controls in a range of brain regions typically associated with monitoring one's own behavior. The researchers concluded that this discrepancy emerged because generating auditory verbal imagery in a particular voice ("You like swimming" or "She likes swimming") required self-monitoring, or keeping track of what one was generating internally. Ordinary inner speech, as defined in this task, was thought to require only low levels of self-monitoring, which is why the two groups did not differ in this condition.

The problem with making sense of these studies is that their definition of inner speech seems far removed from the varied, nuanced phenomena that we have encountered so far. Simply asking people to subvocalize in the scanner does not create a good approximation to ordinary, spontaneous inner speech. There are also problems with the choice of participants for these studies. Most neuroimaging experiments in this area have compared brain activations in schizophrenia patients with those in healthy controls. The weakness of this kind of design is that, if you find differences between the groups, you don't know whether they relate to the hallucinations or the diagnosis. A "schizophrenic" brain might look different from a typical brain for all sorts of reasons, including neuropathology, life experience, and medication. If you are interested in a particular experience—hearing voices—rather than a particular diagnosis, your best bet is to try to find participants who have the experience but no psychiatric diagnosis, with all the complicating factors of medication and institutionalization that can come with that. Researchers interested in auditory verbal hallucinations have argued that this approach gives a clearer picture of what is involved in voice-hearing than studying the brains of people who also have a serious mental illness.

Such studies are still very thin on the ground. The largest to date compared fMRI signals in twenty-one nonclinical voice-hearers from the Netherlands and the same number of voice-hearing patients with psychosis. Kelly Diederen and her colleagues at the University Medical Center in Utrecht found no differences between the groups in brain activations during hallucinations. In a smaller study in Wales, David Linden and his colleagues looked at seven voice-hearers without a psychiatric diagnosis and compared activations when they were hallucinating with those of a separate control group when they were generating auditory imagery (imagining people speaking to them). Both conditions showed activations in the standard inner speech network, but an interesting difference emerged in the activation of the supplementary motor area (SMA), a part of the motor cortex (see Figure 3). When the control participants were imagining speech, activation in the SMA preceded activation in the auditory areas. When the nonclinical voice-hearers were hallucinating, in contrast, both activations occurred simultaneously. This fits with the idea that the SMA is the neural basis of the "voluntariness" of the experience. In

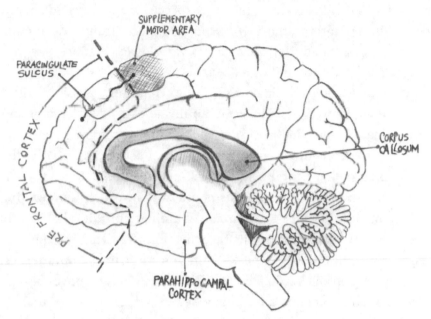

FIGURE 3: Brain regions implicated in voice-hearing. (Note: the length of the paracingulate sulcus is highly variable between individuals.)

the case of ordinary imagining, the SMA fires first, as if to send a clear signal to say, "I did this." In the voice-hearers, the signal that denotes that the stimulus was generated intentionally is caught up with the perception of the resulting voice.

This apparent role of the SMA in auditory verbal hallucinations is supported by an ingenious study from Finland that worked with patients rather than nonclinical voice-hearers. The researchers, Tuukka Raij and Tapani Riekki, compared fMRI activations in two conditions. In one, participants indicated when they were hallucinating by means of a conventional button press. In the other, they were asked to *imagine* the hallucination they had previously experienced. The nice thing about this design, as compared to the Welsh one, was that the imagery condition involved something much more like actual voice-hearing. Rather than a somewhat artificial condition of imagining being addressed by another person, the Finnish participants had to replay their own voices speaking to them.

As with the Welsh study, the inner speech circuit activated in both conditions. However, the SMA responded more strongly during the imagery task than during the auditory verbal hallucinations, suggesting, again, that this kind of hallucination has less of the "I did this" quality that attends ordinary imagining. Here's one possible difference, then, between conjuring up an image of a pink elephant and hallucinating one. The first experience comes with something of the brain activations involved in producing an action voluntarily; the second lacks that neural badge of self-authorship. The writer Daniel B. Smith points out that this is one way in which the puzzling phenomenon of voice-hearing can illuminate profound scientific problems: in this case, how neural activations translate into the subjective qualities of experience. "With voice-hearing," Smith writes, "the brain pops its head, like the Loch Ness monster, above the surface. For an instant one can actually 'see' or, rather, 'hear' the brain."

Despite the limitations of existing research, the inner speech model has provided a useful framework for making sense of neuroscientific findings concerning voice-hearing. Some of the most impressive evidence has come from findings of structural differences between people who hear voices and those who don't. The inner speech model has often been translated into neuroscientific language in terms of the connection between the part of the brain that generates an inner utterance (particularly the left inferior frontal gyrus, or Broca's area) and the region that perceives it (part of the superior temporal gyrus, or Wernicke's area). Recall that, in the model of action monitoring put forward by Chris Frith and colleagues, a signal is sent from the system that produces inner speech to the speech detection areas of the brain, effectively saying, "Don't pay any attention to this; this is *you* speaking." In schizophrenia, Frith argued, something goes wrong with the transmission of this signal. The "listening" part of the brain doesn't expect the signal that is coming, and so it processes the signal as an external voice.

Studying connectivity between these areas of the brain should allow us to see whether this kind of transmission error is occurring.

Neuroscientists make a broad distinction between two kinds of brain material: gray matter, which takes its name from the cell bodies of the neurons, or nerve cells, that color it; and white matter, which consists of the parts of the nerve cell that communicate with other nerve cells (roughly, the brain's wiring). Studying the integrity of white matter can tell you something about how different parts of the brain are talking to each other, or at least how they are wired up to talk. To make an analogy, you can learn a lot about the structure of a communications system—a telephone exchange, for example— simply by studying how it is connected up, even if no signals are actually flowing through the system.

For the inner speech model of voice-hearing, one tract of white matter has been of particular interest. It's the stretch of neural wiring that (very roughly) joins Broca's area to Wernicke's area, the area in the superior temporal gyrus that perceives speech. This group of fibers is called the arcuate fasciculus. Recall that an utterance in inner speech is supposedly generated, but the speech perception area doesn't get the usual tip-off about it. In Frith's theory, this happens because Broca's area usually sends a copy of the instruction to Wernicke's area, effectively telling it not to listen for what's about to happen. That so-called "efference copy" is sent along the arcuate fasciculus.

The integrity of this tract of white matter has indeed been linked to auditory verbal hallucinations. Along with looking at the physical structure of the pathway, researchers have used neurophysiological methods, such as electroencephalography (EEG), to find out whether communication between these brain regions is disturbed. Judith Ford and her colleagues at Yale University showed that the usual "dampening" that occurs in Wernicke's area as a result of receiving the efference copy does not occur so markedly in patients with schizophrenia. That interpretation gained support from an fMRI study looking at how patients' brains responded when they were perceiving external speech in comparison to when they were generating inner speech. The "listening" areas of the control participants' brains activated less when they were imagining sentences than when they were hearing sentences spoken out loud. The difference was significantly less noticeable in the schizophrenia patients' brains, suggesting a problem with the transmission of the efference copy between Broca's and Wernicke's areas.

It may seem counterintuitive, but another way to find out how different neural systems are talking to each other is to look at a brain that is not being asked to do anything at all. It was discovered around the turn of the millennium that the brain is anything but silent when a participant in the scanner is ostensibly doing nothing. Instead, there are organized patterns of communication between brain systems (commonly considered as a "default network") that seem to reveal something important about the functional organization of the brain. A brain that is ticking is a finely tuned—and highly active—machine.

To investigate these activation patterns, neuroscientists use what they term a "resting state" paradigm, which typically involves having a participant lie in the scanner and stare at a fixation cross. There is no task, no instructions are given, and often no psychological or behavioral data are gathered. Looking at the spontaneous activations that occur during the resting state can give us information about how different brain regions talk to each other when the individual is not busy with a task (an electrician will use a multimeter to test connectivity between the parts of a circuit in a similar way). The findings of such studies have indicated subtle differences in resting connectivity in the brains of schizophrenia patients who hear voices and the brains of control subjects. These findings can be best summarized as showing unusual patterns of connectivity between frontal and temporal regions in the schizophrenia patients. The results generally support the idea that in the patients, the frontal areas, like Broca's, fail to communicate correctly with the speech perception areas in the temporal lobe.

The inner speech model has also been tested by techniques that can artificially modify, for short periods of time, the activity of a volunteer's brain. One problem with fMRI studies is that they can only demonstrate correlations, not causation. A particular pattern of activation might occur at the same time as a particular psychological state or cognitive function, but you can never know which has caused which. If you can go in and change how neurons are firing, and show that particular psychological changes follow from that, you can be pretty sure that the brain changes are a cause, not a result, of the psychological change.

There are obvious ethical issues in using such techniques to induce hallucinations in volunteers, even if the methods are safer and more reliable than those used by Penfield to stimulate his patients' exposed brains. Instead of trying to make people hallucinate, though, can changing the electrical activity of the brain switch off hallucinations in those who are having them? One method, known as *transcranial magnetic stimulation* (TMS), involves applying a rapidly changing magnetic field to an area on the scalp in order to induce an electrical current in the cortex. A version of TMS that delivers a repetitive stimulus has shown some success at treating hallucinations when applied to regions such as the left temporal cortex, although the effects are not long-lasting. An alternative method, known as *transcranial direct current stimulation* (tDCS), produces more persistent changes in brain activations, with effects lasting fifteen minutes or so. In this method, the volunteer wears a headband containing two electrodes, one of which delivers an electric current to a particular part of the brain. My graduate student Peter Moseley used this method to test the idea that the superior temporal gyrus (STG) is involved in the kind of source-monitoring judgments thought to be important in auditory verbal hallucinations. In a sample of healthy volunteers, he applied currents to the left posterior STG in order to increase its activity and showed that it made participants more susceptible to errors on an auditory signal detection task of the kind previously implicated in voice-hearing.

These are early days for the neuroscience of auditory verbal hallucinations. At least some kinds of voice-hearing experiences seem to involve atypical processing of inner speech. But what kinds of inner speech, exactly? As we've seen, brain researchers have hardly begun to address the variety of the ordinary voices in our heads. Furthermore, if hallucinated voices stem from misattributed inner speech, then why aren't *all* bits of inner speech misattributed? Why aren't those who hear voices hearing voices all the time? Some voice-hearers are troubled by almost continual hallucinations, but they are the exception rather than the rule.

The answers must lie beyond the standard language system of the left hemisphere. One region in which unusual activations have been found in voice-hearing is the area of the cortex around the hippocampus, the powerhouse of memory in the brain. Using fMRI, Kelly Diederen and her colleagues in Utrecht showed that neural signals in a region known as the parahippocampal cortex decreased just before patients with schizophrenia heard a voice. Why should memory systems be involved in a process that supposedly involves the misattribution of inner speech? As we'll see, there are good reasons to think that at least some voice-hearing experiences have more to do with remembering the past than with talking to oneself in the present.

And then there's the evidence for activation differences on the opposite side of the brain from where language functions are typically housed. Recall that, for most people, language processing is centered primarily in the left hemisphere, in regions like Broca's area and the speech perception areas of the superior temporal gyrus. Paradoxically, a couple of studies have shown activation of *right*-hemisphere language regions when people hear voices in the scanner. Iris Sommer and her group at Utrecht found that experiencing voice hallucinations in the scanner was associated with more activity in the right-hemisphere language-related regions than in the left hemisphere (including Broca's area, which is often activated during voice-hearing experiences). Although the right hemisphere's language regions do not usually have much to do with language production, they are not entirely without effect, particularly in patients affected by aphasia (language loss) resulting from brain damage. In such patients, right-hemisphere language regions have been associated with the production of "automatic speech," which involves short utterances that are often abusive and repetitive. (One such patient could say nothing but the word *motherfucker*, but he said it fluently and with appropriate emphasis.) Perhaps voices—particularly those that are short, brutish, and repetitive—result when these right-hemisphere language regions chip in with their characteristic utterances, a result of a failure of the processes that would usually inhibit this area and keep language on the dominant side. Simon McCarthy-Jones has suggested that the findings of anomalous activation in right-hemisphere language regions lend some support to the otherwise far-fetched theory of Julian Jaynes regarding this typically silent half of the brain.

There is still much to learn about how auditory verbal hallucinations arise in the brain. Some will argue that the neuroscience will never prove anything useful about auditory verbal hallucinations, because it describes biological processes when we need to be interested in experience. But probing voice-hearing in the brain helps us advance in our scientific thinking about the issue in many ways, and it certainly does not entail a reductionist view in which voices are "only" neural activations. For one thing, the complexities of research in this area provide a bracing reminder of how important it is to pay careful attention to the "What is it like?" questions. There are different kinds of voice-hearing experiences, and, as we will see, some of them don't seem to have much to do with inner speech at all.

Voice-hearing keeps raising big questions. What does it mean to generate an action intentionally, to behave under the impression that one is exercising one's free will? What are the implications for understanding why some things that our brains and bodies do seem to happen outside of our voluntary control? We've probably all had the experience of saying something spontaneously that surprises us, or of a thought or memory coming to mind that we ourselves don't seem to have authored. Could the feeling of having done something involuntarily really be as simple as a case of one part of the brain not talking to another? Imagine a world in which, without the voices of the gods to guide them, Homer's heroes would (in one writer's phrase) "stand frozen on the beaches of Troy, like puppets." Jaynes's theory might be riddled with holes, but his analysis invites us to imagine. If important parts of our experience are not consciously willed, what does that mean for how we captain the ship of the mind? Who is in charge up there, and how do we cope with the fact that we—sometimes—are not?

12

A Talkative Muse

I DO NOT HEAR VOICES. I never hear words being spoken and then turn to look where they might be coming from, only to find nothing there. I have had the reasonably common experience of hearing a voice calling my name when there was no one around, and I have quite often hallucinated the presence of one of my children at my bedside, particularly when they were small. I have a vivid inner life, but I always know where the chatter of my internal conversations is coming from. I am not a hallucinator.

I hear people speaking, though, people who aren't there. They don't address me directly, but I can hear how their voices sound, their accents and tones of expression. I know they are not really there because I have invented them—or at least I have hashed them together as creative composites of lots of different people I have known. I give them names, faces, and histories; I know what music they like listening to, how they dress on a lazy day, and what they keep on the sill of their bath. On the pages of a novel, I can tell them what to do. (That doesn't mean they can't sometimes surprise me.) I never mistake these fictional characters for real people, but I do hear them speaking. You could say that I *need* to hear them. I have to get their voices right—transcribe them accurately—or they will not seem real to the people who are reading their stories.

One fiction writer put it like this: "As the writer it is as if I am eavesdropping on a conversation, or conversations. I don't make up the dialogue. I hear the characters speak and write down what they say—like a shorthand typist taking dictation." For another writer, communing with fictional characters is a more subtle process of "tuning in": "It is intimate, like being let in on their thoughts. They don't speak to me, I don't speak to them. It's more like being given access to their interior lives."

The characters will say what they will say. And so will the story. I remember laughing out loud, that day on the Tube train, at the line about the funny slices of cheese at Wembley Arena. The thought came unbidden, so much so that it surprised me into a public display of mirth. But how? You can't tickle yourself, because you know (probably through the same kind of efference-copy transmission that usually ensures that you know that your inner speech is your own) that it is you who is performing the action. If you already know the joke, you shouldn't laugh at it—unless perhaps it's a reliable classic that has made you chuckle before. If I'm making myself laugh, there must be some element of surprise—but how, if I have generated the idea myself? Surely I know what I'm going to think. I'm choosing these words, aren't I?

THE IDEA THAT THERE is a connection between madness and creativity has a long history. In ancient Greece and Rome, creativity was divine intervention, a bursting-through of the supernatural into the human—a transmission error that was also seen as one of the causes of insanity. In the Romantic period of John Keats, William Wordsworth, and Samuel Taylor Coleridge, creativity was seen as the work of a less heavenly set of muses. Later, Freudian psychoanalysis regarded mental fecundity as resulting from the tapping of unconscious forces, which would explain how the conscious ego could be surprised at what was being delivered to it. Creative individuals, said the wisdom of the day, could tune in to these voices that seemed to come from outside the self.

The most creative people are susceptible to all sorts of unusual experiences—just as ordinary people are—but studies have shown a particularly high prevalence of psychiatric disorders (particularly mood disorders) in those of proven creativity. One explanation for this connection is a genetic one. If psychotic experiences have a hereditary component (as they have been amply shown to have), then they must bring some selective advantage, something that balances or protects against their negative implications for fitness and survival. Otherwise, the genes that make someone prone to paranoia, hallucinations, or mood swings would have been eradicated from the gene pool long ago. Perhaps those unusual patterns of thought confer benefits in making the individual more creative: more able to make unusual connections, or to think outside established strictures.

Writers are as susceptible to these unusual experiences as any other original thinkers are. And yet there seems to be something specifically voice-like about the ordinary madness of a writer's creativity. A writer makes narrators and characters speak, and throughout history people have expressed the view that creativity results when another voice is let into the writer's own flow of emotion and thought. In the literary scholar Peter Garratt's words, "to write means having one's voice disrupted, taken over, rendered by another."

Charles Dickens was one such writer. Toward the end of his career, Dickens undertook grueling reading tours in which he would give voice to his famous characters (between 1853 and his death in 1870, he was reported to have performed nearly five hundred times). As well as ventriloquizing his invented characters in these unique performances, Dickens also construed the act of creation as the reception of a voice. "When, in the midst of this trouble and pain, I sit down to my book," he wrote to his friend John Forster in 1841, "some beneficent power shows it all to me, and tempts me to be interested, and I don't invent it—really do not—but see it, and write it down." The book in question was *Barnaby Rudge*. Dickens's American publisher, James T. Fields, recalled Dickens saying "that while the *Old Curiosity Shop* was in process of composition Little Nell followed him about everywhere; that while he was writing *Oliver Twist* Fagin the Jew would never let him rest, even in his most retired moments; that at midnight and in the morning, on the sea and on the land, Tiny Tim and Little Bob Cratchit were ever tugging at his coat-sleeve, as if impatient for him to get back to his desk and continue the story of their lives."

Other writers have given comparable accounts of the voices of their creativity. In an 1899 letter to William Blackwood, Joseph Conrad complained of his desertion by his critical, self-editing muse: "You know how desperately slow I work. Scores of notions present themselves—expressions suggest themselves by the dozen, but the inward voice that decides:—this is well—this is right—is not heard sometimes for days together. And meantime one must live!" The literary scholar Jeremy Hawthorn points out that this is an inner voice that is genuinely *heard*. Whatever is voicing this utterance is not the thinking subject, but a voice that comes to the writer involuntarily and expresses a wisdom that he himself could not have come up with.

Virginia Woolf had a much more tangled relationship with voice-hearing. In Woolf's 1927 novel *To the Lighthouse*, Mrs. Ramsay is sitting and knitting when a voice, speaking in her head apparently against her will, intones, "We are in the hands of the Lord": "What brought her to say that: 'We are in the hands of the Lord?' she wondered. The insincerity slipping in among the truths roused her, annoyed her. She returned to her knitting again. How could any Lord have made this world? she asked." Although we should resist inferring from fictional renditions of voice-hearing that the writers responsible for them had the same experiences, in Woolf's case art and life did align. Writing of one of her early breakdowns following her father's death in 1904, Woolf referred to "those horrible voices." Her 1941 suicide note mentioned them as a cause of her final unbearable distress: "I begin to hear voices, and cant [*sic*] concentrate. So I am doing what seems the best thing to do."

Woolf related her own voice-hearing experiences to early traumas, including childhood sexual abuse, bullying, and the deaths of her mother and siblings. In her 1925 novel *Mrs. Dalloway*, she gave a fictional rendering of voice-hearing in the experience of the shell-shocked war veteran Septimus Smith. Traumatized by the death of his friend Evans, Septimus hears not only his slain companion's voice but also (echoing an experience that Woolf herself reported) the birds singing in Greek. Woolf saw creative inspiration as involving "the voices that [flew] ahead" of her thoughts, likening it to another entity speaking through her, whose influence could be expunged by the creative act. *To the Lighthouse*, for example, came to her in a "great, apparently involuntary rush" as she walked around London's Tavistock Square: "I wrote the book very quickly; and when it was written, I ceased to be obsessed by my mother. I no longer hear her voice; I do not see her."

Voice-hearing in fiction can do humor as well as tragedy. In Hilary Mantel's novel *Beyond Black*, the protagonist, Alison, comes to terms with an abusive childhood by reinventing herself as a Victorian-style medium: she "performs" the voices she hears with a theatricality that Dickens himself might have recognized. Mantel takes the stuff of a misery memoir and puts it to the service of an inventive black comedy, some of it focused on a two-foot-high "fiend" named Morris who hangs around Alison's dressing room playing with his trouser zip. The demons of Alison's trauma are externalized as visions and voices. Discussing how writers make use of voice-hearing, the literary scholar Patricia Waugh notes that we should approach the ordinary madness of the novelist as attempting to understand "the relation between the inner voices that bring into being the work of fiction, and those that threaten to destroy the very integrity of the self." Whether or not they hear frank hallucinated voices, novelists use fictional depictions of the experience to harness that controlled dissolution of the self that we can all enact when we read fiction.

Mantel wrote autobiographically about the relations between voices, illness, and writing in her essay "Ink in the Blood," which was inspired by a hospital stay characterized by psychotic experiences: "My internal monologue is performed by many people—nurses and bank managers to the fore. There is a breathless void inside me, and it needs to be filled." In an interview, Mantel said that she sees the apprehension of what she terms "hearsights" as central to the creative process: "Only the medium and the writer are licensed to sit in a room by themselves with a whole crowd of imaginary people, listening and responding to them." The science fiction writer Philip K. Dick reported hearing voices coming from his radio at night and wrote a million-word document, "The Exegesis," to try to explain the sense he had of receiving messages from a spiritual entity. In a 1982 interview shortly before his death, he described hearing a female voice that had spoken to him sporadically since his schooldays: "It's very economical in what it says. It limits itself to a few very terse, succinct sentences. I only hear the voice of the spirit when I'm falling asleep or waking up. I have to be very receptive to hear it. It sounds as though it's coming from millions of miles away."

"ALL WRITERS HEAR VOICES," said another science fiction writer, Ray Bradbury, in a 1990 interview. "You wake up in the morning with the voices and then when they reach a certain pitch you jump out of bed and try and trap them before they get away." Bradbury's idea is commonly heard in discussions of creativity. In Siri Hustvedt's memoir *The Shaking Woman*, the novelist writes of an experience akin to the "automatic writing" that so fascinated Victorian spiritualists: "When I am writing well, I often lose all sense of composition; the sentences come as if I hadn't willed them, as if they were manufactured by another being. . . . I don't write; I am written."

But what are these "voices" actually like? Do they have anything in common with the intrusive voices heard by Jay or Adam, or by those with a diagnosis of schizophrenia or another psychiatric disorder? In classical accounts of inspiration, the voices of creativity were literally *heard*: the shepherd Hesiod's hearing of the Muses on Mount Helicon, for example, has been interpreted as a hallucination with genuine auditory properties. But there is also a real risk of making a too-literal interpretation of writers' descriptions of receiving inspiring voices—what might ultimately be no more than a useful metaphor for describing the ineffable processes of creativity.

The only way to answer this question is to pay much closer attention to the experience. Do writers' voices have sensory qualities, like many auditory hallucinations clearly do? Beyond anecdotal accounts, there is almost no hard evidence on the quality of writers' voices of creativity. A group of us from Hearing the Voice set out to plug this gap in a 2014 collaboration with the Edinburgh International Book Festival. More than eight hundred writers were due to pass through the three-week festival; we would ask them about the voices they heard. Is the idea that writers "hear" the voices of their characters anything more than a cliché or a metaphor?

All of the writers participating in that year's festival were first invited to fill in a questionnaire about their experience of the voices of their characters. Ninety-one professional writers—with different specialities, such as fiction for adults, fiction for young people, and nonfiction—completed the questionnaire. When asked, "Do you ever hear your characters' voices?" 70 percent of the writers answered yes. In response to the question, "Do you have visual or other sensory experiences of your characters, or sense their presence?" most also replied in the affirmative. A quarter of the writers said they heard their characters speaking as if they were in the room, while 41 percent said they could enter into dialogue with their characters. Many writers, however, denied that tuning in to the voice of a character was like hallucinating a voice. One writer of fiction for adults said, "I 'hear' them speak about themselves within the world of the story or speak dialogue with other characters. But they don't 'speak' to me as such. I don't think they know I exist. I eavesdrop on them." For one children's writer, in contrast, the voice was sometimes experienced in external space: "Occasionally when I am writing or when I am working on a story, I can hear the voice of the most important character, just as if they are a real person in the room talking to me. It feels slightly mad, but it never disturbs or upsets me, because I just think this is part of my own creative process, triggered by using imagination and by writing."

Writers reflected on how the experience differed from their ordinary inner experience: "It's not much different from how I hear my own voice in my head (when I'm thinking, I mean, not when I'm talking aloud). So, their voices are just there, mixed up with everything else in there. Though, now I think about it, their voices are always on the right-hand side, low down, by my right shoulder. I don't think I ever hear them on the left." Another wrote: "It actually sounds like my own voice in my head, but coming from an entirely different person. Not unlike those terrifying adverts for Haribo featuring adults speaking with kids' voices."

Around twenty of the writers who filled in the questionnaire also volunteered for a follow-up interview to explore these ideas in more depth. The interviews were led by postdoctoral researcher Jenny Hodgson, who described the process as revealing "a rare and at times startling picture of the mysterious workings of the writerly imagination." Almost all of the writers Jenny interviewed recognized the experience of tuning in to a character's voice as an essential part of the process. One successful novelist said, "I can't really write the work until I hear the character's voice. I have to be able to hear their voice, how they sound, what they say, the style and content of their remarks. Then you try to sort of fan that and hope that it develops a little bit more." Another observed: "The characters often start with a voice—the voice is what usually brings me into the character. Sometimes I might have a general idea about a kind of character, but the voice is what leads me in. . . . It comes when I'm writing. It's actually the process of writing when the voice comes through. I don't know if it's instantaneous, but I can hear the voice."

The follow-up interviews also revealed teasing differences in how writers experience primary and secondary characters. Most of the writers said that they would inhabit the mind of a protagonist and look out at the world through that character's eyes. Secondary characters, in contrast, would tend to be experienced visually, and in more distant, objective ways. One novelist observed: "Physically they present themselves as there. I can see them, I can describe them. . . . I can hear how they speak but I don't inhabit them." In line with that idea, several of the writers said they were unable to see the faces of their protagonists, and instead had to construct a visual appearance for them, with some effort, almost as an afterthought. One writer commented: "When a character comes to me, I can hardly ever see their face. . . . It's as if it was just a blur, like a kind of silhouette. . . . It's like a gap where the face should be."

All in all, our findings suggest a great deal of variability in writers' experiences, but they also show support for the idea that creating both fictional and nonfictional prose is like "tuning in" to a voice or voices, even when the experience is not intrusively received (as it is in some cases of full-blown voice-hearing). The poet Denise Riley has written extensively on internal speech and how writers navigate the line between the inner and the outer. When I discussed our Edinburgh findings with her, she told me of the "almost embarrassing sense of *hearing* a voice as a writer, of tuning in to something that is not the speaking self."

ARE THESE LITERARY VOICES a kind of inner speech? In some sense they must be. None of the writers we spoke to genuinely thought that their creativity emanated from somewhere other than their own organism. (Most voice-hearers also recognize that their experiences must be of their own making; the problem is that the voices don't *feel* as though they are.) But many of the writers we talked to also said that it was like tuning in to another's voice, one that was "speaking through" them. Is our ordinary inner speech ever more like hearing than speaking?

The findings from DES suggest that it can be. Over the decades in which he has been developing his method, Russ Hurlburt has described several cases in which people reported something like inner speech, but with a quality that suggested they were hearing it being delivered rather than actively speaking it. In finessing the distinction between what he calls "inner speaking" and "inner hearing," Russ uses the analogy of recording and listening back to one's own voice on a tape recorder. Inner speaking is the sense of generating the language that is being produced, as in speaking into the microphone of the recorder, and it is the more common form of inner speech. Inner hearing is something more receptive, like listening to one's own voice speaking when the recording is played back. Far from all DES participants describe moments of inner hearing (recall that some DES interviewees report no inner speech at all), but a sufficient number of cases have been observed to make it appropriate to distinguish it from episodes of inner speaking.

Our participant in Berlin, Lara, reported several such experiences. One of her beeps caught her describing to herself, silently, an almost out-of-body experience: "It's like watching my hands through a TV." She had been sitting at her desk, looking at her left hand and the pattern of light and dark caused by the activity of the desktop scanner positioned next to it. On another occasion, lying in the MRI machine, she heard herself saying, "Still worth it," in relation to a problematic collaboration with a colleague. In this example, she felt that what she was experiencing was more like hearing than speaking, although there was an element of both. Like other DES participants, Lara reported that the "speaking–hearing" distinction was not always clear cut, and that her experiences could often be placed along a continuum between those two extremes.

Lara had been recruited to a sample of five volunteers whose role was to help us find out whether the DES method could be integrated with neuroimaging. The two methods had never been combined before, and doing it properly meant ensuring that participants were fully trained in the DES method and able to report consistently and clearly on their own experience before they tried to repeat the trick in the scanner. Lara had four full days of sampling in her natural environment before, in the week that followed, she was beeped in the scanner. During these periods, she was given no specific tasks to do: she simply had to lie there with her eyes open and think about nothing in particular (this is the neuroscientist's standard "resting state" paradigm). Although she had to keep her head entirely still, we set it up so that she could jot down notes on a notepad by seeing what she was writing through the careful placement of some mirrors. At four points during each twenty-five-minute session, she heard a random beep and had to note down her impressions of the moment before the beep, just as she had been trained to do. After that, we pulled her out of the scanner and interviewed her about those beeps in the usual way. Finally, she had another session of being beeped in the scanner as the last requirement of the day. That pattern of two scanner sessions a day was repeated over five days in total.

Because Lara experienced quite a few instances of inner hearing, we were able to compare activations in her brain when she was innerly hearing with moments when she was innerly speaking. As expected, there was less activation in her Broca's area when she was hearing than when she was speaking. This fits with the idea that Broca's area does the "speaking" bit of inner speech. Although we can't draw any conclusions about how inner hearing might work in the brain on the basis of a single case study, this methodological integration felt like a bit of a breakthrough, showing us how neuroimaging studies might in the future be able to zoom in on such moments of experience as they occur naturally.

Are there any other ways of getting at the experience of inner hearing without relying on the slightly unwieldy method of DES? Inspired by Russ Hurlburt, we added to our questionnaire some new items designed to tap into these qualities of inner speech. When presented with the statement, "When I think in words, it feels more like I am speaking than listening," around 90 percent of our 1,400 participants endorsed it in some way. In response to the statement "When I think in words, it is like listening to a recording of my voice," around a fifth of our participants said it was like this "very often" or "all the time." Only around a quarter said they never had this experience. However, the new "inner hearing" items did not cohere into any specific factor, meaning that this quality of inner experience is either not common enough to be picked up by a self-report measure like our questionnaire, or that it requires a more sensitive method, such as DES, to pick it up.

At least some of us, it seems, experience our own inner speech in a similar way to Beckett's Unnamable, as both the speaker and the listener in the narrative of our consciousness. There is much more research to be done on the question of how inner hearing works in the brain, and also whether the experiences of Lara and others match up with what writers describe when they hear their creative voices. Russ is currently on the lookout for professional novelists who might be willing to undertake DES with him in order to help us address this question. He has also done plenty of sampling with people who do not write professionally, but who nevertheless have much to say about how inner speech sounds out in the head during the writing process. Although he has not yet studied it systematically, many years of observations suggest that inner speech is very common when people are writing. Children are often seen mouthing the words, or even saying them out loud, when they are setting them down. Before she could do any actual writing, my daughter Athena would talk to herself as she practiced scribbling on the page, saying repetitive things like, "one, two, three, four," and "Mummy, Daddy, me," even though the marks she was making with her crayon were not yet anything like written language. This suggested to me that she understood the connection between speech and the process of making marks on paper, an understanding that would serve her well when she began to study writing more formally at school.

These casual observations are backed up by more substantial research on the role of inner speech in the writing process. Vygotsky's celebrated student, the neuropsychologist A. R. Luria, observed that, when children were asked to inscribe with the mouth open or with the tongue held between the teeth, their writing errors increased. Vygotsky himself noted that inner speech could serve a crucial function in preparing one for speaking out loud, and also that it could serve as a prelude to composition: "Frequently, we say what we will write to ourselves before we write. What we have here is a rough draft in thought." The process of writing is a process of re-expansion of that fragmentary, condensed language of inner speech.

In fact, one important psychological model of writing holds that it is completely underpinned by spoken language processes, meaning that inner speech should be going on when it is happening. Sure enough, children's developing writing skills seem to lag behind their spoken language, suggesting that the latter needs to be in place before the writing skills can develop. Studies of brain damage also show that writing deficits tend to follow on from impairments in spoken language, although not in every instance. In the case of the patient described earlier who lost his ability to speak as a result of a stroke, inner speech wasn't necessary for reading—but neither was it for writing. A more striking example comes from the study of a "co-operative and lively" thirteen-year-old from Sardinia who had complete oral apraxia—a total inability to speak or produce any vocal sounds. The boy had nevertheless acquired normal reading and composition skills, and over the next ten years he continued to develop typically, obtaining a diploma in agriculture and then holding down a job as a clerk in a local administrative office. Given how unlikely it is that he could have developed inner speech, his case strongly suggests that the ability to talk to oneself is not a prerequisite for writing.

It may not be essential, but inner speech is undoubtedly a useful tool in the writing process. In a study designed to probe this connection further, James Williams at the University of Southern California identified two groups of students as either above average or below average on a standardized test of writing skills. The participants had to write for fifteen minutes on two topics in succession. The first task was to recount everything that had happened from the moment they entered the lab; the second was to discuss how they would have resolved the hostage crisis with Iran (the study was conducted shortly after the 1979–1981 Tehran crisis). While the students were silently writing and thinking, Williams measured electromyographical activations of the articulatory muscles of the tongue, lower lip, and larynx, and took them to indicate the use of inner speech.

The rationale was that the students would vary in how much they used inner speech to plan out their sentences, and that this usage would correlate with their writing skills. As predicted, the below-average-ability group showed less electromyographical activation during pauses in the task, the very moments when a skilled writer might be expected to be using inner speech to plan out his next bit of writing. It wasn't simply that the weaker writers were less likely to use inner speech in general, as their activations were actually higher during the writing itself. All of this fits with the idea that covert speech, as measured by electrical activity in the relevant muscles, eases the process of producing written sentences. The more you use inner speech for discourse planning, the higher the quality of the prose you will produce.

Many authors say that they need silence in order to write. I myself can't compose text with music on, and any spoken language distracts me (as I frequently observe when I am trying to work on my laptop in the "quiet coach" of a train). One reason might be that the sounds of other people talking around us, or the sung words on a piece of vocal music, create what psychologists call the *unattended speech effect*, whereby even speech that is not being listened to can block the phonological loop component of the working memory system, and thus interfere with our ability to create inner speech. Instrumental music, because it does not trigger our brains' automatic processing of words, might have less of an effect. For me, though, even the rhythms of instrumental music disrupt the patterns of the language I am trying to produce in my head. Some less fussy writers say that they can work perfectly well with music on, even music with words. It is possible that they have a more visual mode of writing that is less susceptible to verbal interference, or some other way of focusing that allows them to screen out what others are saying. In any case, it would be dangerous to assume that these processes work in the same way for all writers, professional or otherwise.

We should also not forget that a huge part of writing is reading—not just reading the books that are already out there, but one's own stuff, too. In an essay on the creative writing process, the novelist David Lodge observed that "90 per cent of the time nominally spent 'writing' is actually spent reading—reading yourself. . . . It is essentially what distinguishes writing from speaking." Part of the value to a writer of reading her own work, particularly after something of a gap, is that it gives her a chance to assess its effect on the reader. Several of the writers in our survey said that they needed to hear their characters' voices sounding out in their heads before they knew that they had gotten them right, and that reading back is one important way of performing that check. Virginia Woolf used to do this in her own private speech. Louie Mayer, for several decades the Woolfs' cook and housekeeper, recalled overhearing Virginia talking to herself in the bath upstairs, trying out the sentences she had written the night before: "On and on she went, talk, talk, talk, asking questions and giving herself the answers. I thought there must be 2 or 3 people up there with her." Woolf's husband, Leonard, explained to the baffled housekeeper that Virginia was simply trying her prose out loud. She would repeat her sentences to herself because "she needed to know if they sounded right."

Writers have complex relationships with the voices of their creativity, and they will use different methods to "defamiliarize" their own prose and see it through the eyes of a new reader. And yet, as we have seen, there are many ways in which writers can be surprised by the words that come to them. Several of our respondents in the Edinburgh study observed that the experience was in some ways out of their control. Fictional characters seem to acquire an agency of their own, an existence that continues once they have been thought up by the mind that created them; like the voices heard by voice-hearers, they seem largely beyond the author's own command. Dickens spoke to his American publisher, Fields, on this topic, saying that "when the children of his brain had once been launched, free and clear of him, into the world, they would sometimes turn up in the most unexpected manner to look their father in the face." On one occasion, Fields recalled Dickens exhorting him to cross the road with him so that they should not bump into Mr. Pumblechook or Mr. Micawber.

In the previous chapter, we began to explore what this experience of alien agency can tell us about how inner speech and voice-hearing work in the mind and brain. One way of thinking about this question is in relation to another kind of hallucination, usually considered to be an entirely benign one. Between the ages of around four and ten, something between one-third and two-thirds of children play with, talk to, and have adventures with people who are not there. Once considered a phenomenon that parents ought to be worried about, engaging with imaginary friends is now seen as a completely normal aspect of a child's development (so much so that, when I mention it in talks, parents sometimes ask whether they should be alarmed by the fact that their child does *not* have an imaginary friend). To what extent are the characters produced by an adult novelist like the child's imaginary playmates?

This question was addressed by one of the world's leading experts on imaginary companions, Marjorie Taylor of the University of Oregon. After many years of investigating the phenomenon in children, Taylor turned her attention to whether imaginary friends persisted into adulthood, particularly among creative people. There is some limited evidence linking pretend companions to imaginative processes. In one study, students who recalled having a make-believe friend in childhood scored higher on a self-report measure of creativity. In a separate sample of students, those who had had an imaginary companion obtained higher scores on a personality dimension that relates to how absorbed one gets in one's own acts of imagination.

One thing Taylor had noticed about children's imaginary companions was that they were often badly behaved or resistant to their child creator's demands. Taylor and colleagues observed that this same quality of noncompliance characterizes how some adult novelists describe their relationships with their characters. Philip Pullman, for example, has described having to negotiate with a particular character, Mrs. Coulter, to allow him to put her in a cave at the beginning of *The Amber Spyglass*. Recalling the writing process for his novel *The French Lieutenant's Woman*, John Fowles noted: "It is only when our characters and events begin to disobey us that they begin to live. When Charles left Sarah on her cliff-edge, I ordered him to walk straight back to Lyme Regis. But he did not; he gratuitously turned and went down to the Dairy."

Taylor went on to interview fifty writers about how they experienced the agency of their characters. Most reported some cases of characters behaving in ways that went beyond the author's control, or what Taylor termed the "illusion of independent agency." Forty-two percent reported that they had had imaginary companions as children, a higher proportion than usually emerges when adults are asked this question. Five of the fifty writers said that they still had their imaginary friends from childhood. Having a history of imaginary companions did not predict how susceptible the writer would be to noncompliant characters, but that might have been because the illusion of independent agency was so prevalent in this sample. Writers who were published were slightly more susceptible to the illusion than those who had not yet seen their work in print, although the difference was only marginally significant.

Although we were asking about fictional characters rather than imaginary companions, this quality of noncompliance also emerged in our interviews with writers. One writer of fiction for adults said, "To my delight, my characters don't agree with me, sometimes demand that I change things in the story arc of whatever I'm writing, and generally talk as if they were only having to speak to me to kind of keep me happy." One of the ways in which writers felt that they could "get it wrong" was by trying to put words into a character's mouth that were not the kinds of things that character would say. Few of the writers interviewed, however, felt that they could enter into a genuine dialogue with their characters. They might pose a question to the character—"Why are you doing that?" or "What are you doing now?"—without really expecting, or getting, a response.

That slightly one-sided nature of the relationship came to the fore for many writers when the relationship ended. Some of our interviewees had something like a feeling of bereavement when the book was finished and the voices went silent—if indeed they did. One children's writer described the voices of certain characters intruding into storyworlds to which they did not belong: "I might be working on a book from one series, and suddenly hear (in my mind) a comment from another character from a different series. Or I might be writing a situation and suddenly I'm hearing/thinking what the different characters might respond to it. Even if they don't belong in that book or series." The playwright Nick Dear said that he wrote his monologue on George III, *In the Ruins*, after completing another piece on the subject and finding that "the old boy would not shut up." In a radio interview, the screenwriter Sarah Phelps described it like this: "You do feel this absolute, black sense of bereavement, that these people who were so alive and so full of blood and so full of urgency are now not there. . . . The people in your head are sometimes more real than the people you encounter day to day. Sometimes it does feel like a form of madness."

Hallucinated voices can have a similar role in populating the imaginary landscapes that people move through. The academic Lisa Blackman described to me how the voices that her mother heard furnished her fantasy world as a child. They became her playmates: familiar visitors and interlocutors. Her mother was being treated with Largactil (also known as chlorpromazine) and electroconvulsive therapy, and as a teenager Lisa was offered genetic counseling (which she refused). As a child, she played with a box of colored pencils of different sizes and shapes, giving each a name and a distinct character and personality based on her mother's voices. "I would spend hours in my room," she told me, "constructing different settings and scenarios. I would simply lie on the floor and pick up different pencils and move them as they were speaking to each other. This was my fantasy life." Despite the difficulties of growing up in a house with a parent with these mental health issues, Lisa felt that she learned more about her mother during her psychosis than at any other time. She now describes herself as an "honorary voice-hearer," attuned to the rich fascination of auditory verbal hallucinations through a particular kind of personal experience.

Just as writers use the multiple voices of inner speech to construct their fictional worlds, so they can make meaning out of more frankly hallucinated voices. For Patricia Waugh, novels are "fictional worlds built out of voices": both the ordinary voices of inner speech and the more intrusive, foreign ones of auditory hallucination. Depicting the voices of absent entities can be a powerful fictional device. In Salman Rushdie's novel *Midnight's Children*, the protagonist, Saleem Sinai, hears the voices of all the other children who were born on the stroke of midnight on the day when India was partitioned; they become literally a chorus speaking for a divided nation. William Golding's

novel *Pincher Martin* uses indistinguishably internalized and externalized voices to re-create the consciousness of its drowning protagonist. In her first novel, *The Comforters*, the Scottish novelist Muriel
Spark used the hallucinated voice of a tapping typewriter to create a
storyworld in which the protagonist, the writer Caroline, hears her
own activities being narrated back to her. Like Woolf before her,
Spark was writing from personal experience. Around the time of her
conversion to Catholicism in the early 1950s, she became convinced
that the poet T. S. Eliot was trying to communicate with her through
coded messages, evidence of the same confusion between fictional
and real worlds that besets Caroline in her novel.

You don't have to have heard hallucinated voices yourself,
though, to be able to harness their power in creating fiction. Many of
the writers Jenny Hodgson interviewed spoke of hearing the voices
of their characters, but rarely as overtly as the experiences that Spark
and Woolf described. Is all this talk of the "voices of creativity" anything more than a metaphor? It is wise to be cautious. Daniel B.
Smith has proposed that when you take the long view of how these
ideas have been expressed in Western culture, the voices of inspiration appear to have become less physically substantial than those
that resonated for Hesiod on Mount Helicon. The artist and poet
William Blake spoke often of hearing the voices of the entities that
inspired him, including the ghost of his dead brother: "With his
spirit I converse daily & hourly. . . . I hear his advice & even now
write from his Dictate." Contrary to some modern claims that the
artist genuinely hallucinated, Smith argues that Blake was speaking
metaphorically in an attempt to make artistic inspiration more easily
comprehensible to less gifted others, and probably with some nostal-
gia for a time when the Muses *were* genuinely heard out loud.

It's time to circle back to the question with which we began,
and ask again whether these voices of creativity really have anything
in common with the voices that psychiatric patients complain of
hearing. The restrictive label "hallucination" is certainly of limited
use here. A hallucination is supposed to be involuntary, beyond the

control of the person who experiences it—and yet it's unclear whether a noncompliant imaginary companion or a disruptive fictional character could necessarily be excluded from that definition. Plenty of voice-hearers say, like Jay, that they have some control over their voices, and can occasionally even order them to go away and come back at particular times. Even some classical hallucinations, therefore, do not really justify the term, as Oliver Sacks pointed out in relation to the many experiences in varied modalities that blur the boundaries between hallucination, delusion, and illusion. You could say that someone like Jay, who knows what is happening to him and can control his reaction to it, simply has an "insight" that other people lack. The problem is that, in the absence of any objective definition of insight, such reasoning is circular.

One thing we can say about writers' experiences is that in some sense the authors go looking for them. Having recently finished writing a novel, I can think of many occasions when I actively put myself in the way of those voices. Like Julian of Norwich with her revelations, writers make themselves open to the experience in ways that patients who are troubled by auditory hallucinations really do not. It is well known that effortful imagining can blur the boundary between fantasy and reality, as evidenced by findings that imagining events that never happened increases the likelihood of having false memories of them. Given the large role that active imagination plays in the process, it's even more essential not to rush uncritically to the conclusion that writers are having the same kind of experiences as voice-hearers. That was one reason why Jenny Hodgson's face-to-face interviews with the professional writers were so valuable: they may have teased out a more sober account of the creative process than would have resulted if we had relied on questionnaires or publicity interviews alone.

We should think about the voices of creativity as a fertile inner dialogue, a dialogue in which perspectives from experience and memory come together in varied, troublesome, regenerating ways. That interpretation works, I think, even when the sense is of eavesdropping on a voice rather than actively engaging it in a conversation. Although they can very often carry a strong flavor of "other," the voices come from within—all of them. Fitting them together is something akin to assembling a self: "not as an endocrine system," in Patricia Waugh's words, "but as an experience straddled across body, mind, environment, language and time." Hilary Mantel expresses this act of self-creation beautifully: "Sometimes I feel that each morning it is necessary to write myself into being. . . . When you have committed enough words to paper you feel you have a spine stiff enough to stand up in the wind. But when you stop writing you find that's all you are, a spine, a row of rattling vertebrae, dried out like an old quill pen."

It's appropriate that the last word for now should go to another novelist. Jeanette Winterson wrote of her own experiences in her memoir, *Why Be Happy When You Could Be Normal?*: "I often hear voices. I realize that drops me in the crazy category but I don't much care. If you believe, as I do, that the mind wants to heal itself, and that the psyche seeks coherence not disintegration, then it isn't hard to conclude that the mind will manifest whatever is necessary to work on the job." In a 2004 interview, she said, "Writers have to have a knack for listening. I need to be able to hear what is being said to me by the voices I create. Just on the other side of creativity is the nuthouse—and I often notice people looking at me strangely when I am talking out loud, but there is no other way."

13

MESSAGES FROM THE PAST

"I DON'T KNOW. It sounds daft, but sometimes he says things that are really funny."

The speaker is Margaret, a woman in her seventies with a bright, open face and a gentle smile. She has come along today with her daughter, who is desperate for advice on helping her mother to cope with her frequent voices. There are around twenty of us in the room. Apart from a couple of clinical psychologists and a few of us from the academic team, everyone here is an expert by experience. We are gathered in a conference suite at Durham University on a cold, sparkling spring afternoon. We are hosting the event with our special guest Jacqui Dillon, chair of the UK Hearing Voices Network and an old friend of our project.

"Yeah, mine say funny things, too."

Before Margaret came into this room, she had never met another voice-hearer. Now she is surrounded by them. I see her deep in conversation with Julia, a writer of a similar age who has come to talk to us several times about her experiences. Two elderly ladies, sipping tea and chatting about the voices in their heads. Julia is an old hand, but Margaret is in entirely new territory. She looks radiant, transformed. I have the sense that a life could be changing in front of my eyes.

I'm not having a dull day, either. I've spoken to a middle-aged man with a dark complexion who has a habit of laughing along to himself as he speaks. He says that his voices have saved his life—twice. (He doesn't expand.) Alison has also been saved by a voice. She is in her forties, with cropped gray hair and a severe expression that transforms, when you engage her in conversation, into a generous smile. In a former life she was a shoplifter, and on one occasion she heard a voice yelling "Stop!" as she fled down a street away from the scene of a theft. She pulled up short, and as she rounded the next corner she saw a car smashing into the wall just ahead of her, destroying a lamppost. Alison believes that some of her voices have an internal origin, and that others result from connecting with what she calls "cosmic consciousness." She says that our minds and those of all living beings are connected in a single unity of being. I'm not sure that I share her view, but I believe in her explanation. I believe that she believes it, and that it is helpful to her.

Today is a networking event, set up for people who experience voice-hearing but do not yet attend a hearing voices group. There is a lot of talk about taking the opportunity to set up new groups, and phone numbers are exchanged. Hearing voices groups are set up and run by people who have had the experience for themselves—which excludes me—and so this is as close as I will get to attending a group in person. Across the room from me is Simon, who has learning difficulties caused by fragile-X syndrome. His caregiver tells us that Simon gets frustrated because he assumes that everyone else can hear his voices, and that the people around him are pretending they can't hear them in order to wind Simon up. The caregiver is from a charity group that works with people with intellectual disabilities, but she, like most of her colleagues, has no training or experience in voice-hearing. She has come along to try to gather some ideas about how to help Simon manage his voices. Simon laughs when Adam, telling the group about his experiences, swears under his breath as he describes the kinds of things the Captain gets up to. Adam is also an old friend of our project, and he is speaking to the new faces as an expert—someone, like Jacqui, who has been through the psychiatric system and has come out on the other side to live comfortably, if not always exactly happily, with his voices.

Another participant, Richard, started hearing voices after having a conversation at work. The people who had been speaking had moved on across the office, but their voices stayed with him. They were saying things about his wife and the affairs she had supposedly been having behind Richard's back. He left the office and headed home to confront her. A heated argument ensued, and Richard ended up in a police cell, where the voices continued. He later became delusional, and he was eventually diagnosed with paranoid schizophrenia. He sees his two episodes of psychosis as resulting from stress, including the fallout of a difficult marriage and the pressures of supporting a young family. When he heard the voices, it was like listening to someone in the same room with him. As part of his recovery, he was invited to write a narrative of his experiences. "I remember sitting eating my tea at my mum's when all of a sudden a voice appeared in my mind. It was a [street] address and it was clear. . . . I can remember looking up, as though looking into my brain, and laughing. I remember saying, 'You're having a laugh' as though to tell my brain/ mind off. I wondered what the hell was going on because the voices were so clear, almost booming into my head."

Many people at today's event have stories to tell about stress and trauma. Groups like this come together around a starting assumption that voices are meaningful, and that they convey valuable emotional messages. The idea that voices can have profound human significance has deep roots, featuring, for example, in the psychoanalyst Carl Jung's argument that hallucinations contain a "germ of meaning" that, if identified accurately, can mark the beginning of a process of healing. But that notion is antithetical to the traditional biomedical view in psychiatry, which has tended to see voices as neural junk, meaningless glitches in the brain. In Eleanor Longden's gripping and heartrending book *Learning from the Voices in My Head*, based on her popular TED talk, she describes how her psychotic breakdown as a student led to a diagnosis of schizophrenia, from which she was told there would be no recovery. The first voice that Eleanor heard was benign, commenting on her actions in the third person: "She is leaving the building"; "She is opening the door." The voice remained neutral but increased in frequency, and occasionally it mirrored Eleanor's own unexpressed emotions, taking on a tone of irritation, for example, to reflect its host's suppressed anger. When Eleanor mentioned her voice to a friend, the beginnings of a positive relationship with the voice began to unravel. Eleanor was urged to seek medical help, and her college doctor referred her to a psychiatrist—the beginning of a journey from straight-As student to cowering, degraded psychiatric patient. One consultant psychiatrist told Eleanor that she would have been better off with cancer than schizophrenia, "because cancer is easier to cure."

Like countless others, Eleanor has benefited from the alternative framework of understanding that the Hearing Voices Movement has given her. After her grim days in the hospital, she was seen by an enlightened psychiatrist, Pat Bracken, who helped her to understand her voices not as symptoms of disease but as survival strategies. She had been brutalized by her experiences, and her psyche was struggling to adapt. Eleanor began to understand her voices as resulting from the horrific and organized sexual torture she had suffered as a small child. "It was a blasphemy," she wrote of her abuse, "a desecration beyond expression; and it left behind a tiny child whose mind broke and shattered into a million tiny pieces." Eleanor grew into an academically successful, organized young woman and became adept at presenting a serene face to the world. Behind the façade, though, was a mind torn apart by a "psychic civil war."

With Bracken's help, Eleanor resolved to make sense of her voices. She learned of the Dutch psychiatrist Marius Romme's claim that voices are messengers communicating important information about unresolved emotional problems. In Romme's metaphor, it makes no sense to shoot the messenger just because the content of the message is unpleasant. Instead, the Hearing Voices Movement approach is to encourage voice-hearers to try to understand the events that led to the emotional distress that the voices are expressing. "The question we should be asking," Longden says, "is not 'What's your problem?' It's 'What's your story?'"

The movement has its origins in a particular therapeutic partnership between Romme and one of his patients, a young Dutch woman named Patsy Hage. As a conventionally trained physician, Romme's instinct was to see Hage's destructive, troubling voices as meaningless symptoms of a biomedical illness. But Hage insisted that her voices were as real and significant as the deities to whom those around her prayed. She was influenced by Julian Jaynes's theory of how our ancestors in the era of the *Iliad* had experienced the gods speaking to them, and she was reassured by the closeness of her experience to what Jaynes claimed was once the default mode of thought. As she put it to Romme, her epiphany in understanding her alien voices was a simple realization: "I'm not a schizophrenic, I'm an ancient Greek!"

Romme's view of his patient started to change, and he began to take her testimony more seriously. When they appeared together on Dutch television to discuss the work they had been doing and to appeal for voice-hearers to contact them, there was an overwhelming response. Around 150 of the people who contacted them had found ways of living contentedly with their voices. As the movement grew, its basic tenets began to cohere: that hearing voices is a common aspect of human experience, which can be distressing but is not inherently a symptom of illness; and that voices bear messages about emotional truths and problems that can, through taking the voices seriously and with appropriate support, be resolved. In Lisa Blackman's words, voices "speak the unspeakable." However unpleasant and distressing, they often carry information that needs to be heard.

The method that Romme and his co-researcher, Sandra Escher, developed in working with voice-hearers has become known as the Maastricht approach. "We ask about the meaning of the voices," Romme told me, "with a focus on their particular characteristics." Escher picks up the story: "In our first studies we asked about what the voices said, who they represented, and how they had developed.

And we then tried to relate that to what had happened in the person's life and how emotionally it had influenced the person. About 90 percent of the people we worked with had clear emotional problems." The Maastricht Interview asks questions about the different voices heard, the age at which they first appeared, personal experiences of adversity, and how the appearance of the voices is set off by different triggers. I have used the interview with a voice-hearer myself, as part of the training that Escher led when she and Romme were guests of ours in Durham, and it is far more detailed than most of the other instruments designed to assess the experience. Particularly notable is the fact that it asks for voice-hearers' own interpretations of the origin of their voices, with response options including that the voices emanate from a real person; that they are supernatural entities, such as gods, ghosts, angels, spirits, or devils; and that they express the pain felt by other people. The interview's ultimate goal is to create what Romme and Escher call a "construct," a detailed description of that voice-hearer's experiences and their relation to events from the individual's life.

Seeking the origins of their experiences in traumatic events is a powerful approach for many voice-hearers. After early experiences of being bullied as a schoolboy, which had confirmed his own impression of himself as a sensitive, thoughtful person, Adam joined the Royal Artillery. Almost overnight, the fragile schoolboy was being asked to become an aggressive man. During his training he began to have problems controlling his anger, smashing up his room on several occasions and punching the floor in his fury. Instead of taking the anger management classes he was enrolled for, he volunteered for Iraq, taking a role in his battery commander's escort and providing top cover for his signal sergeant as he moved around the south of the country. He received great support and helpful psychiatric treatment during his tour, but things really deteriorated after he returned from Iraq in 2004. He left the army in 2007 and took a job as a foundry operative making specialized gas and oil pipelines. Although he enjoyed the work, his voices returned with renewed force.

They were mean and critical, particularly the Captain. He has never left Adam's side since.

Adam took part in Sandra Escher's training course in Durham, which culminated in a public event in which voice-hearers told the stories of their recovery. Even as Adam was typing out his story, expressing the hope that one day he would be able to banish his voices, the Captain was trying to persuade him to delete what he had written: "Fuck off, I'm here for life." Through working with Sandra, Adam began to understand his experiences as stemming from the bullying he had suffered in his schooldays. For him, the recovery journey went further. With our support, he made a short film of his experiences, *Adam Plus One*, which we have since shown in many contexts to try to reduce stigma about voice-hearing. When the BBC presenter Sian Williams asked Adam what kind of person he would be without the Captain, he had no answer. "All I know now is that I'm a voice-hearer. . . . That's who I am. And I don't think anybody would want to strip their own identity away. I don't think I would want a space where he wasn't there. Sometimes, yes, he is very annoying, he makes me very uncomfortable. But I have no idea who I would be without him."

The Hearing Voices Movement approach is, in Jacqui Dillon's words, "spreading like wildfire." The movement currently has networks in 23 countries, with more than 180 groups in the United Kingdom alone. The movement is also becoming established in the United States. When I went on National Public Radio's *Radiolab* in 2010 to talk about voice-hearing, the producers struggled to find someone from a hearing voices group to talk to them—there were no such groups in New York City. By early 2015, there were six. The organization has well-developed plans to create regional networks and stimulate the movement's growth. With this progress in the heartland of biological psychiatry, it has become a truly worldwide phenomenon.

ONE OF THE CORNERSTONES of the movement that Jacqui Dillon and Eleanor Longden are so closely associated with is a particular idea about where voices come from: that they have their roots in traumatic events that have led to unresolved emotional problems. At first glance, this looks utterly different from the idea that voices result from atypical processing of inner speech. Rather than pointing us to the processing of language and the speech perception networks in the brain, it suggests that we should look for a link with traumatic memories. Clinically, and from the evidence of personal testimony, their theory makes perfect sense. What scientific support, though, is there for the idea that voices are about memories of the past?

One way of addressing this question is to ask whether some voice-hearing experiences have the quality of memories. Simon McCarthy-Jones and colleagues analyzed in-depth phenomenological interviews with nearly two hundred people with auditory hallucinations, most of whom had a diagnosis of schizophrenia. More than a third of the voice-hearers reported that their voices seemed in some ways to be replays of previous conversations with other people. But only a minority of this group thought that their voices involved literal reproductions of the earlier experiences; most claimed that the things they heard were only "similar" to them.

An alternative approach is to see whether those who hear voices show any differences in how they process memories. Flavie Waters and her colleagues at the University of Western Australia have proposed that auditory hallucinations result from a failure to inhibit memories that are not relevant to what the person is currently doing. The idea, which has gained support from Waters's experimental studies, is that people who have such experiences are particularly bad at keeping irrelevant information out of consciousness. Coupled with a problem with context memory—which refers to the ability to recall the details of the context in which an event happened—this can lead to memories intruding into consciousness shorn of the contextual anchors that would usually allow us to recognize them as a memory rather than a hallucination.

Another line of evidence comes from associations with trauma. There is now very strong evidence for a link between hearing voices and early adversity, particularly childhood sexual abuse. In one recent study led by Richard Bentall, childhood rape was strongly and specifically associated with hallucinations later in life. To give an indication of the strength of the relationship, Bentall likened it to that between smoking and lung cancer. A dose-response relationship was also observed, meaning that the more adversity the individual faced, the greater his or her risk. "Dose-response relationships are thought to be quite good evidence that an effect is causal," Bentall told me, "because they are not easily explained away in other ways. So the finding that children who experience multiple traumas are more likely to experience voices than children who only experience a single traumatic event makes us more confident that the trauma plays a causal role."

There are still reasons for caution, however. "Cause is a tricky thing to pin down," Bentall explained. "In this case we can be pretty confident, even if not to 100 percent certainty, that the effect is causal. But of course this is not to say that trauma always causes voices, or that it is the only cause of voices." Although the literature on memory for trauma is highly complex, the causation view is supported by evidence that images and impressions from horrific events can remain in a free-floating state, ready to intrude upon consciousness detached from the contextual information that would typically allow them to be recognized as a memory.

Another advantage that the memory account has over the inner-speech one is that the latter struggles to explain nonverbal auditory hallucinations such as music, the barking of dogs, screaming, clicks, humming, watery sounds, or the murmuring of crowds. In Simon McCarthy-Jones's study, a third of participants reported that kind of hallucination. Unless one wants to claim that ordinary inner experience also incorporates such sounds, it is hard to see how hallucinations like these could result from misattributed inner speech.

But the memory account faces serious problems as well. For one thing, it has to explain how memories of horrible events can lie dormant for so many years before resurfacing in early adulthood—the peak time for the diagnosis of disorders like schizophrenia. Another problem is that memory simply doesn't work like that. Creating a memory is a reconstructive process that involves bringing together

lots of different sources of information, some of which are erroneously included, having not figured in the original event at all. We are
particularly bad, even over a short period, at recalling the exact words
that people say to us: we tend to recall the gist of messages rather
than their verbatim information. That would be problematic if we
wanted to propose that voices are literal reproductions of earlier conversations. In general, the idea that a traumatic memory can faith-
fully reproduce the details of an event and then be reactivated decades
later doesn't fit with what is known about how we remember.

The missing link between trauma and voice-hearing might be a
psychological phenomenon known as *dissociation*. First described by
the French psychiatrist Pierre Janet toward the end of the nineteenth
century, the term refers to the phenomenon whereby thoughts, feelings, and experiences are not integrated into consciousness in the
usual way. The connection with hearing voices comes through the
finding that people who live through horrific events often describe
themselves dissociating during the trauma. Splitting itself into separate parts is one of the most powerful of the mind's defense mechanisms. It is as though there is some drastic attempt by the psyche to
remove itself from the horror that is unfolding: drastic because it effectively involves the psyche cleaving itself into pieces.

Scientific research has suggested that dissociation might act as a
bridge between trauma and voice-hearing. A study by Richard Bentall's group asked patients with a schizophrenia spectrum disorder
and non-patient controls about susceptibility to hallucinations, dissociative tendencies, and childhood trauma. The analysis confirmed
previous findings that childhood sexual abuse related to hallucinations, but it also showed through statistical analysis that the relationship was "mediated" by dissociation. *Mediation* is a statistical term
that refers to how three variables, or factors, can be related to each
other in a particular way: essentially, factor A is related to factor C
because of how they both relate to factor B. Bentall's analysis is consistent with (although doesn't prove) the idea that trauma (factor A)
causes dissociation (factor B), which then causes hallucinations (factor C), rather than that trauma causes hallucinations directly.

Researchers have also made use of the fact that dissociation varies in the general population, just like voice-hearing does. In a study with our inner-speech questionnaire, we asked undergraduate volunteers to also complete an instrument called the Dissociative Experiences Scale, which asked them to rate their experience of a range of dissociative states (for example, having no memory of an important event such as a wedding or graduation). We found that dissociation mediated the link between proneness to auditory hallucinations and two of our inner-speech factors: specifically, the one that relates to evaluating one's own behavior, and the one that describes the presence of other people in one's inner speech. That is, certain inner-speech characteristics (factor A) related to dissociation (factor B), which in turn related to voice-hearing (factor C). Although in this case we didn't set out to measure childhood trauma (a very difficult thing to do in a questionnaire study), our findings supported the idea that dissociation is an important mechanism in explaining why some people hear voices.

Dissociation perhaps just describes an extreme version of what is normal in the rest of us. Eleanor Longden is now a postdoctoral researcher specializing in how the psychological processes of dissociation might help to explain the occurrence of trauma-related voices. When I spoke with her recently, she agreed with me that there is an important conceptual problem with replacing the idea of a unitary self with an account that proposes multiple selves—all of which are still conceived as having the basic structure of an ordinary self, but just in the plural rather than the singular. "I think we all have multiple *aspects* of self," Eleanor observed, "and that this is an experience most people will relate to: a part that's very critical, a part that wants to appease everyone, a part that is playful and irresponsible, and so on. Voices feel more disowned and externalized in most cases, but essentially I think they represent a similar process."

Voices, then, might give us important clues about the fragmentary constitution of an ordinary human self. Dissociation makes sense as a natural reaction to horrific events, an argument that Eleanor can make from personal experience: "Some of the most dramatic memories of dissociation I have are acute ones, during actual trauma exposure—the sense of seeing myself on the floor, as if I was just floating above the horror happening below, completely separate from it. It's like your mind knows that the time has come when it's better to lose touch with what's happening to your body and simply breaks free: mental flight." This view of a dissociated self is already paying dividends in research on voice-hearing, although much remains to be done in explaining exactly what these fragments of self look like, and how they operate and behave. A dissociation account is still some way from explaining how traumatic memories become transmuted into hallucinations—and in particular, why those experiences are so often verbal—but it is a promising avenue for future research. It might provide a partial answer to the puzzle of how a voice can be both "me" and "not me."

At the same time, these arguments don't mean that we should reject the inner speech model. Rather, they push us to recognize that voices take different forms; that they may have different cognitive and neural mechanisms underpinning them; and that we therefore may need different explanations of their causes and different theories about why they persist and how they can be managed. Some of the voices that people report may well have their roots in inner speech, while others might be best described as intrusions from memory. Unless we are more careful about how we listen to voice-hearers describing their experiences, we will miss distinctions that could turn out to be critical.

PERHAPS THE MOST IMPORTANT reason to think about voice-hearing in this way is that it has implications for managing the experience. If voices are at least partly about things that happened to the hearer, then they give the hearer something to work with. They hold out the prospect of recovery.

This is an idea that the Hearing Voices Movement has used to powerful effect. When Eleanor Longden offered forgiveness to her most unpleasant voice, the tone of its communications with her changed. "Essentially," she told me, "it was a process of making peace with myself, because the negative voices embodied so many painful memories and unresolved emotion. A turning point was coming to the realization that the voices weren't the actual abusers; rather, that they represented my feelings and beliefs about the abuse. So while they appeared incredibly negative and malicious, they actually embodied the aspects of me that had been hurt the most profoundly, and as such needed the greatest amounts of compassion and care."

Just as it was beneficial in thinking about the psychological processes underlying voices, a comparison with memory can be useful in working out how to help people with distressing voices. Voices may not be memories in the literal sense, but we can learn much about methods for dealing with them by looking at how people learn to live with memories of horrible events. Therapy for traumatic memories, such as those that characterize posttraumatic stress disorder, involves encouraging the sufferer not so much to try to forget the event as to remember it more accurately. That means fitting it into a network of memories in such a way that it can become less intrusive, distorted, and autonomous.

As far as voices are concerned, that means recognizing that one's voices are strange, disruptive, twisted facets of the self—but they are still parts of the self. If they're in some sense about memory, the voice-hearer can come to terms with them in the same way that an individual can come to terms with unpleasant memories: by integrating them back into the psyche from which they have become split away.

One way to ease the process of integration is to give the voices some concrete external reality. Some voice-hearers have told me that they use puppets to represent the things their voices say in order to detach themselves from them and make them easier to deal with. In another technique favored by many in the Hearing Voices Movement, the voice is brought directly into the therapy session. Known as Voice Dialogue or Talking with Voices, the method involves the facilitator asking the voice-hearer whether she can speak directly to the voice. In one of Eleanor Longden's case studies, the psychotherapist, Dr. Dirk Corstens, asks to speak with one of the participant's dominant voices. The participant's name is Nelson; the voice goes by the name of Judas. For Nelson, Judas seems well-meaning, but he also has a dominant, frightening manner. After establishing contact with Judas, Nelson adopts a military stance and begins pacing around the room (Nelson had previously served in the army) while speaking in Judas's voice, with its characteristic abrupt sentences. Judas turns out to be an overprotective, paternal figure who is making excessive demands of Nelson (forcing him to go to nightclubs in order to meet women, for example). He wants Nelson to accept him, not push him away. The aim of the technique is to find out more about Judas and what he wants, so as to give Nelson some options for how to deal with him. At the end of the session, Nelson comes back into himself and reports that he was aware of everything that went on. He was intrigued by Judas's explanation of his name, which drew on an association of Judas as a protector of Christ from early gnostic works. The therapy had positive and lasting effects. It helped Nelson find a new rapport with his mental visitors—and, crucially, effected a rapprochement between his distinct voices—and thus parts of his self—which had previously been at war.

Another technique that involves externalizing a voice bears several parallels with Voice Dialogue, although it emerged from a rather different quarter. The English psychiatrist Julian Leff was responsible for some groundbreaking work in the 1970s on social factors triggering relapse in schizophrenia. More recently, he had the idea of setting up a therapeutic situation in which patients who heard voices could interact with them through a computer-based avatar. Using face-generation software, patients are first asked to create a face that matches the voice they want to work with, then to use voice-synthesis software to construct a voice to go with it. The therapist, sitting in another room, then speaks to the patient in the voice of the hallucination, with the face of the avatar animated in sync, although at the flick of a switch he can flip back to being the comforting, guiding therapist. Typically this method involves encouraging the patient to stand up to the voice and challenge what it is saying. A pilot study showed impressive results, with reductions in both the frequency of

voices and the patients' beliefs in their malevolence and omnipo-
tence. Three out of sixteen of the patients in the pilot trial stopped
hearing voices altogether. Leff believes that the visualization of the
hallucinatory experience allows patients to gain control over their
voices, particularly when they are frightened about how the voice
might react if it is confronted or challenged.

Jacqui Dillon points out that there is nothing particularly new in
this approach. When I meet her for lunch on a sunny November day
at the Barbican Centre in London, she tells me that the Avatar project is thoroughly well meaning but appears to lack theoretical foundations. "It does seem to be making the whole thing much more
convoluted and technologically heavy than it needs to be," she explains. "Because essentially what seemed to be working was that
you're taking these things as being real and meaningful to me, and
you're kind of having a conversation with me about them. The fact
that you've got to go in another room and do that, through an avatar
that we have to create, seems to me a bit of a palaver, really. Why
can't we just sit in the same room and have that conversation?"

Jacqui explains that the Hearing Voices Movement is partly about
who has the right to tell people what their experiences mean. "It is
about power, and it's about who's got the expertise, and the authority." She contrasts the approach with cognitive behavioral therapy
(CBT), the system of thought- and behavior-modification that has
benefited Jay. "One of the criticisms about CBT is that it's about an
expert doing something *to*, and of course the whole hearing voices
approach is about doing *with*, and it's not about an expert in that
way. . . . People with lived experience have a lot to say about it, know
a lot about what it's like to experience it, to live with it, to cope with
it. If we want to learn anything about extreme human experience, we
have to listen to the people who experience it to learn more."

I've known Jacqui for several years. She was the first person I ever
met who I knew for a fact to be a voice-hearer. Those were early days
for me in researching this topic, and I still felt apprehensive about
how someone with such an unusual experience would behave. If I
had the impression that Jacqui was approaching me with suspicion,

she probably was. She is a highly influential figure in the mental health world, traveling frequently to give talks about her own life and experiences and her role in the growing international movement. As our project has developed and she has seen that we are genuinely interested in understanding voice-hearing, we have become friends, although there are still a few things that we disagree about. Like many others in the Hearing Voices Movement, Jacqui is skeptical about the inner speech model of voice-hearing, because it seems not to do enough justice to the meaning of the experience. Catching up with her today is partly about persuading her that my being interested in how voices work—wanting to understand their mechanisms in the mind and brain—doesn't entail trying to explain them away. Or even wanting to make them *go* away, in the sense of stopping them altogether. Admitting that, as a scientist, I want to know how things work is not the same as saying that I want to deny the significance of the individual's experience, or to make everyone's voices vanish.

I suspect that some of the antipathy to the inner speech model stems from overlooking the complexity of the phenomenon. "How can it just be inner speech?" people ask me. I respond that there is nothing "just" about inner speech. As we have seen, the voices in our heads contain multitudes: not just a considerable variety of forms, but also diverse voices in dialogue, representations of remembered events, interactions with visual imagery and other sensory experiences, and so on. That fear of reductionism is understandable, but in this case it is misguided. Saying that inner speech cannot explain why voices are meaningful only makes sense if you hold that inner speech is not meaningful. As I hope to have shown, nothing could be further from the truth.

A pluralistic view seems both possible and necessary. Rachel Waddingham, who has done groundbreaking work in Camden, London, with young people who hear voices, thinks that inner speech might have a role as one of many mechanisms. The danger is that people might assume that it is the only possible one. When Marius Romme was a guest of Durham's Institute of Advanced Study at our invitation in 2011, he and I had several conversations about whether an inner speech model could be integrated with a trauma one. Like many others in the movement, Romme was skeptical about the inner speech model's ability to explain the relationship of voices with past trauma. But he did think there might be a role for inner speech in engaging silently with one's own voices, learning about them, understanding them better, and thus aiding their reintegration into the self. Jay, for example, says that he never speaks to his voices out loud, but only silently in his head, and then only at certain times of the day. Even if it doesn't explain the phenomenon, inner speech can provide a channel for keeping in touch with one's voices.

Some kind of rapprochement between the two models will clearly be needed, but things are going to have to get even more complex first. At some basic level, voices *must* be about inner speech, simply because of the definitional point that they are about language sounding out silently in the head. Jacqui hears more than a hundred different voices, and she is far better placed than I am to say whether the scientific theories make sense. She has described hearing a voice as being like receiving "a telephone call from your unconscious." It's a message that, however horrible and disruptive, you feel compelled to listen to. "It's an aspect of self, isn't it?" Jacqui tells me. "Even if it's an unpleasant aspect. I find this with a lot of people who hear voices—when you really ask them, they don't really want them to go away. They don't want them to be as distressing, but there's this sense that they're part of me in some way, even if they're saying these really troubling, upsetting things."

Exactly the same question comes up when we ask about how people relate to traumatic memories. Some research from Elizabeth Loftus's lab at the University of California, Irvine, has shown that people feel very strongly attached to their memories, even traumatic ones. In one experiment, Loftus presented participants with a scenario in which one could take a (hypothetical) drug to erase the memory of a trauma. Eighty percent of people said that they would not take the drug; they would rather keep the horrible memory. Even when memories are terrible, we seem to want to hang on to them. They are parts of our selves, even if they are aspects that we can only look upon with horror.

But therapy can help with traumatic memories. It can lead them to be reprocessed in such a way that they become less intrusive, disruptive, and distorted. When I was researching my book on the topic, I talked to a lorry driver, Colin, who had had his horrific and distorted memories of a road traffic accident reshaped by a method called *eye movement desensitization and reprocessing* (EMDR). During the worst phase of his posttraumatic stress disorder, he would have given anything to make the memories go away, but now, after therapy, he accepts them as part of himself. I would say the same thing about a couple of highly distressing memories that I myself have. They're horrible, but they are mine. Isn't this precisely what some people say about their voices?

Jacqui agrees. The experience of hearing distressing voices is not something that can be best dealt with by banishing them. Voice-hearing can enrich a person. The process of mastering them changes us. "It deepens us as human beings," Jacqui says. "It impacts on a whole load of levels in terms of capacity to feel things, or capacity to feel a connection with other suffering beings." And not only are voices comprehensible on an analogy with traumatic memories, they also *are* traumatic memories in many cases, or at least reconstructions of them. The puzzle for me, I tell her, is how to account for the fact that this awful thing that happened to a person is coming back as a voice. That is very difficult to explain purely in terms of a conventional view of memory. Dissociation might be part of it, but you've still got to get to language. You've still got to explain why you're hearing it as a voice.

In a way, that was also at the heart of my disagreements with Marius Romme. I suggested to him that we could both be right—we might just be working on different aspects of the same problem. For Romme, the key thing to explain was how a trauma could lead to the emotional messages that were now crying out to be heard. For me, it was how and why that message was being heard as a voice rather than as something else. Memory is useful as a model here, because memory is reconstructive. It changes as we do. Even if the event happened in the distant past, the story we construct about it is shaped by who we are now: what we want, what we believe, and what has happened in the interim. Pursuing this analogy further might help us to understand how voices change over a person's lifetime, with some growing older with the voice-hearer, and others frozen in time.

When you misremember the past, one reason is that the old version doesn't fit with your story now. So you change the facts to fit the story. I put it to Jacqui that voice-hearers are doing something similar with their pieces of remembered experience: they are reshaping them into a story that is not quite as shattering to their sense of who they are. This chimes with her intuitions as a voice-hearer: "I suppose I would see those as aspects of a person's self," she responds, "and the analogy I would often use is family therapy. . . . It's a dysfunctional family. I would see them as fragments of a self, and those aspects make up a person."

And we are all fragmented. There is no unitary self. We are all in pieces, struggling to create the illusion of a coherent "me" from moment to moment. We are all more or less dissociated. Our selves are constantly constructed and reconstructed in ways that often work well, but often break down. Stuff happens, and the center cannot hold. Some of us have more fragmentation going on, because of those things that have happened; those people face a tougher challenge of pulling it all together. But no one ever slots in the last piece and makes it whole. As human beings, we seem to want that illusion of a completed, unitary self, but getting there is hard work. And anyway, we never get there.

In the meantime, people like Jacqui are left with the voices. Joking with her at the café at the Barbican, I can tell she's happy with the company. "Most of the time they make me laugh," she said later in an interview. "They're actually hilarious. We have a good old laugh together. They're insightful, they're loving, they're comforting, and they help me to feel less alone. They know me better than anybody else and they're always there for me."

14

A Voice That Doesn't Speak

A former voice-hearer—let's call her Rumer—was telling me about how her voices disappeared for good. Her main voice was a female one, and it was connected with her eating disorder. It would tell Rumer that she was fat and ugly, and point out things that she should and shouldn't eat. And then one day it wasn't there anymore. At the time that I spoke to Rumer about it, a few months had passed since she had last heard a voice. She found it difficult to pin down the exact moment, and she still wasn't certain that the voice had gone away forever. But the interesting thing was how Rumer knew that it had disappeared. It was a feeling that her social environment had changed, like the way you know that someone has left a room in which you are sitting even if there isn't an explicit goodbye. Rumer found it hard to put into words, but it was the sense of the passing of a person who had stopped speaking some time ago. This wasn't the cessation of an auditory experience; it was the end of a feeling of being inhabited.

This is not an uncommon story among people whose voices go away. Someone is there, and then they're not there anymore. I was reminded of what I had been told about the initial onset of voice-hearing: how it can be like dialing into a transmission that has always been present. "Once you hear the voices," wrote Mark Vonnegut of his experiences, "you realise they've always been there. It's just a matter of being tuned to them." If you can tune in to something, then perhaps you can also tune out.

That sense of a presence is also there in Jay's testimony. At the moment when he was hearing the voice of the Doctor outside of Wetherspoons, Jay knew that one of the other characters he sometimes heard was there even though he wasn't hearing that character's voice at that time. In the moment in the railway tunnel, Jay could hear the Witch, but he could not feel her presence. And yet he knew that both of his other voices were there even though they weren't saying anything. So the voices can be split apart from the feeling of a presence: a voice-hearer can at times hear the voice without feeling the presence, and at other times can feel the presence without hearing the voice.

There has been a small amount of research on the psychological experience of the "felt presence." A common version of it, among new parents, is the feeling that your baby is there in the bed with you. Feeling the presence of someone who has recently died is also a frequent occurrence among people who have been bereaved. Felt presence features in various neurological disorders, including epilepsy, and often it accompanies the more common experience of sleep paralysis, in which one has a fleeting experience of being paralyzed at the moment of falling asleep or waking up. The feeling of a benign presence is of course a typical feature of religious experience. Many people feel that they have guardian angels who are looking out for them, and such entities are by no means always vocal ones.

In more extreme circumstances, a felt presence can seem to have a more direct involvement in one's survival. The polar explorer Sir Ernest Shackleton wrote of how, on his perilous journey with two companions across the mountains and glaciers of South Georgia, he often felt that a fourth traveler was accompanying them. "I said nothing to my companions on the point, but afterward [Frank] Worsley said to me, 'Boss, I had a curious feeling on the march that there was another person with us.'" The presence was a guiding, protective one. Extremes of cold, exhaustion, and isolation are also fertile ground for hearing voices, as the mountaineer Joe Simpson discovered during the events described in his bestseller *Touching the Void*. Although Simpson does not describe the sense of a presence that Shackleton noted, he found that the voice had a guarding, motivational function. Some have argued that these experiences might even be a basic survival mechanism that evolved to keep us safe when our lives are in danger.

How common is it for people to feel a presence when they hear a voice, and how is that feeling, in turn, connected to the feeling that an entity is trying to communicate with them? One problem has been that, when researchers or clinicians ask about voices, they have tended not to ask about the other experiences that accompany them. This blind spot has been lamented for a long time by people in the Hearing Voices Movement, and many hearing voices groups explicitly acknowledge it in their names and publicity material (the full title of the Hearing Voices Network in England, for example, adds "for people who hear voices, see visions or have other unusual perceptions"). This neglect of concomitant experiences is arguably a by-product of how voice-hearing has assumed such an important role in the diagnosis of schizophrenia. When you're dealing with the sacred symbol of the sacred symbol, it can be easy to miss the other crucial clues that accompany it.

We set out to ask about these additional aspects of the voice-hearing experience in a large Internet-based study led by Angela Woods, a medical humanities researcher and codirector of Hearing the Voice. Voice-hearers were asked anonymously to answer questions such as, "How, if at all, do your voices differ from thoughts?" and, "Does it feel as though the voice(s) that you hear have their own character or personality?" One group of questions focused on what other sensations were associated with the individual's unusual experiences. The results from around 150 voice-hearers showed that the experience is decidedly not just about hallucinated sounds. Fewer than half of our respondents reported experiences that had exclusively auditory features. Two-thirds of the voice-hearers who responded reported bodily sensations accompanying their voices, such as a feeling that their brain was on fire or that they were cut off from their body. There was a tendency for these changes in bodily experience to be associated with voices connected with violence and abuse. "The results are clear," Woods explains. "Voice-hearing is anything but an exclusively auditory experience."

That is not the same question as whether voice-hearing is always a *verbal* experience. We have already seen plenty of examples of nonverbal, and yet still auditory, "voices." In a seminal study of the phenomenology of auditory hallucinations, Tony Nayani and Anthony David at the Institute of Psychiatry found that two-thirds of their sample of voice-hearers (most of whom had a diagnosis of schizophrenia) heard nonverbal auditory hallucinations along with their verbal voices. Experiences described included whispers, cries, clicks and bangs, and musical hallucinations, particularly of choral music. Many voice-hearers spontaneously classify nonverbal auditory hallucinations as voices, and the experiences can often co-occur or even merge into each other. Margery Kempe heard the voice of God as the sound of a bellows, the voice of a dove, and the chirp of a robin. Julian of Norwich similarly reported experiences that were not always clear, intelligible voices, but instead (on at least one occasion) an indistinct murmuring in which specific words could not be distinguished.

All of which suggests that we could widen the net even further to catch phenomena that are not even auditory. Some experiences that are perceived as voices do not have any acoustic elements at all, such as the voices that both Margery and Julian received with their "ghostly understanding"—words implanted in the mind without any auditory concomitant. The twelfth-century German mystic Hildegard of Bingen wrote of hearing words that were "not like those which sound from the mouth of man, but like a trembling flame, or like a cloud stirred by the clean air." Soundless voices also crop up in more modern psychiatric reports, such as in the "vivid thoughts" described by some patients of Eugen Bleuler at the turn of the twentieth century. In one of Bleuler's case studies, a patient reported: "It was as if someone pointed his finger at me and said 'go and drown yourself.'" It does not seem too far a stretch, therefore, to include other unusual perceptions, such as visions, feelings of a felt presence, and additional sensations. There may be nothing particularly "voicey" about hearing a voice.

For a different approach, we can turn again to those medieval accounts of voice-hearing. The testimonies of Joan of Arc, Margery Kempe, and Julian of Norwich all point to an experience that was much more like perceiving a presence in all its facets: the visual and bodily as well as the auditory. I mentioned earlier that one reason for this might be a social or religious one: if you are really going to be visited by the Holy Ghost, you're likely to report an assault on all your senses (especially if you suspect that people might have trouble believing you). Perhaps people who hallucinate voices are actually hallucinating *people*—in a way that can make them manifest in one of several possible sensory modalities.

Take Adam as an example. "It's not a voice," he tells us about the Captain. "It's a person." Rather than the Captain being an auditory experience, let's suppose that Adam's mind is creating a representation of an individual who does not actually exist. Sometimes that person appears as a voice, sometimes he is felt as a presence, sometimes as a visual image. The idea that voice-hearers are hallucinating people rather than sensory data helps to explain why voices can have so much about them that is not voice-like. Perhaps the most striking demonstration of this point comes from cases of voice-hearing in people who have never heard anything at all.

A TWENTY-EIGHT-YEAR-OLD Danish woman was admitted to the psychiatric hospital in Aalborg, Denmark, complaining of hearing voices urging her to harm herself. She was profoundly deaf from a congenital hearing impairment that was diagnosed when she was two, and she started learning sign language at age ten, having previously gotten by with lip-reading and speaking. From the time she was around sixteen or seventeen years old, she had begun hearing her parents' encouraging voices in her right ear, sounding loudly and "quite musically" in her head. Shortly after that she began having visual and olfactory hallucinations of her recently deceased cousin, perceiving him in external space and hearing his voice at different volumes and levels of clarity. After a traumatic physical assault in her mid-twenties, she began to hear a male voice commanding her to hurt herself or others—urging her, for example, to take a knife and stab herself. She heard the voice in both ears. It was quite loud, and had a higher pitch than her own voice. She was prescribed the antipsychotic drug aripiprazole and, without much delay, the voice went away.

Schizophrenia and other psychotic disorders seem to be just as prevalent in the deaf community as they are among hearing people, with roughly half of deaf people with the diagnosis reporting "voices." The first case in the literature dates from 1886, in a report of a deaf-mute woman with a condition known as *folie circulaire* (an early description of bipolar disorder). From the 1970s onward, a series of reports appeared of such hallucinations in individuals including those who were congenitally deaf, and thus could not have had any prior auditory experiences. In one 1971 study, a man who had become deaf as a one-year-old reported hearing the voice of God; he even proceeded to draw the entity involved—including an elaborate arrangement of wires, connected to different parts of his body, which drew the communicative signals up to his ear.

There is a certain amount of controversy about how much these reports of "voice"-hearing really capture something akin to the experiences of hearing people. On the skeptical side, it has been proposed that reports of deaf voice-hearing actually reflect a *desire* to be able to hear—a kind of wishful thinking. Another view is that such individuals are actually misdescribing other, nonauditory experiences, such as anomalous perceptions of air currents or vibrations. Some have argued that these reports are more about the preconceptions of the people doing the interviewing than about the actual experiences of deaf people. On the other hand, several detailed reports exist of deaf individuals using signs that are unambiguously about hearing. One British study interviewed seventeen profoundly deaf individuals with a diagnosis of schizophrenia, of whom ten reported currently hearing voices whose content they could describe. Five had been profoundly deaf from birth, discounting the possibility that some limited experience of hearing very early in life could explain the findings. One thirty-three-year-old woman, never able to perceive sounds, could nevertheless hear a man's voice saying bad things constantly in her right ear. Describing herself as "completely deaf," she remained fully aware that she couldn't physically hear her own or other people's voices.

The accounts emphatically referred to hearing voices rather than some other experience; several of the patients used the sign for talking. But when the researchers posed the awkward question, "How can you be hearing voices when you have never heard anything at all?" the patients' responses were strangely uninformative. "Most commonly," the authors wrote, "the patients merely shrugged, gave a 'don't know' reply, or indicated that they could not understand the question. Others made attempts at explanation which were superficial, facile or otherwise unsatisfactory, such as 'maybe talking in my brain,' or 'sometimes I'm deaf, sometimes I hear.' . . . One patient, who was diagnosed as deaf at the age of 2 years, stated that she could hear before the age of 5 years, but then she hit a brick wall and became deaf. One patient believed that his hearing had been restored by God." In another study, a different researcher asked deaf people with schizophrenia about the acoustic properties of their voices (pitch, volume, accent) and was met with tart responses, including the unanswerable: "How do I know? I'm deaf!"

This vagueness about the nature of the experience should not lead us to conclude that these reports are not genuine. Someone hearing for the first time—even if the experience was totally hallucinatory—would doubtless lack an appropriate frame of reference for communicating that experience to a hearing person. But another intriguing fact of these accounts is that they often include experiences in other modalities, such as a sense of being signed or fingerspelled to, or visual hallucinations and vibrations experienced within the body. In the British study, several of the deaf voice-hearers also saw things like flashing lights, images of the devil, and even, in one case, a "panoramic vision of heaven." Hallucinated smells included smoke, mint, and rotten eggs, while bodily hallucinations included abdominal twisting and bursting sensations as well as the sense that there were other people inside the patients' bodies.

For the London-based psychologist Joanna Atkinson—herself profoundly deaf since childhood—these nonauditory concomitants of deaf voice-hearing give us a clue to the puzzle of how those who cannot perceive sounds can nevertheless sometimes hear things that aren't there. On a visit to our research group in Durham, Joanne explained to me that a version of the inner speech model may be able to help us understand voice hallucinations in deafness, but only with some important modifications. My meeting with Jo was the first time I had interacted at length with someone who was deaf, and I found myself struggling with the timing of the interaction, and with dividing my attention between her and her interpreter. I felt embarrassed that I wasn't able to sign to her, although I did a good enough job of conquering my usual tendency to mumble, allowing her to lip-read me easily. Jo has pioneered new methods for assessing whether what deaf hallucinators hear is really a voice. In one of her studies, she developed picture cues that allowed people to refer to their experiences without having to translate them into formal sign language or English (which for many deaf people is not their first language). For example, one picture showed a head with a thought bubble emanating from it, within which two hands were actively signing. This particular image depicted the statement (also reproduced in English on the card), "When I experience voices, I can see someone signing to me in my mind."

The standard inner speech model would predict that heard voices would take the form of an individual's ordinary inner communication. So the first question is whether deaf people experience anything that equates to a hearing person's ordinary inner speech. When this question was asked recently on the online forum Quora, there were thought-provoking responses from several deaf people. One contributor stated, "I have a 'voice' in my head, but it is not sound-based. I am a visual being, so in my head, I either see ASL [American Sign

Language] signs, or pictures, or sometimes printed words." For this individual, sound was not a feature of the experience. Another respondent experienced a mix of modalities: "My inner voice is figuratively speaking to me and I hear it as well as lipread it." In this case, the experience had both auditory and visual properties. One contributor who lost his hearing at age two said that he thought in words, but words without sound, while another individual with early hearing loss described "hearing" a voice in dreams in the absence of signs or lip movements. All the evidence suggests that the inner voice serves similar functions for deaf people as for hearing individuals. For example, inner signing seems to play a role in short-term memory in signing individuals, just as inner speech mediates short-term remembering in hearing people.

Perhaps deaf voices occur, then, when ordinary inner signing becomes misattributed as an experience from elsewhere. Just as with auditory inner speech, the internal version does not have to "sound" exactly the same as the external one—in fact, it is very likely not to, perhaps because of processes like condensation. Some descriptions of deaf voices fit this account. Several individuals, for example, have described being fingerspelled to by a persecutor without any clear visual perception of the movement of the hands, or lip-reading without any direct view of the communicating agent's face. But it would be a mistake to assume that deaf voices activate visual parts of the brain in the same way that hearing people's voices activate auditory parts. In fact, inner speech and inner signing seem to share neural resources. Language processing in deaf people seems to be based in regions very similar to those activated in hearing individuals, and covert signing in the deaf seems to recruit a classic "inner speech" network.

These findings suggest that our brains code information about communication in a way that is not specific to any particular sensory channel. That would explain why deaf people who report hearing voices often report a mix of experiences, and it also fits with observations that voices in hearing people are often accompanied by experiences in other senses. In one of Jo Atkinson's studies, for example, there was no difference between samples of hearing and deaf voice-hearers in the extent to which their experiences were accompanied by visual imagery. The groups might have relied on quite different sensory channels for most of their communication (auditory for hearing, visual for deaf), but they were equally susceptible to visual experiences when they were hearing voices.

The question then moves on from the puzzle of how a person who has never heard anything could possibly "hear" a hallucinated voice. It becomes a question of how people—deaf or hearing—could have the experience of being communicated with *in the absence of any sensory input at all*. In fact, we're back to something very like the experience of a felt presence. Some have argued that felt presence should be properly understood as a delusion, because it seems not to involve any sensory perception, phantom or genuine. But a more useful way of thinking about it is as a hallucination of a social agent with communicative intentions. When you sense the presence of your baby in your bed, or feel that your deceased partner is in the room with you, you are effectively hallucinating a person: not the person's voice or face, but his or her entire being. The reason might be that there is, or was, a real person there whose presence you have been tracking, just as a shopkeeper might track the movements of a suspicious-looking customer, or a parent might track the whereabouts of an inquisitive toddler. Research in developmental psychology has shown that the ability to keep track of social agents develops very early in babyhood, or may even be innate. In the case of bereavement, a person whose presence you have been monitoring for a long time, perhaps decades, is suddenly not there anymore. But your brain keeps on expecting their presence and filling in the gap that has been left. It's no wonder that hearing voices is so common in people who have recently lost a loved one.

The phenomenon of felt presence turns out to be a powerful idea for understanding the complexities of voice-hearing. A voice is heard, and it has various sensory properties associated with it. But an entity, like a person, is felt as well. That's how Adam knows that the Captain is there even when he is not speaking, and how Rumer knew that her voice had gone away. Many voice-hearers report an aware-ness of a particular presence before the voice occurs. The artist Dolly Sen described it in an interview in terms of being able to get a sense of a person even without perceiving the person directly: "It's a bit like when you're on a bus and somebody sits next to you; you can't see them but you kind of guess what they are like just from them be-ing next to you."

Ultimately, a heard voice is something that communicates, and an entity that communicates can be represented separately from its actual utterances. If I'm on the phone to someone and there's a pause in the conversation, I can still represent my interlocutor mentally even though I'm not hearing her voice. Voices are more than frag-ments of sensory perception or intrusions from memory. As Rachel Waddingham explained to me: "They're kind of like people, really." And the communicative agents that are experienced or hallucinated have intentions—they want things that don't necessarily map onto what the voice-hearer wants. As we've seen, something similar can happen with imaginary companions, and with the fictional creations that a novelist comes up with.

These descriptions of voices as having agent-like properties occur right through the history of voice-hearing. Take this exchange in the 1890s between a patient and the pioneering psychiatrist Pierre Janet: "I am spoken to all the time. . . . I am told I need to go and ask the Pope for a pardon.—Do you recognize the voice that speaks to you?—No, I don't recognize it, it is not the voice of anybody.—This voice, is it far or near?—It is neither far nor near, it is as if it is in my chest.—Is it like a voice?—Not really, it is not a voice, *I do not hear anything*, I sense that I am spoken to." When we asked people about their voices in our online survey, we found cases where the commu-nicative and emotional urgency of soundless voices was as clear as if there had been an auditory stimulus. "It's hard to describe how I could 'hear' a voice that wasn't auditory," wrote one respondent, "but the words used and the emotions they contained (hatred and disgust) were completely clear, distinct and unmistakeable, maybe even more so than if I had heard them aurally."

From our initial focus on voices as misrecognized inner speech, we've arrived at a rather different way of looking at things. When an individual is hearing a voice, he or she is experiencing an intention to communicate. The term "auditory verbal hallucination" starts to look like a misnomer. We should move on from our fixation on the auditory qualities of the experience and focus instead on some neglected facts: that voices are entities that can be interacted with, that voice-hearers can often readily answer a question like "How many voices do you hear?" and that they can even find them good company. These are strong signs that some voice-hearers experience their mental visitors as hallucinated people. That doesn't mean that voices won't differ in their agent-like properties. The philosopher Sam Wilkinson and the psychologist Vaughan Bell have described four levels of voice-hearing experiences, from those that have very little agency attached to them (such as hallucinated screams or groans) to those where the voice-hearer can identify the specific individual who is speaking. Around 70 percent of the people in our survey reported that their voices had consistent identities.

If we adopt this different view of voice-hearing, many new questions arise. Instead of asking why inner speech might be misattributed, we should instead ask why there are these changes in the way that social agents are tracked. We know a fair bit now about the cognitive and neural systems that underlie our representations of social beings. Does voice-hearing stem from those processes going awry? Not according to the current neuroimaging evidence, which shows no strong signs of abnormality in how social cognition operates during voice-hearing. But there are interesting leads. Damage to the temporoparietal junction (TPJ), an area strongly linked with theory-of-mind abilities, has been associated with a feeling of felt presence in some cases of brain injury, and artificial stimulation of this area has been shown to induce a feeling of felt presence in ordinary volunteers. Intriguingly, an area close to the right TPJ showed up in our study of the neural signature of dialogic inner speech. Our finding that internal conversation recruits parts of the theory-of-mind system might open up a new way of understanding how social processing might interact with the inner speech network in the experience of hearing a voice.

Asking how voices develop over time could also give us some valuable clues. In a case like Jay's, did the distinct social characters of his voices (the Doctor, the Witch) appear fully fledged at the beginning, or was there something less person-like that kicked them off, only gradually acquiring the properties of social beings? Eleanor Longden's experiences progressed from voices that commented rather blandly on her behavior to hallucinated agents with specific, often unpleasant intentions. But it would be a mistake to suggest that this progression happens in all cases. Working out the varied ways in which voices might develop is a tricky challenge, and at the very least we will need to conduct sensitive longitudinal research that follows individuals through the course of their unusual experiences for a period of time.

This new perspective on voice-hearing also points us to some lively puzzles about the social nature of inner speech. When we talk to and listen to ourselves in our own ordinary voices, do we sense the presence of a social agent? Could our multivoiced inner speech even be one of the ways in which we represent such agents for ourselves, as we fill our minds with the voices of the people we carry with us? Is that "you" in your head really like a person who is communicating with you? If so, what does that mean for what you know of yourself, and for the challenge of keeping track of who you are?

One way into this question is to ask whether our inner speech has a tone of voice, or any of the other qualities that make a voice into something like an agent, capable of expressing emotions and intentions. Try, for example, asking whether your inner speech can ever be sarcastic or insincere. (I, for one, am fairly sure I've said to myself things like "Today is going *really* well," when I actually meant the exact opposite.) Can you lie to yourself in inner speech, or say to yourself something that you don't really mean? The evidence on the dialogicality of ordinary inner speech certainly suggests that our speaking selves have that multiplicity. And yet these selves don't feel alien; we don't feel that we have been colonized, inhabited, or taken over, as many voice-hearers do. What makes our speaking selves seem like "us" in the typical case? Whatever it is, its disturbance makes for a thoroughly disorienting experience.

It is also important to bear in mind that for many voice-hearers the distinction between voices and thoughts is not always clear-cut. In our survey, a third of the sample reported either a combination of auditory and thought-like voices, or experiences that fell somewhere between auditory voices and thoughts. One of our respondents said, "The voice I heard was always inside my own head. I didn't hear it as a noise, it was like how you hear your own thoughts, except louder and more powerful than your own thoughts and usually running alongside."

If voices are one-half of an internal dialogue, then this gray area between thoughts and voices makes more sense. Adam, quite under-standably, called it "confusing," but I think it's also highly revealing about how our stream of consciousness flows, both in the typical and the unusual cases. Thinking about voices as communicative acts gives us a clearer sense of how our consciousness is peopled by social agents. Complaining that something important is lost by viewing voices as "only" inner speech misses the fact that internal self-talk has its origins in interactions between people, and that it represents the different perspectives of the social agents that constitute it. Still, inner speech can only be part of the story. We need to account for the other auditory and nonauditory experiences that accompany inner dialogue, and we need to understand that, like voice-hearing, inner dialogue is bigger than mere language.

Construing voice-hearing as a communicative act also helps us to understand how people can become emotionally involved with their voices in all sorts of ways. As we've seen, heard voices give us plenty of clues to the social identities behind them. Where there are people, there is the possibility of attachments and even sympathy. "I've had a terrible time," complains Margaret's voice as it keeps up its almost incessant monologue. When I spoke to the former voice-hearer Ru-mer, she sounded faintly regretful that her mental companion was no longer there. She missed her slightly, even though what the voice had said was mostly negative.

Adam fears that the Captain might one day go away for good. He would miss the banter, cruel though it often is. Take the time Adam was talking to a member of his mental health team and saying, "I would be terrified to be a schizophrenic," and the Captain said, "You can hear *me*, you fucking idiot, of course you're a schizophrenic!" Your friends can tease you, cheat you, and be irritating beyond belief, but they're still your friends. "There is a feeling of safety to a degree," Adam told the BBC. "Sometimes he'll come across and he'll stand with a big giant pair of Acme-type binoculars. It feels like you've got a mate looking out for you as well, making sure you're okay."

15

TALKING TO OURSELVES

"NICE TO BE THE INTERVIEWER."

Susan is lying in the brain scanner at the Max Planck Institute in Berlin. She is thinking back to the moments before she was inserted into the magnet, when she was asking Russ Hurlburt some questions about his family. She likes the idea that it is she, Susan, who is asking Russ the questions, rather than the other way round. At the moment of the beep, a song is in her head, playing lightly in the background. It is REM's "Ignoreland" and she is hearing it just the way the band played it, with the jangly guitar music and Michael Stipe's singing. When the beep goes off she is saying to herself, "Nice to be the interviewer." She has been feeling pretty good all morning, but that isn't in her experience at the moment that DES has sampled.

Susan's silent, private utterance strikes her as the outpouring of a happy soul, spoken by herself in one voice, rather than directed back to its originator with some separation between speaker and listener. "I wasn't saying it to myself, like I was two people. I was saying it as one person making an exclamation." It's hard to construe Susan's inner speaking as an attempt to direct her own behavior, or to encourage, motivate, or admonish herself. If it has any function, it might simply be to express a satisfied thought. It is a fairly unexceptional bit of inner speech, like my thought on the Tube train—an aspect of our experience whose very ordinariness can make us hardly notice or pay attention to it. "The fact of its insistent indwelling," notes the poet Denise Riley about inner speech, "can blind us to its peculiarities."

When we look at what was going on in Susan's brain at the time, we observe that this everyday phenomenon is anything but simple. One of the aims of our Berlin study was to see whether the kind of inner speech that results from participants being instructed to produce it bears any resemblance, in terms of neural activations, to the kind that occurs naturally. Three of us in the research team gathered together all of the DES vignettes and, working independently, made sure that we could settle on a subset that unmistakably involved inner speech. We then did the same with the remainder of the beeps, identifying those that clearly did *not* include inner speech. Any vignettes for which there was any ambiguity about the degree of inner speechiness were excluded from our analysis.

We then looked back at some brain-imaging data we had acquired when each volunteer began to participate. In this part of the study, we asked people to say words silently to themselves: effectively, we instructed them to do inner speech on demand, as the researchers did in all of the previous neuroimaging studies on the topic. Our analysis focused on two areas of the brain that had been identified by earlier research as potentially important: Heschl's gyrus, which is usually associated with auditory perception, and an area roughly equating to Broca's area (which, as we have seen, is often activated in inner speech studies). We then compared those activations to the ones we saw when we captured inner speech occurring spontaneously using DES.

The patterns were strikingly different. When people were instructed to use inner speech, Broca's area burst into life—as you would expect on the basis of the previous studies that asked people to do similar things—but the auditory perception area (Heschl's gyrus) was *de*activated. In complete contrast, when inner speech was caught occurring naturally, Broca's area was only slightly excited, and instead the auditory perception area showed major activation. The two kinds of inner speech produced the opposite patterns of neural activity. As we've seen throughout this book, inner speech is a slippery phenomenon: these findings show that it's difficult to get volunteers doing it in any naturalistic way. You can't assume that people have done it just because you have asked them to. A worrying implication is that, if our findings are confirmed, we will have to question anew how to interpret the studies (including those that purport to reveal the neural bases of auditory verbal hallucinations) that have simply asked people to go into the scanner and produce inner speech on demand.

The science of inner speech has made great strides since I started thinking about it as a doctoral student in the 1990s. From a phenomenon that was supposedly impossible to study, internal self talk has become a productive area of research. A review article that Ben Alderson-Day and I published in 2015 contained around 250 references to published research, covering topics from child development to brain damage. No one will ever again tell a graduate student that inner speech is not a topic worth pursuing because it cannot be studied empirically.

We have made progress methodologically, and we have learned a lot, but there is a long way to go. We particularly need to tread carefully when it comes to thinking about the relationship between internal self talk and the tricky topic of voice-hearing. The inner speech model has been criticized on various grounds, and it undoubtedly does not provide a complete account of auditory hallucination. Not least among those objections is the fact that it is criticized by those whose experiences it is supposed to explain. "As a society," Rachel Waddingham told me, "we are biased toward biochemical and psychological models, and we need to work hard to make sure that other, more diverse understandings get a look-in." While scientific tests should be the ultimate arbiters of a scientific inquiry, any theory that does not ring true for those who have had the experience should be viewed with skepticism; their criticism is itself a clue that we have missed something important about the phenomenology of the experience and its significance in people's lives. If the science simply ignores their experience, then it is not good science.

The inner speech model will also have to work hard to explain other kinds of phantom perceptions. Although voice-hearing is the dominant form of hallucination in schizophrenia, individuals with the disorder also have hallucinations in other modalities. Musical hallucinations, for example, are reasonably common. When we asked ordinary people about this in an Internet survey, more than two hundred responded, with around forty describing their experiences as musical hallucinations. One respondent said, "It's like an internal iPod. Any music I've ever heard can come back." For another, the hallucination of "a heavenly choir" was "so clear I thought I'd left the car radio on." We need to explore whether a version of the inner speech model can work for hallucinations of this type. Many of us experience a kind of "inner music"—Susan reported it in her moment in the scanner described above. Perhaps musical hallucinations, or at least some forms of them, occur when that inner music is misattributed to an external source.

Hallucinations in other modalities might turn out to be more difficult to explain. One problem is in working out, for any particular sensory channel, what the equivalent of inner speech is supposed to be. In each case, you would want to propose that there was some ongoing stream of experience in that modality: a flow of visual images, for example. While the stream of consciousness undoubtedly unfolds in multiple media (I certainly experienced visual images in my mirthful moment on the Tube train), a flow of inner visual imagery, analogous to inner speech, has not so far figured in much scientific theorizing. It's hard to see how something we might call "inner vision" could fulfill the varied functional roles that our internal conversations have. Making the model fit would be even harder work in the case of olfactory or somatic hallucinations, such as experiences of spectral smells or of feeling things crawling on one's skin.

At the same time, there is growing support for the idea that hearing voices involves some kind of confusion between internal and external sources of information. In an episode of *Father Ted*, Ted draws Dougal a helpful diagram to help him to distinguish what arises from within his own head (in this case, a bizarre dream of a creature called the Spider Baby) from what's really out there in the world. We are all prone to making mistakes like this, as you will know if you have ever confused a dream for something that actually happened. Unsurprisingly, the capacity to distinguish between internal and external events (technically termed *reality monitoring*) is thought to play a key part in hallucinations.

Researchers are beginning to understand how these processes operate in the brain. Marie Buda, a student of the cognitive neuroscientist Jon Simons at the University of Cambridge, showed that reality-monitoring abilities relate to variation in a specific structure in the medial prefrontal cortex, a fold in the brain's surface known as the paracingulate sulcus (see Figure 3 in Chapter 11). Around half of us have a fairly prominent one of these, and its presence indicated, in Buda's study, that these people would do better on reality-monitoring tasks. In a recent study, another of Simons's students, Jane Garrison, looked at a more sensitive measure of this brain fold, painstakingly measuring its length on structural brain scans from a large sample of schizophrenia patients. She showed that the length of the fold in the left hemisphere was the best predictor of whether a patient would hallucinate—including when the analysis controlled for various other factors, such as the overall amount of brain folding and the volume of the brain. In fact, Jane could put a number on it: for every one-centimeter reduction in the length of the fold, the chances of that individual having hallucinations increased by nearly a fifth.

Crucially, the relationship she found between fold size and proneness to hallucinations did not depend on what modality the experience was in. Sulcus length was essentially the same for voice-hearers and other hallucinators. If this part of the brain is involved in distinguishing internal from external events, it seems to relate to a general tendency to hallucinate, rather than being specific to auditory happenings. And yet hearing voices is rather more common an experience than hallucinations in other sensory channels. It may be that the brain system that generates inner speech is strongly linked to this prefrontal reality-monitoring system, so that any disruption to the communication between those systems would be especially likely to lead to a voice being heard, rather than to an experience in some other modality. There is already strong evidence that the resting brains of those who hear voices are connected up differently from the brains of those who do not, specifically between the temporal regions implicated in inner speech and the frontal regions that support reality monitoring.

Accounting for why some people hear voices would thus involve a number of different processes. In many voice-hearing experiences, inner speech might be the internal event that gets misattributed and accordingly perceived as a voice. But such attributions are not made in a vacuum. In the reality-monitoring framework, deciding whether an event is internal or external is influenced by a host of other factors. General biases toward making one kind of interpretation rather than another might relate to certain expectations about where information is likely to come from. Someone who has heard voices in the past, and is distressed by them, might be on the lookout for it happening again, which may bias their interpretations and make their apprehension about voice-hearing a self-fulfilling prophecy.

One class of auditory hallucinations seems to illustrate this kind of general bias. "When people feel threatened," the clinical psychologist Guy Dodgson told me, "evolution has enabled them to be hypervigilant for signs of danger, which can lead people to incorrectly 'hear' the threat they were anticipating." Such "hypervigilance" hallucinations illustrate a classic distinction in psychology between bottom-up processes, which are driven by data coming in from the environment, and top-down processes, in which the individuals' beliefs and emotions can shape what is perceived. Under the right kinds of stresses and expectations, people can quite readily perceive communicative intentions in signals such as cell phone ringtones or pager bleeps. One recent study showed that it is not uncommon for nursing mothers to hear voices and other sounds in the noise of their breast pumps, including repeated, alarming utterances like "Snap my arm."

A literary example of this kind of skewed perception comes from the novelist Evelyn Waugh, who dealt with the experience of voice-hearing in his 1957 novel *The Ordeal of Gilbert Pinfold*. Under the influence of a mixture of alcohol and a sleeping draft, the eponymous middle-aged writer begins to hallucinate human voices coming from the pipes of a ship. In his book *Hallucinations*, Oliver Sacks explains that on one level, Pinfold's ordeal was an autobiographical account of Waugh's own toxin-induced delirium, but that more generally, the account also provides a demonstration of how hallucinations are "shaped by the intellectual, emotional, and imaginative powers of the individual, and by the beliefs and style of the culture in which he is embedded." Cultural beliefs can exert top-down effects on hallucinatory experiences in many different ways. In a recent review of the evidence, my colleagues and I concluded that an individual's cultural (including religious) background affects what counts as "reality," shapes how a hallucination is experienced, and influences the meaning that is attributed to it. For example, a study by the Stanford anthropologist Tanya Luhrmann showed that voice-hearing patients in Ghana and India were more likely than those from a group in California to identify the voices they heard as people they knew and to engage them in conversation—a finding that is difficult to reconcile with a view that hallucinations can be entirely explained in terms of biological mechanisms.

It's not only the top-down processes that are influenced by an individual's cultural background. Vygotsky's view was that inner speech is shaped by the social dialogues from which it derives, which in turn are influenced by cultural norms about how people should interact with each other. Particularly relevant are interactions between children and their caregivers in the period in which private speech is being internalized. There has been very little cross-cultural work on variations in private speech development. My graduate student Abdulrahman Al-Namlah studied samples of children from England and Saudi Arabia, predicting that differences between the cultures in how children were encouraged to participate in adult conversations would pan out in the private speech of the children. In line with our hypotheses, Saudi children did not show the sex difference in private-speech use (boys talking more than girls) that was shown by their English counterparts. We argued that this result might reflect Saudi girls' opportunities to express themselves in female-only social groups, compared to the expectation that Saudi boys will listen in to male-only discussions, but not actively contribute.

So far, this limited research interest in cultural differences in private speech has not carried over to the study of internal self-talk. We need to learn much more about how particular languages confer specific properties on inner speech, and how they might even open up patterns of thought that would not be possible in other languages. Beyond personal accounts—such as Aamer Hussein's description of the difference between thinking in Urdu and in English—there is next to no research on this topic. We also need to discover more about the processes through which inner speech is shaped by its social context, asking deeper questions about exactly *how* language is transformed as it makes the journey inside. A distinct challenge is to learn more about the processes of condensation. As we've seen, the transition from condensed to expanded inner speech is likely to be a particular flashpoint for the misattributions that are believed to lead to voice-hearing. One question for the future is whether the stripped-down, telegraphic nature of condensed inner speech protects it from being misattributed, so that it's only the expanded form of internal self-talk that risks being erroneously attributed to another entity. If that prediction held out, it would in turn help us to solve the puzzle of why, despite these supposedly general processing biases, only some inner-speech utterances are mistakenly perceived as external voices.

The personified, characterful nature of many voices would also need to be explained. One possibility is that something goes awry with the usual processes of representing and keeping track of the mental states of others: that group of psychological capacities known as social cognition or theory-of-mind. In the model that Ben Alderson-Day and I have been developing, these aberrant theory-of-mind processes throw up social representations that capture the "open slot" of dialogic inner speech, putting a character into the internal dialogue who wasn't previously there.

Much of the mystery of voices is about how the inner speech network collaborates with other brain systems. We saw earlier that inner speech appears to "plug into" other cognitive systems, such as those so-called executive functions that allow us to plan, control, and inhibit our behavior. The system in the brain that keeps us focused on executive tasks is often seen as working in opposition to the brain's default mode or resting network. Roughly speaking, when one network is on, the other is off, and vice versa. But inner speech can also plug into the default network, which is believed to underpin those aspects of our thinking, like daydreaming and mind-wandering, that are not focused on specific tasks. Although it is early days for this research, it is clear that much mind-wandering is verbal in nature, and that large parts of it can be described as essentially daydreaming in inner speech. So the inner speech network can interact separately with two systems that are usually seen as working in opposition to each other. The words in our heads can control and direct, but they can also fashion fantasies and dream of other realities.

While we're thinking about the future of research on inner speech, we should not forget those voices of the past. Perhaps the most important role for the default network is in autobiographical memory: our ongoing weaving of stories about our past lives. The interaction between the inner speech system and the default network might explain how many hallucinated voices relate to memory processes. Rather than seeing the divide between "inner speech" and "memory" voices as a distinction between two separate systems, it might make more sense to think of the inner speech network as a channel through which dormant memory representations, such as of trauma, become reactivated—sometimes decades after the terrible events took place. Again, much remains to be worked out about the process through which horrible memories can resurface as words in our heads.

The voices of our consciousness are powerful experiences. Even ordinary inner speech can have a salience that outreaches the banality of what it can sometimes be heard to say. That's arguably part of the force of the device of the cinematic voiceover—the verbal commentary that is almost like the inner speech of a movie. In the Oscar-winning 2014 black comedy *Birdman*, the voiceover is literally a hallucinated voice: the commentary of the protagonist's superhero alter ego. Before the talkies came along, moviegoers had much more work to do in making meaning out of the images on the screen. For the Russian literary theorist Boris Eikhenbaum, inner speech was part of the mechanism through which a viewer could make sense of the discontinuities in the visual flow of a silent picture. The sociologist Norbert Wiley has flipped this around, proposing that inner speech interprets the stream of our ordinary consciousness, just as the internal self-talk of those ancient moviegoers would make meaning out of the flickering on the screen. "Life," Wiley writes, "is something of a silent movie, and inner speech makes it hang together."

For many reasons, inner speech is the predominant mode in which we communicate with ourselves, just as external speech is our default channel for interacting with others. If something changes in that process of internal communication, then unusual and even distressing experiences can follow. For voice-hearers with some forms of the experience, that view of what is happening—that it is a distorted instance of what the self would have been communicating to itself anyway—can be a comforting, even liberating thought.

WHAT HAVE WE GAINED from thinking about inner speech as a conversation with the self? From the self-regulatory exhortations of a professional athlete to the divine revelations of a medieval English mystic, I have suggested that focusing on the voices in our heads as internal dialogues can illuminate some enigmatic features of our mental lives. I set out to persuade you that our mental voices have diverse functions that relate to their varied forms, that these in turn are shaped by the development of inner speech in childhood, and that talking to ourselves betrays its social origins at every turn. Having explored inner speech as a counterpart to the more unusual experience of voice-hearing, we are now in a better place to appreciate how the latter, in turn, is also an experience that can take many different forms. We can now better understand the commonalities and differences between inner speech and voice-hearing, and we can reach a deeper understanding of their personal, cultural, and psychological significance.

Some of the experiences I have included seem to stretch the boundaries of what we would define as internal dialogue. The creative thoughts of a novelist, for example, seem to have more in common with overhearing or eavesdropping than with engaging in reciprocal conversation. Our writers rarely said that they communed directly with their characters. As far as my own fiction-writing is concerned, I feel (perhaps superstitiously) that talking back to my characters might disrupt what is gently being revealed to me. The model of the open slot would likely need to be refined, so that voices can come into the mind (perhaps through some anomalous activation of a social representation) without, once they are present, having to be dialogically engaged. Arguably, you can only let other voices into your head like this because you have that dialogic structure of internal conversation, and that structure in turn is a function of how you developed as a human being. We just don't know. But this is at least a new way to think about the long-mysterious processes of creativity.

A model of dialogic inner speech is useful, too, in making us think differently about those who hear voices in a spiritual context. Although her experiences are illuminating for understanding voice-hearing today, we should be wary of taking Margery Kempe and her kind too literally as examples of individuals struck by hallucinations. There is a very strong need to normalize such experiences and reduce stigma around them, but there is also a risk—potentially harmful to both sides—of trivializing phenomena that are powerful, profound, and often catastrophically debilitating.

Rather, we can think of Kempe's experiences, and those of others like her, as parts of an internal dialogue. Was Margery praying to a deity, or was she talking to herself? Your answer will depend on your own cosmology. Without denying the spiritual significance of her experiences, I think we can get a long way by taking the tack of inner dialogue, especially if we also distinguish its condensed and expanded versions. In her everyday condensed inner speech, Margery is having a conversation with God, but in a stripped-down, abbreviated form that approaches the stage of "thinking in pure meanings" that Vygotsky described. When that inner dialogue is expanded, the voice of God sounds out in Margery's head. Conceiving of her ordinary state of "being with" her Lord as a form of condensed inner dialogue, as opposed to an explicit conversation, gives us a rather different way of thinking about the psychology of spiritual meditation.

Adopting a dialogic framework also brings us somewhere close to the testimony of voice-hearers, even those who might vigorously reject the standard inner speech model. It reflects the understanding of many voice-hearers that their voices are a conversation, often a troubled one, between different aspects of the self. Those facets might be disconnected or even alien, and it may take a courageous effort on the part of the voice-hearer to recognize them as part of who they are, but this understanding can be a valuable way of making sense of the experience. Seeing voice-hearing as a conversation with the self does not commit us to a simplistic model of inner speech; nor does it force us to dismiss the vibrant complexities of the experience.

At the same time, voice-hearers can usually distinguish their ordinary inner speech from their voices, and the two can be quite different. Jay, for example, told us that his voices spoke more slowly than he did. Given that he also said that his inner speech was generally like his external voice, it follows that his voices spoke more slowly than his inner speech. Adam, in contrast, regards his voices as part of his thoughts, but thoughts that can nevertheless comment on themselves. When we were doing DES, for example, the Captain occasionally chipped in. "I'm aware of what you're saying," he said at one point, when Adam was describing a fairly ordinary and voice-free moment of experience. Over time, Adam has given up trying to distinguish between the two kinds of experiences. "I don't have thoughts," he told us. "I have a voice." In old-school psychiatry, this would mean that Adam wasn't really hearing voices, but suffering from a *pseudohallucination* (that is, a hallucination that he recognized as a hallucination). That almost completely meaningless term is falling from favor, to the relief of many. Adam's experiences are real to him, and dismissing them as a false version of a false experience does not really help anyone.

What can we conclude, then, about the importance of these conversations in our heads? We can fairly easily reject the idea that human beings need language in order to be intelligent. There is an agonizingly complicated philosophical literature on whether thinking depends on language, and my own view should now be plain. For a start, we can't have that conversation unless we are willing to be much clearer on what we mean by *thinking*. For many of the activities we call thinking, the use of self-directed language provides a massive boost, but it is by no means essential. Inner speech is the way in which humans happen to do much of it, but it is by no means the only way.

We also need to be clear on what we mean by *language*. For Vygotsky, words function as psychological tools: they are capable of enhancing the range of things that can be done with one's mental capacities. But that role can be fulfilled by any sufficiently sophisticated system of signs and is certainly not restricted to the verbal or auditory realms. Deafness affects language use in many ways, but there is no reason why deaf people could not do their internal communication in sign language. Many deaf people are in fact bilingual, and bilingualism in all its forms raises profound questions about our inner conversations. A favorite trick when I'm giving talks is to ask if anyone in the room speaks two languages. A few people usually put their hands up, at which point I ask one at random, "So what language do you think in?" People always respond to this inquiry in delightful and varied ways, but for me the interesting thing is that the question makes sense. If thinking was not verbal, people would presumably respond to that question with a look of bafflement.

Examples of thinking in the absence of *any* language are a bit more complicated. In cases of aphasia, people typically lose their language functions (through brain damage or disease) after they have learned to speak—and thus, presumably, after they have had a chance to learn to talk to themselves. Studying cognitive functions in aphasia is thus not a critical test of the model, because the structures necessary for dialogic thinking will have developed during the period in which language was intact.

Developmental disorders such as autism are different again. We don't know much about inner speech in autism, partly because the disorder is defined in terms of problems with language and communication, meaning that getting autistic people to describe their inner experience is going to be difficult. The little evidence that we have suggests that people with autism do use inner speech, but that it appears not to have the dialogic, self-communicative qualities that it has in neurotypicals. That might be a function of how the disorder limits autistic children's opportunities for social interaction as they are growing up. If you are not participating in social dialogues, you cannot really internalize them.

Asking how thinking is affected by the various language deficits that characterize disorders like autism and aphasia also tells us something about why inner speech might have evolved. Whether you see language more as a biological refinement or a cultural creation doesn't really matter too much—what's at stake is whether using internal language confers benefits on an organism. As we saw earlier, one view is that inner speech plays a role in pulling together the many different things that the brain does. A brain that has evolved to fulfill many varied functions will require some way of integrating these different information-processing systems. According to some scholars, language became involved in human cognition (ultimately, in the form of mental voices) because it was able to bind together the outputs of separate, autonomous brain systems. To switch the metaphor, think of inner speech as the thread of a necklace. Different experiences flow through our consciousness: visual images, sounds, music, feelings. But it is inner speech that strings them all together, allowing distinct neural systems to talk to one another by virtue of the way in which the internal language network plugs flexibly and selectively into other systems.

If inner speech has this kind of usefulness, then it is bound to be a boon. If it can actually have a survival function—as suggested by the voice-hearing experiences of those in extreme situations—then there is even more reason to think that it will stick around in the face of natural selection. Many voice-hearers can link their experiences to specific episodes of trauma. "My voices saved my life," said the artist Dolly Sen in an interview. "I could have just said, 'It's not worth living, my dad tried to kill me, nobody cares, better to die.' And, you know, I could have committed suicide. What my voices did was protect me. . . . I couldn't look at the truth directly at the time, so voices helped me not to do that." The founders of the Hearing Voices Movement, Marius Romme and Sandra Escher, eloquently summed up the dual role of voices as tormentors and protectors. The experience, they write, "is both an attack on personal identity and an attempt to keep it intact." If we insist on telling people that their voices are neural junk, then a profound part of the experience, and a possible route to relief from its distress, are lost.

Our inner voices can help to keep us safe. Doing that internal speaking *silently* will also have clear evolutionary benefits. Talking to ourselves won't be much good if it betrays our position to a predator or enemy—one reason why my thought on the Tube resulted in no loss of social capital. The pressures to keep a lid on our inner conversation might be social as well as evolutionary. One reason why private speech "goes underground" in middle childhood is probably that talking to yourself out loud is rarely sanctioned in Western schools. There is nevertheless a growing recognition that audible self-talk can remain valuable well into adulthood, which is certainly a change from the way grown-up private speech was perceived in Jean Piaget's day. "To say nothing of internal speech," wrote the great developmental psychologist, "a large number of people, whether from the working classes or the more absent-minded of the *intelligentsia*, are in the habit of talking to themselves, of keeping up an audible soliloquy." Fine for dustmen and absent-minded professors, but Piaget clearly thought that chatting to yourself was not what civilized people do.

The list of things that inner speech can do for us is already a long one, and it is likely to grow as research on it continues. For one thing, I suspect that inner speech will turn out to have a substantial role in memory. We have seen how verbal rehearsal of material is an important part of the human working memory system (think of that shopping list you recite to yourself as you walk around the supermarket). On a much longer time scale, talking to ourselves might be a big part of how we keep a grip on the past. Children's development of autobiographical memory is known to be influenced by the kinds of conversations that parents have with them about past events. If children are exposed to talk in which adults elaborate on details, such as the emotions and feelings of the protagonists in the events, they go on to produce richer autobiographical narratives of their own. In a study using the Tower of London task, Abdulrahman Al-Namlah found that children who produced more self-regulatory private speech also produced more sophisticated autobiographical narratives. There is also evidence that the memories of adults are mediated by inner speech. Bilingual people find it easier to recall events if they are asked about them in the language they spoke at the time of the event, as compared to a language they might have learned more recently. This finding fits with the idea that we code memories verbally, so that they are sensitive to the kind of language with which they are probed.

Such a prominent role for internal language would arguably give it a role in how we become aware of our own selves. "Our inner speech," writes Denise Riley, "is at least faithful to us. It is reassuringly or irritatingly there on tap. . . . It offers us the unfailing if ambiguous company of a guest who does not plan to leave." The Canadian psychologist Alain Morin has shown that people who talk to themselves more frequently also score better on measures of self-awareness and self-evaluation. Supporting the idea that the narratives we spin about ourselves play a role in anchoring those selves, the study of aphasia has shown that the condition can be accompanied by a diminution of the sense of who one is. Dr. Jill Bolte Taylor, for example, who temporarily lost her ability to speak following a stroke, wrote of "the dramatic silence that had taken residency inside my head," which accompanied the dwindling of her sense of individuality and ability to retrieve autobiographical memories. When we lose the ability to talk to ourselves, we might also lose something of the sense of who we are.

Another area in which inner speech might turn out to be important is in our reasoning about right and wrong. I myself am most likely to experience a full-blown inner conversation when I am grappling with a dilemma. There is almost no research on this topic, although one study has looked at how children use out-loud private speech to think through moral problems. One eight-year-old American girl described how she grappled with keeping control of her younger sister when the adults were out of the house:

> Well, yeah, I do it, 'cause sometimes my grandmother and my mom and dad are gone, and she like goes in places that she's not supposed to, and I say, "no, you're not allowed," and then I say to myself, before I say "okay" or "no"—then I just say to her . . . well, I say to myself first, "well, I don't know, I'll have to think about it," . . . and then she sits down for a while until I say something, and then I say "no," because I don't know where she's going to go or something, she might even go outside.

This inner conversation seems to have a moral function: helping the child to tell right from wrong. Perhaps that to-and-fro of perspectives continues to be valuable later in life. In Christopher Isherwood's memoir *Christopher and His Kind*, the young Isherwood has an angry conversation with himself about his own homosexuality: "Couldn't you get yourself excited by the shape of girls, too—if you worked hard at it? Perhaps. And couldn't you invent another myth—to put girls into? Why the hell should I? Well, it would be a lot more convenient for you, if you did."

In Russ Hurlburt's work with DES, full-blown moral debates are rare, although fragments of them appear. In one sample, a woman was reading an article and thinking about a row she had had with her husband earlier that day. She was going through the argument and wondering indignantly about how he could have said some of the things he'd said. She reported no clear words, more a sense of recapping something that was hurtful and unpleasant. A more concrete case of inner speech came in the case of a woman who was having a discussion with her sister about the rights and wrongs of cheating on her Spanish homework. At the moment of the beep, she was saying to herself internally: "It's easy."

Perhaps these positive effects of inner speaking improve our chances of dealing with the negative ones when they occur. Auditory verbal hallucinations are not the only pathological experience in which inner speech has been implicated. *Rumination* refers to an obsessive dwelling on the reasons for distress or unhappiness, and it has been associated with several psychiatric symptoms, including hallucinations. There have been almost no attempts to investigate whether rumination is a specifically verbal phenomenon, although it seems likely that it is in many cases. The auditory modality might be a particularly suitable channel for dwelling on miserable things. You can have a self-sustaining dialogue with an auditory representation, for one thing—particularly one that takes the form of a characterful, agentic "other"—in a way that would be difficult with a visual image. Verbal rumination might therefore be the dismal counterpart to creative, open-ended inner dialogue.

Perhaps this is even a way of understanding the perspective from the Hearing Voices Movement that voices are a safety mechanism. If negative emotions are channeled into the auditory modality, it might make them slightly easier to deal with. Voices and negative ruminations might be unpleasant, but at least they can be engaged with. In which case, the dominance of inner speech might ultimately reflect its evolved role in making the organism resilient to distress. In a similar way to avatar therapy, giving the troublesome thought a material, external form may make it easier for the sufferer to engage with it, thus reducing the unhappiness it can cause.

This view is certainly in keeping with some of the principles of cognitive behavioral therapy. If you are prescribed CBT for depression, you are encouraged to document your negative thoughts—by, for example, recording them in a diary, and then subjecting them to scrutiny to see whether they hold up. CBT for voice-hearing works in a similar way. In the package we have been developing at Durham, we have focused on helping the client to understand where inner speech comes from and why it has the properties it has. One patient was encouraged to visualize the sinister psychologists who he believed were tormenting him and then reshape their voices in his imagination, turning them into comedy characters who were harder to take seriously. "It was about transforming his voices so that they seemed less threatening," explains one of the creators of the CBT manual, David Smailes. "The patient learned that he was able to exert some control over his voices in much the same way that he could control his inner speech." The result was that the voices seemed less powerful, which was a key to making the experience less distressing for him.

Another aspect of this work is helping people to recognize that the thoughts that come into their heads—verbal and otherwise—are often not under their control. The issue is not whether the intrusive cognitions occur: they will do that inevitably, and in the pathological case of conditions like obsessive-compulsive disorder, they cause significant distress. The important thing seems to be how the individual responds to these rogue thoughts when they do crop up. My favorite example of the power of these interpretations is a historical one. Beset by doubts and apprehensions, the eighteenth-century English writer Samuel Johnson was likened by his biographer James Boswell to a gladiator fighting back wild beasts. Survival involved a desperate fight for self-control. "All power of fancy over reason is a degree of insanity," Johnson wrote, "but while this power is such as we can control and repress, it is not visible to others, nor considered as any depravation of the mental faculties: it is not pronounced madness but when it comes ungovernable, and apparently influences speech or action." Johnson worried deeply about his sanity, and anything that did not stem from the forces of rationality was a threat to the delicate mental balance he so highly prized.

Boswell, in contrast, embraced the chaotic, the intrusive, and the random. The literary scholar Allan Ingram notes that Boswell was fascinated by the workings of his own mind, and he greeted the unruly thoughts that Johnson so feared—"the whims that may seize me and the sallies of my luxuriant imagination"—with gleeful enthusiasm: "I am really pleased with myself; words come skipping to me like lambs upon Moffat Hill; and I turn my periods smoothly and imperceptibly like a skilful wheelwright turning tops in a turning-loom. There's fancy! There's simile! In short, I am at present a genius." Boswell knew a similar "melancholy" to that faced by Johnson, a similar assault by the forces of mental chaos, but he responded to them quite differently. Two literary giants with very similar experiences; two very different attitudes toward them.

A more drastic approach to quelling the inner conversation is to try to abolish thinking completely. In one episode of *The Simpsons*, Homer takes his daughter Lisa to try out a sensory deprivation tank. While Homer attains an empty-headed nirvana as soon as the lid of the tank is closed, Lisa finds it more of a struggle to switch off: "It's so hard to turn off my brain. I have to stop thinking, starting . . . NOW. Hey, it worked! Oh no, that's thinking." I have spoken to some practitioners of meditation who say that they are able to empty their minds completely: no words, no images, nothing. In the Christian church, the tradition of apophatic prayer, or *via negativa* (the negative way), encourages its practitioners to approach the perfection of God by attaining a true internal silence—as set out in Margery and Julian's time in the anonymous *The Cloud of Unknowing*. More popular these days is the Buddhism-inspired mindfulness meditation, which does not try to banish thought so much as allow the thinker a new perspective on it. When a thought comes by, the mindful meditator can stand outside it, much as a voice-hearer undergoing CBT can learn to adopt a critical distance from the voice that is bothering him.

Another way to attain that distance is to understand the voice as coming from a nonphysical entity. More people make sense of their voice-hearing experiences within a spiritual framework than they do within any other, whether neuroscientific, trauma-related, or anything else. Given how the feeling of a communicating agency seems so central to voice-hearing, a spiritual interpretation would seem to flow naturally. I am not a religious person, and yet it seems plausible to me that many believers would see some of their ordinary thoughts as having a supernatural origin, even if they do not describe them in terms of voice-hearing.

We have already seen this spectrum of experience—from out-loud voices to divinely implanted thoughts—in the work of the fifteenth-century mystics. In a later era, John Wesley's hymns provide many examples of a yearning for the "small inward voice . . . that whispers all my sins forgiven." It's important to be on guard here against metaphorical uses of *voice*, just as caution has been urged in interpreting the voice-hearing experiences of famous figures such as William Blake. People often speak of a "voice" of conscience that guides us on our moral obligations. For Sigmund Freud, this was the utterance of the superego, which could in certain circumstances manifest as a hallucination (such as, Freud believed, when people with schizophrenia heard voices commenting on their behavior). Following the triumph of her Congress Party in the 2004 Indian general election, Sonia Gandhi announced that she would not take office as prime minister because of her "inner voice." That possibly metaphorical use can be contrasted with that of her namesake Mahatma Gandhi, whose guiding inner spirit had a much more substantial quality. Struggling with a dilemma about a fast, Gandhi heard a voice "quite near," "as unmistakable as some human voice definitely speaking to me, and irresistible. . . . I listened, made certain that it was the Voice, and the struggle ceased."

Studies of the psychology of prayer have found that many religious people have vivid experiences of spiritual voices. A study by the anthropologist Simon Dein involved in-depth interviews with twenty-five Pentecostal Christians in northeastern London who reported God's voice answering their prayers. Fifteen of the congregants stated that they had sometimes heard the voice aloud from an external location. They clearly distinguished their own thoughts from the divine voices, which sometimes had the homeliest human qualities—one member of the congregation heard God speaking in a

Northern Irish accent. Many of the respondents reported having a conversation with their divine voices in which they were able to question them and ask them for clarifications. "What does God's word say?" a voice asked, when one congregant questioned whether she really had to pay a big tithe. Her answer was that God's word was to give a tenth of her income as a contribution to the church. "Well, you know what to do, then," said the voice.

God's instructions are not always carried out as obediently as they were in this case. In a subsequent study of evangelical Christians in London, Dein and the theologian Chris Cook asked eight congregants about their experience of the deity communicating with them. Far from the compliance that Margery Kempe showed when God instructed her to visit Julian in Norwich, all of the participants reported that they retained their own agency in these interactions and could choose to obey the voice or not. The anthropologist Tanya Luhrmann has also discovered that, when God speaks, human beings don't always act. She has conducted intensive studies of hearing the voice of God in the Vineyard churches (a neocharismatic evangelical Christian denomination), and tells of one woman who heard God giving her one very specific instruction:

> "The Lord spoke to me clearly in April, like May or April. To start a school."
>
> "You heard this audibly?"
>
> "Yeah."
>
> "Were you alone?"
>
> "Yeah, I was just praying. I wasn't praying anything really, just thinking about God, and I heard, 'Start a school.' I immediately got up and it was like, 'Okay Lord, where?'"
>
> But she never did. She never felt she had to.

WHAT IS THAT VOICE in your head? The one you hear when you're slicing carrots in the kitchen, waiting for a bus, clicking through your emails, or grappling with a dilemma. Is it *you* speaking to *you*, or are *you* the thing that is endlessly spun by that conversation? In which case, where do you go when the voice stops? Does it ever stop? Who is the "me" or "you" to whom a young child speaks aloud, and who is the speaker—especially in the stage when that fragile self is still in the process of being formed? Who speaks to the novelist in her study, or to the psychiatric patient in his hospital room? To the churchgoer, praying silently in her pew, or to the ordinary voice-hearer, listening in to the transmissions of a fractured self? What are the tattered, dissociated fragments that auditory verbal hallucinations bring into being, protect against, and help us to understand? "It is entirely a matter of voices," Beckett's Unnamable reminds us; "no other metaphor is appropriate."

I sit in my study, typing these words. I hear the next sentence resonating in my head, and a voice repeats it back at me as I watch it taking shape on the screen. I stop, listening to the winter wind howling outside. I look out of the window at the bright February afternoon. The voice is quiet now, a shadow of the urgent chatter of a moment ago, but it is still there. I mutter aloud to myself, sounding out the sentences I am grappling with. Am I in my head, a product of my restless brain, or am I the echoes of what I hear coming back at me, part of the process by which all of this—my self, these words, this reality—is constructed? There's a brief silence; I've been working hard and I am very tired. But I know that it will start up again before too long: softly, inconspicuously, intimately familiar. The voice in my head will not frighten or demean me, although it will occasionally chastise me and urge me to do better. It will tell me things I didn't know. It will surprise me and make me laugh, and above all, it will remind me of who I am. I have heard it before.

Acknowledgments

Many people have helped me in the research for this book. I owe specific debts to several members of the Hearing the Voice team: Jo Atkinson, Ben Alderson-Day, Vaughan Bell, Marco Bernini, Alison Brabban, Matthew Broome, Felicity Callard, Chris Cook, Felicity Deamer, Guy Dodgson, Paivi Eerola, Amanda Ellison, Peter Garratt, Jane Garrison, Lowri Hadden, Jenny Hodgson, Russell Hurlburt, Renaud Jardri, Nev Jones, Joel Krueger, Simone Kühn, Frank Larøi, Jane Macnaughton, Simon McCarthy-Jones, Peter Moseley, Victoria Patton, Ami Plant, Hilary Powell, Mary Robson, Corinne Saunders, Sophie Scott, Jon Simons, David Smailes, Flavie Waters, Patricia Waugh, Susanne Weis, Sam Wilkinson, and Angela Woods. Other collaborators involved in the research described here include Abdulrahman Al-Namlah, Lucy Firth, Emma Fradley, Robin Langdon, Jane Lidstone, Elizabeth Meins, Jenna Robson, Paolo de Sousa, and Adam Winsler. I received helpful information and advice from Micah Allen, Ian Apperly, Paul Carrick, Mary Carruthers, Jules Evans, Usha Goswami, Jeremy Hawthorn, Sara Holloway, Allan Ingram, Andrew Irving, Phil Johnson-Laird, Laurie Maguire, Sara Maitland, Ron Netsell, Dan O'Connor, Edward Platt, Joshua Wolf Shenk, Jonny Smallwood, Jon Sutton, and Norbert Wiley. I owe particular debts of gratitude to two mentors, collaborators, and friends. My former PhD supervisor, Jim Russell, first turned me on to the writings of Vygotsky, Luria, and Piaget, and he has been an intellectual inspiration to me for more than twenty-five years. Richard Bentall has been unfailingly generous with his time and encouragement in helping me to understand the shifting truths of madness and sanity.

The following kindly gave up their time to be interviewed for the book: Lisa Blackman, Jacqui Dillon, Sandra Escher, Aamer Hussein, Eleanor Longden, Denise Riley, Marius Romme, and Rachel Waddingham. I am especially grateful to all those who were interviewed anonymously. The book first took shape when I was a fellow of the Institute of Advanced Study at Durham University, and I have received invaluable support and guidance from that quarter from Tom McLeish, Veronica Strang, Ash Amin, and the Centre for Medical Humanities. At the Wellcome Trust, I have benefited from the wisdom and generosity of a great many people, particularly Chris Chapman, Lauren Couch, Nils Fietje, Chris Hassan, Harriet Martin, Clare Matterson, Dan O'Connor, Bárbara Rodríguez Muñoz, and Kirty Topiwala. My Hubbub colleagues Felicity Callard, Claudia Hammond, Daniel Margulies, Kim Staines, and James Wilkes have been patient and supportive as I have multitasked projects. The book has been enriched by collaborations with Nick Barley, Roland Gulliver, and Janet Smyth of the Edinburgh International Book Festival; Jad Abumrad and Pat Walters at Radiolab; Sam Guglani at Medicine Unboxed; and Claire Armitstead, Marta Bausells, and James Kingsland at the *Guardian*. I am grateful to all those who completed questionnaires and participated in experimental studies. Several people read and commented on parts of the manuscript: Marco Bernini, Chris Cook, Jane Garrison, Jenny Hodgson, Russ Hurlburt, Simone Kühn, Corinne Saunders, Jon Simons, Pat Waugh, Sam Wilkinson, and Angela Woods. Ben Alderson-Day read the entire manuscript and saved me from several mistakes. Needless to say, all errors and omissions are my own.

I am grateful to my editors at Profile Books, Mike Jones and Nick Sheerin, and to Daniel Crewe and Andrew Franklin for initially seeing the book's potential. Their colleagues at Profile have been generous with their support at every stage: Penny Daniel, Anna-Marie Fitzgerald, Hannah Ross, and Valentina Zanca. Mary Robson prepared the diagrams with flair and grace, and Sally Holloway made a pleasure from the process of copyediting. My editors at Basic Books, TJ Kelleher and Hélène Barthélemy, made the preparation of the US edition a great pleasure, and I have benefitted too from the generosity and expertise of George Lucas, Lara Heimert, Elisabeth Asher, Allison Finkel, Sarah Hausman, Cassie Nelson, Shena Redmond, Kathy Streckfus, and Liz Tzetzo. My agent, David Grossman, has been a source of unfailing support and friendship for many years. To Lizzie, Athena, and Isaac: thank you.

Notes

There are several online resources available for those seeking information about voice-hearing and other unusual experiences. See the "FAQs" and "Looking for Support?" pages of our Hearing the Voice blog at http://hearingthevoice.org.

Suggestions for further reading are marked in **boldface type**.

I. Funny Slices of Cheese

4 *degenerative brain disease:* Robert B. Zipursky, Thomas J. Reilly, and Robin M. Murray, "The Myth of Schizophrenia as a Progressive Brain Disease," *Schizophrenia Bulletin* 39 (2013): 1363–1372.

4 *"psychic civil war":* **Eleanor Longden, *Learning from the Voices in My Head*** (New York: TED Books, 2013).

4 *the negative connotations of "hallucination":* A hallucination is defined as a compelling perceptual experience in the absence of any external stimulus. See p. 120.

5 *the voices of morality:* For a discussion of the "voice" of conscience, see p. 245.

6 *"something that it is like":* Thomas Nagel, "What Is It Like to Be a Bat?," *Philosophical Review* 83 (1974): 435–450. There is a lively debate in philosophy of mind about whether thinking has a phenomenology—that is, whether there is "something that it is like" to be doing it. For a view in favor of cognitive phenomenology, see Terence Horgan and John Tienson, "The Intentionality of Phenomenology and the Phenomenology of Intentionality," in David J. Chalmers, ed., *Philosophy of Mind: Classical and Contemporary Readings* (Oxford: Oxford University Press, 2002). For a case against, see Peter Carruthers and Bénédicte Veillet, "The Case Against

Cognitive Phenomenology," in Tim Bayne and Michelle Montague, eds., *Cognitive Phenomenology* (Oxford: Oxford University Press, 2011).

6   *inner experience:* I use the term "inner experience" to refer to the contents of consciousness, including thoughts, emotions, sensations, perceptions, and other experiences. It can be taken to equate to the terms "conscious experience" and "phenomenal consciousness." See **Russell T. Hurlburt and Eric Schwitzgebel, *Describing Inner Experience? Proponent Meets Skeptic*** (Cambridge, MA: MIT Press, 2007).

7   *if a lion were able to speak:* "If a lion could talk, we could not understand him." Ludwig Wittgenstein, *Philosophical Investigations*, G. E. M. Anscombe, trans. (Oxford: Basil Blackwell, 1958), II, xi, p. 223.

7   *thinking has a linguistic quality:* As will become clear in the chapters that follow, I am not claiming that language has what philosophers would term a "constitutive" role in thinking. That is, language is not *necessary* for thinking; rather, it happens to be a tool that many human thinkers use much of the time.

8   *the magic of thinking is that it can be pointless:* Philip N. Johnson-Laird, *The Computer and the Mind: An Introduction to Cognitive Science* (London: Fontana, 1988).

8   *what exactly they mean by "thinking":* Ray Jackendoff, *A User's Guide to Thought and Meaning* (Oxford: Oxford University Press, 2012), chap. 15; Charles Fernyhough, "What Do We Mean by Thinking?," blog post in The Voices Within, *Psychology Today*, August 16, 2010, https://www.psychologytoday.com/blog/the-voices-within/201008/what-do-we-mean-thinking. Daniel Kahneman's bestselling book *Thinking: Fast and Slow* (London: Penguin, 2012) adopts a liberal definition of "thinking" that includes nonconscious (or fast-acting, System 1) cognition. My use of the term is closer to the deliberate, effortful processes of Kahneman's System 2. See also p. 106.

9   *the idea of an "inner voice":* In this book I am interested in experiences that have something of the linguistic, acoustic, and communicative properties of voices that speak and are heard. See pp. 185, 245.

10   *the "Dialogic Thinking" model:* See Chapter 7 for a discussion of this model.

11   *enchanted loom:* Sir Charles Sherrington, *Man on His Nature* (Cambridge, UK: Cambridge University Press, 1940), 225.

12   *"To think . . . is to talk with oneself":* Miguel de Unamuno, *The Tragic Sense of Life in Men and in Peoples*, J. E. Crawford Flitch, trans. (London: Macmillan, 1931), 25.

2. TURNING UP THE GAS

15   *what kind of activity is thinking?:* Ray Jackendoff, *A User's Guide to Thought and Meaning* (Oxford: Oxford University Press, 2012), chap. 15. See p. 7.

15   *your mind is likely to be anything but silent:* There has been an explosion of interest in recent years in the mental processes that operate when an individual is not busy with any specific task. See Jonathan Smallwood and Jonathan W. Schooler, "The Science of Mind Wandering: Empirically Navigating the Stream of Consciousness," *Annual Review of Psychology* 66 (2015): 487–518. See also pp. 162, 233.

16   *"Why . . . should we not gently and patiently review our own thoughts":* Plato, *Theaetetus,* in *Dialogues of Plato,* Benjamin Jowett, trans., vol. 3 (Cambridge, MA: Cambridge University Press, 1871), 155, p. 376.

16   *Cogito ergo sum:* René Descartes, *Discourse on Method and the Meditations,* F. E. Sutcliffe, trans. (Harmondsworth, UK: Penguin, 1968).

16   *"difficult and fallible":* William James, *Principles of Psychology,* vol. 1 (London: Macmillan, 1901), 191.

17   *two kinds of introspection:* Wilhelm Wundt, "Selbstbeobachtung und innere Wahrnehmung," *Philosophische Studien* 4 (1888): 292–309.

17   *10,000 introspective "reactions":* Edwin G. Boring, "A History of Introspection," *Psychological Bulletin* 50 (1953): 169–189.

17   *babies would make excellent introspectors:* James, *Principles of Psychology,* 1:189.

18   *". . . how the darkness looks":* Ibid., 1:244.

18   *the final nail in the coffin of introspection:* Boring, "A History of Introspection"; Kurt Danziger, "The History of Introspection Reconsidered," *Journal of the History of the Behavioural Sciences* 16 (1980): 241–262; Richard E. Nisbett and Timothy DeCamp Wilson, "Telling More Than We Can Know: Verbal Reports on Mental Processes," *Psychological Review* 84 (1977): 231–259.

18   *"arousal" pill:* Michael D. Storms and Richard E. Nisbett, "Insomnia and the Attribution Process," *Journal of Personality and Social Psychology* 2 (1970): 319–328.

20   *scientists who are rethinking introspection:* Interview with Russell Hurlburt, July 2, 2013.

22   *Descriptive Experience Sampling (DES):* **Russell T. Hurlburt and Christopher L. Heavey, "Telling What We Know: Describing Inner Experience,"** *Trends in Cognitive Sciences* 5 (2001): 400–403; **Russell T. Hurlburt and Eric Schwitzgebel,** *Describing Inner Experience? Proponent Meets Skeptic* (Cambridge, MA: MIT Press, 2007).

25   *"The studies do not suffice . . .":* Nisbett and Wilson, "Telling More Than We Can Know," 246. Emphasis is reproduced from the original quotations unless otherwise noted.

25   *The method is not without its critics:* Eric Schwitzgebel, "Eric's Reflections," in Hurlburt and Schwitzgebel, *Describing Inner Experience?,* 221–250.

26   *into the scanner:* See p. 176.

27   *preconceptions about your own experience:* Hurlburt and Schwitzgebel, *Describing Inner Experience?*

3. Inside the Chatterbox

31   *the ubiquity of inner speech:* Ray Jackendoff, *A User's Guide to Thought and Meaning* (Oxford: Oxford University Press, 2012), 82; Ludwig Wittgenstein, *Philosophical Investigations*, G. E. M. Anscombe, trans. (Oxford: Basil Blackwell, 1958), I, 329, p. 107; Peter Carruthers, *Language, Thought, and Consciousness* (Cambridge, UK: Cambridge University Press, 1996), 51. Note that these philosophers are making points about the relationship between thinking and language, rather than empirical claims about the frequency of inner speech.

31   *"We are a gabby species":* Bernard J. Baars, *In the Theater of Consciousness: The Workspace of the Mind* (Oxford: Oxford University Press, 1997), 75; Bernard J. Baars, "How Brain Reveals Mind: Neural Studies Support the Fundamental Role of Conscious Experience," *Journal of Consciousness Studies* 10 (2003): 100–114.

31   *These views have gained limited empirical support:* One study using a version of experience sampling showed inner speech occurring in around three-quarters of random samples: Eric Klinger and W. Miles Cox, "Dimensions of Thought Flow in Everyday Life," *Imagination, Cognition and Personality* 7 (1970): 105–128. This study is criticized by Hurlburt and colleagues for using inadequate methods for investigating inner experience: **Russell T. Hurlburt, Christopher L. Heavey, and Jason M. Kelsey, "Toward a Phenomenology of Inner Speaking,"** *Consciousness and Cognition* 22 (2013): 1477–1494.

31   *the so-called "resting state" paradigm:* Pascal Delamillieure et al., "The Resting State Questionnaire: An Introspective Questionnaire for Evaluation of Inner Experience During the Conscious Resting State," *Brain Research Bulletin* 81 (2010): 565–573. See Chapters 11 and 12 for further discussion of inner speech in the resting state.

32   *the huge variations among people:* A popular distinction is between "verbal" and "visual" thinkers, but research in this area has generally not measured how much inner speech people in the two categories actually use. See, for example, Alan Richardson, "Verbalizer-Visualizer: A Cognitive Style Dimension," *Journal of Mental Imagery* 1 (1977): 109–125.

32   *self-talk:* The term is widely used in sports psychology, but it has been criticized for typically making no distinction between external (audible) speech and its covert counterpart: Adam Winsler, "Still Talking to Ourselves After All These Years: A Review of Current Research on Private Speech," in **Adam Winsler, Charles Fernyhough, and Ignacio Montero, eds.,** *Private Speech, Executive Functioning, and the Development of Verbal Self-Regulation* (Cambridge, UK: Cambridge University Press, 2009).

33   *"You clumsy ox, your grandmother could play better!":* W. Timothy Gallwey, *The Inner Game of Tennis* (New York: Random House, 1974), 9.

33   *"I mean the conversation which the soul holds with herself..."*: Plato, *The-aetetus*, in *Dialogues of Plato*, Benjamin Jowett, trans., vol. 3 (Cambridge, UK: Cambridge University Press, 1871), 190, p. 416.

33   *listening to a verbal thought as it unwinds*: William James, *Principles of Psychology*, vol. 1 (London: Macmillan, 1901), 281.

33   *dialogue between different aspects of the self*: Charles Sanders Peirce, *Collected Papers of Charles Sanders Peirce*, C. Hartshorne and P. Weiss, eds., vol. 4 (Cambridge, MA: Harvard University Press, 1933), 6; Margaret S. Archer, *Structure, Agency and the Internal Conversation* (Cambridge, UK: Cambridge University Press, 2003).

34   *an internalized "other"*: George Herbert Mead, *Mind, Self, and Society: From the Standpoint of a Social Behaviorist* (Chicago: University of Chicago Press, 1934).

34   *Andy Murray*: "I Talked Myself into Being a Winner, Reveals Murray," *The Times* (London), March 30, 2013.

35   *personal pep talks in sports*: James Hardy, "Speaking Clearly: A Critical Review of the Self-Talk Literature," *Psychology of Sport and Exercise* 7 (2006): 81–97; James Hardy, Craig R. Hall, and Lew Hardy, "Quantifying Athlete Self-Talk," *Journal of Sports Sciences* 23 (2005): 905–917; Whisler, "Still Talking to Ourselves After All These Years."

35   *The pub game of darts*: Judy L. Van Raalte et al., "Cork! The Effects of Positive and Negative Self-Talk on Dart Throwing Performance," *Journal of Sport Behavior* 18 (1995): 50–57.

35   *analysis of gymnasts*: Michael J. Mahoney and Marshall Avener, "Psychology of the Elite Athlete: An Exploratory Study," *Cognitive Therapy and Research* 1 (1977): 135–141.

35   *all the good stuff is kept within*: We shall return to the distinction between internal and external self-talk in Chapter 4.

36   *no opportunity to react consciously*: Peter McLeod, "Visual Reaction Time and High-Speed Ball Games," *Perception* 16 (1987): 49–59; Michael F. Land and Peter McLeod, "From Eye Movements to Actions: How Batsmen Hit the Ball," *Nature Neuroscience* 3 (2000): 1340–1345; John McCrone, "Shots Faster Than the Speed of Thought," *Independent*, October 23, 2011; Frank Partnoy, *Wait: The Useful Art of Procrastination* (London: Profile Books, 2012), chap. 2.

37   *how batsmen really use self-talk*: Adam Miles and Rich Neil, "The Use of Self-Talk During Elite Cricket Batting Performance," *Psychology of Sport and Exercise* 14 (2013): 874–881. For all this study's ingenuity, it is important not to read too much into its findings. First, the participants' reports involved reconstructing what had gone on in their heads a full week after the events, leaving them exposed to the vagaries of memory. There was no way to objectively determine what was said or thought out on the pitch, or whether the batters' reports involved a certain amount of idealized reconstruction. And we also cannot draw any causal

conclusions about what these utterances were achieving. Even if the words were spoken as described, there is no way to tell whether they were effective in controlling attention, action, or motivation. Finally, like pretty much all research in this area (and in fact most questionnaire studies of self-talk more generally), the researchers did not distinguish between overt and covert (silent) speech.

39   *internal interlocutors:* Małgorzata M. Puchalska-Wasyl, "Self-Talk: Conversation with Oneself? On the Types of Internal Interlocutors," *Journal of Psychology: Interdisciplinary and Applied* 149 (2015): 443–460.

40   *the effects of referring to oneself in the first person:* Ethan Kross et al., "Self-Talk as a Regulatory Mechanism: How You Do It Matters," *Journal of Personality and Social Psychology* 106 (2014): 304–324.

4. TWO CARS

44   *Lev is also talking to himself:* Jean Piaget, *The Language and Thought of the Child,* Marjorie and Ruth Gabain, trans. (London: Kegan Paul, Trench, Trubner, 1959 [1926]), 14.

45   *rooted in his own viewpoint:* Jean Piaget and Bärbel Inhelder, *The Child's Conception of Space,* F. J. Langdon and J. L. Lunzer, trans. (London: Routledge and Kegan Paul, 1956 [1948]).

45   *"speech does not communicate the thoughts of the speaker . . .":* Piaget, *Language and Thought of the Child,* 16.

45   *At the same time, in Moscow:* **L. S. Vygotsky, *Thinking and Speech,*** in *The Collected Works of L. S. Vygotsky,* vol. 1, Robert W. Rieber and Aaron S. Carton, eds., Norris Minick, trans. (New York: Plenum, 1987 [1934]), 70. Piaget's label "egocentric speech" has generally been superseded by the term "private speech," which is less theoretically laden: John H. Flavell, "Le Langage Privé," *Bulletin de Psychologie* 19 (1966): 698–701.

47   *a noisy orchestra:* Vygotsky, *Thinking and Speech.*

47   *"parasocial" nature:* Lawrence Kohlberg, Judy Yaeger, and Else Hjertholm, "Private Speech: Four Studies and a Review of Theories," *Child Development* 39 (1968): 691–736.

47   *analyzing children's private speech:* Adam Winsler, Charles Fernyhough, Erin M. McClaren, and Erin Way, *Private Speech Coding Manual,* unpublished manuscript, George Mason University, Fairfax, Virginia, 2004.

47   *"psychological tool":* **L. S. Vygotsky, *Mind in Society: The Development of Higher Psychological Processes,*** M. Cole, V. John-Steiner, S. Scribner, and E. Souberman, eds. (Cambridge, MA: Harvard University Press, 1978 [1930, 1933, 1935]).

48   *cognitive benefit from using private speech:* Charles Fernyhough and Emma Fradley, "Private Speech on an Executive Task: Relations with Task Difficulty and Task Performance," *Cognitive Development* 20 (2005): 103–120.

48   *contracted and abbreviated:* Paul P. Goudena, "The Problem of Abbreviation and Internalization of Private Speech," in R. M. Diaz and L. E. Berk, eds., *Private Speech: From Social Interaction to Self-Regulation* (Hove, UK: Lawrence Erlbaum Associates, 1992); A. D. Pellegrini, "The Development of Preschoolers' Private Speech," *Journal of Pragmatics* 5 (1981): 445–458.

49   *this dialogic quality:* **Charles Fernyhough, "Dialogic Thinking,"** in Adam Winsler, Charles Fernyhough, and Ignacio Montero, eds., *Private Speech, Executive Functioning, and the Development of Verbal Self-Regulation* (Cambridge, UK: Cambridge University Press, 2009); Peter Feigenbaum, "Development of the Syntactic and Discourse Structures of Private Speech," in R. M. Diaz and L. E. Berk, eds., *Private Speech: From Social Interaction to Self-Regulation* (Hove, UK: Lawrence Erlbaum Associates, 1992); Kohlberg et al., "Private Speech."

49   *people continue to talk to themselves as adults:* Robert M. Duncan and J. Allan Cheyne, "Private Speech in Young Adults: Task Difficulty, Self-Regulation, and Psychological Predication," *Cognitive Development* 16 (2002): 889–906.

50   *working memory:* Although defined slightly differently, the construct has generally replaced the more familiar term "short-term memory," partly because it has been more successfully specified in cognitive and neuroscientific terms. Alan Baddeley, "Working Memory," *Science* 255 (1992): 556–559.

51   *the phonological similarity effect:* Alan D. Baddeley, "Short-Term Memory for Word Sequences as a Function of Acoustic, Semantic and Formal Similarity," *Quarterly Journal of Experimental Psychology* 18 (1966): 362–365.

51   *Children below about six or seven:* For example, Sue Palmer, "Working Memory: A Developmental Study of Phonological Recoding," *Memory* 8 (2000): 179–193. For a study that challenges the claim of a qualitative shift in short-term memory strategies, see Christopher Jarrold and Rebecca Citroën, "Reevaluating Key Evidence for the Development of Rehearsal: Phonological Similarity Effects in Children Are Subject to Proportional Scaling Artifacts," *Developmental Psychology* 49 (2013): 837–847.

51   *two schools, one in the United Kingdom and one in Saudi Arabia:* Abdulrahman S. Al-Namlah, Charles Fernyhough, and Elizabeth Meins, "Sociocultural Influences on the Development of Verbal Mediation: Private Speech and Phonological Recoding in Saudi Arabian and British Samples," *Developmental Psychology* 42 (2006): 117–131.

52   *articulatory suppression:* Jane S. M. Lidstone, Elizabeth Meins, and Charles Fernyhough, "The Roles of Private Speech and Inner Speech in Planning in Middle Childhood: Evidence from a Dual Task Paradigm," *Journal of Experimental Child Psychology* 107 (2010): 438–451.

53   *DES-style experience sampling with kids:* Russell T. Hurlburt and Eric Schwitzgebel, *Describing Inner Experience? Proponent Meets Skeptic* (Cambridge, MA: MIT Press, 2007), box 5.8, 111.

53   *what children do and don't understand about inner speech:* John H. Fla-
     vell, Frances L. Green, and Eleanor R. Flavell, "Children's Understand-
     ing of the Stream of Consciousness," *Child Development* 64 (1993):
     387–398; Charles Fernyhough, "What Can We Say About the Inner Ex-
     perience of the Young Child? (Commentary on Carruthers)," *Behavioral
     and Brain Sciences* 32 (2009): 143–144; John H. Flavell, Frances L. Green,
     Eleanor R. Flavell, and James B. Grossman, "The Development of Chil-
     dren's Knowledge About Inner Speech," *Child Development* 68 (2006):
     39–47. Note that the assumption is that the children in these studies
     were at an age where they possessed the machinery to do inner speech,
     including an intact phonological loop, but that they might typically not
     have chosen to use it, or that they might not have known how.

54   *a strange place to be:* Charles Fernyhough, *A Thousand Days of Wonder:
     A Scientist's Chronicle of His Daughter's Developing Mind* (New York:
     Avery, 2009).

55   *". . . like a splash of colour landing on a page":* Edward St. Aubyn, *Moth-
     er's Milk* (London: Picador, 2006), 64.

5. A Natural History of Thinking

58   *one of Russ's participants, Melanie:* Russell T. Hurlburt and Eric Schwitz-
     gebel, *Describing Inner Experience? Proponent Meets Skeptic* (Cambridge,
     MA: MIT Press, 2007), 66–68.

59   *more complex transformations:* L. S. Vygotsky, *Thinking and Speech,* in
     The Collected Works of L. S. Vygotsky, vol. 1, Robert W. Rieber and
     Aaron S. Carton, eds., Norris Minick, trans. (New York: Plenum, 1987
     [1934]), chap. 7.

59   *ten times faster than ordinary speech:* Rodney J. Korba, "The Rate of In-
     ner Speech," *Perceptual and Motor Skills* 71 (1990): 1043–1052.

60   *"Why are you bringing this woman to my attention?":* J. Y. Kang, *Inner
     Experience of Individuals Suffering from Bipolar Disorder,* master's thesis,
     University of Nevada, Las Vegas, 2013. Cited in Russell T. Hurlburt,
     Christopher L. Heavey, and Jason M. Kelsey, "Toward a Phenomenology
     of Inner Speaking," *Consciousness and Cognition* 22 (2013): 1477–1494.

60   *". . . a shower of words":* Vygotsky, *Thinking and Speech,* 281.

61   *the varieties of inner speech:* Simon McCarthy-Jones and Charles Ferny-
     hough, "The Varieties of Inner Speech: Links Between Quality of Inner
     Speech and Psychopathological Variables in a Sample of Young Adults,"
     Consciousness and Cognition 20 (2011): 1586–1593. We actually termed
     the last factor *evaluative/motivational;* for simplicity, I refer to it here as
     evaluative.

62   *patients diagnosed with schizophrenia:* Robin Langdon, Simon R. Jones,
     Emily Connaughton, and Charles Fernyhough, "The Phenomenology of
     Inner Speech: Comparison of Schizophrenia Patients with Auditory

Verbal Hallucinations and Healthy Controls," *Psychological Medicine* 39 (2009): 655–663.

62   *DES findings on inner speaking:* Hurlburt et al., "Toward a Phenomenology of Inner Speaking." Recall that Hurlburt and colleagues refer to certain forms of inner speech as "inner speaking" to emphasize its active nature (see p. 22).

63   *DES might underestimate the frequency:* Ben Alderson-Day and Charles Fernyhough, "More Than One Voice: Investigating the Phenomenological Properties of Inner Speech Requires a Variety of Methods. Commentary on Hurlburt, Heavey and Kelsey (2013), Toward a Phenomenology of Inner Speaking," *Consciousness and Cognition* 24 (2014): 113–114.

64   "*... motor habits in the larynx*": John B. Watson, "Psychology as the Behaviorist Views It," *Psychological Review* 20 (1913): 158–177, 174.

64   *the nerve poison curare:* Scott M. Smith, Hugh O. Brown, James E. P. Toman, and Louis S. Goodman, "The Lack of Cerebral Effects of *d*-tubocurarine," *Anesthesiology* 8 (1947): 1–14.

64   *the motor simulation hypothesis:* The motor simulation hypothesis of inner speech links to a wider group of "embodied simulation" theories which hold that processes such as word understanding and mental imagery essentially represent attenuated actions or perceptions. For a recent summary, see Benjamin K. Bergen, *Louder Than Words: The New Science of How the Mind Makes Meaning* (New York: Basic Books, 2012).

65   *asked participants to read limericks:* Ruth Filik and Emma Barber, "Inner Speech During Silent Reading Reflects the Reader's Regional Accent," *PLOS ONE* 6 (2011): e25782. See also Charles Fernyhough, "Life in the Chatterbox," *New Scientist*, June 1, 2013.

66   *inner speech shares many of the properties of external speech:* See, for example, Melanie's description of her "inner thought" voice: Hurlburt and Schwitzgebel, *Describing Inner Experience?*, box 4.2, 62; **Ben Alderson-Day and Charles Fernyhough, "Inner Speech: Development, Cognitive Functions, Phenomenology, and Neurobiology,"** *Psychological Bulletin* 141 (2015): 931–965.

66   *people who stutter:* R. Netsell and E. Ashley, "The Rate of Inner Speech in Persons Who Stutter," *Proceedings of the International Motor Speech Conference*, 2010.

66   *two kinds of errors:* Gary M. Oppenheim and Gary S. Dell, "Inner Speech Slips Exhibit Lexical Bias, But Not the Phonemic Similarity Effect," *Cognition* 106 (2008): 528–537; Martin Corley, Paul H. Brocklehurst, and H. Susannah Moat, "Error Biases in Inner and Overt Speech: Evidence from Tongue Twisters," *Journal of Experimental Psychology: Learning, Memory, and Cognition* 37 (2011): 162–175; Gary M. Oppenheim and Gary S. Dell, "Motor Movement Matters: The Flexible Abstractness of Inner Speech," *Memory & Cognition* 38 (2010): 1147–1160. For further discussion, see Alderson-Day and Fernyhough, "Inner Speech."

69   *Put your hand to your skull:* A good way to get a feel for the three-dimensional layout of these brain regions is through an online brain atlas or a smartphone app. 3D Brain is a good app for smartphones.

70   " . . . *what happens when people run through dialogues*": Ben Alderson-Day, Susanne Weis, Simon McCarthy-Jones, Peter Moseley, David Smailes, and Charles Fernyhough, "The Brain's Conversation with Itself: Neural Substrates of Dialogic Inner Speech," *Social Cognitive & Affective Neuroscience* 11 (2016): 110–120.

6. VOICES ON THE PAGE

75   " . . . *It was never otherwise*": St. Augustine of Hippo, *The Confessions*, Maria Boulding, trans. (Hyde Park, NY: New City Press, 1997), book 6, chap. 3, pp. 133–134. The translation is discussed in Mary Carruthers, *The Book of Memory: A Study of Memory in Medieval Culture*, 2nd ed. (Cambridge, UK: Cambridge University Press, 2008), 213, n. 63.

76   *"I snatched it up, opened it . . ."*: St. Augustine, *The Confessions*, book 8, chap. 12, p. 224.

76   *Ambrose's innovation:* Alberto Manguel, *A History of Reading* (London: Flamingo, 1997); A. K. Gavrilov, "Techniques of Reading in Classical Antiquity," *Classical Quarterly* 47 (1997): 56–73; M. F. Burnyeat, "Postscript on Silent Reading," *Classical Quarterly* 47 (1997): 74–76; James Fenton, "Read My Lips," *Guardian*, July 29, 2006; Sara Maitland, *A Book of Silence* (London: Granta, 2008), 151. Another view, from the medievalist Mary Carruthers, is that Augustine was writing at a time when he himself had come to understand the pressures of being a bishop and having one's opinion sought constantly, and so his emotional reaction is one of empathy rather than astonishment. If anything surprises Augustine, it is that Ambrose is only ever seen reading silently in these situations, and never in "the other way" (i.e., aloud), even though people are present. See Carruthers, *Book of Memory*, 212–216.

77   *one critic of the Ambrose story:* Gavrilov, "Techniques of Reading in Classical Antiquity."

77   " . . . *the essential characteristics of the original*": Edmund Burke Huey, *The Psychology and Pedagogy of Reading* (New York: Macmillan, 1980), 117–123. These "essential characteristics" are explored in more detail below.

78   *words and non-words:* Marianne Abramson and Stephen D. Goldinger, "What the Reader's Eye Tells the Mind's Ear: Silent Reading Activates Inner Speech," *Perception & Psychophysics* 59 (1997): 1059–1068.

78   *Even skilled readers move their tongues when reading:* H. B. Reed, "The Existence and Function of Inner Speech in Thought Processes," *Journal of Experimental Psychology* 1 (1916), 365–392.

78   *a behaviorist view of inner speech:* See p. 64.

78   *reading may be a special case:* W. D. A. Beggs and Philippa N. Howarth, "Inner Speech as a Learned Skill," *Journal of Experimental Child Psychology* 39 (1985): 396–411.

78   ". . . *the lips are seldom moved* . . .": Huey, *Psychology and Pedagogy of Reading*, 122.

78   *Findings from Hurlburt's DES method:* Russell T. Hurlburt and Eric Schwitzgebel, *Describing Inner Experience? Proponent Meets Skeptic* (Cambridge, MA: MIT Press, 2007), 101.

79   *mute as a result of a stroke:* David N. Levine, Ronald Calvanio, and Alice Popovics, "Language in the Absence of Inner Speech," *Neuropsychologia* 20 (1982): 391–409.

79   *inner speech that is stimulated when you read:* Brianna M. Eiter and Albrecht W. Inhoff, "Visual Word Recognition During Reading Is Followed by Subvocal Articulation," *Journal of Experimental Psychology: Learning, Memory, and Cognition* 36 (2010): 457–470.

79   *voices of two speakers:* Jessica D. Alexander and Lynne C. Nygaard, "Reading Voices and Hearing Text: Talker-Specific Auditory Imagery in Reading," *Journal of Experimental Psychology: Human Perception and Performance* 34 (2008): 446–459.

79   "*the experience of a relationship in silence*": Adam Phillips, *Promises, Promises: Essays on Psychoanalysis and Literature* (London: Faber and Faber, 2000), 373.

80   *a character's private thought processes:* Dorrit Cohn, *Transparent Minds: Narrative Modes for Presenting Consciousness in Fiction* (Princeton, NJ: Princeton University Press, 1978).

81   *the voices of fictional characters:* Ben Alderson-Day, Marco Bernini, and Charles Fernyhough, "Uncharted Features and Dynamics of Reading: Voices, Characters, and Crossing of Experiences," manuscript under review.

81   *hearing voices when reading:* Ruvanee P. Vilhauer, "Inner Reading Voices: An Overlooked Form of Inner Speech," *Psychosis* 8 (2016): 37–47. Note that Vilhauer's data collection involved starting with a text search for "hearing voices" and then adding the modifier "read*."

82   *direct speech is generally perceived as more vivid:* Elizabeth Wade and Herbert H. Clark, "Reproduction and Demonstration in Quotations," *Journal of Memory and Language* 32 (1993): 805–819.

82   *neural basis for the observation:* Bo Yao, Pascal Belin, and Christoph Scheepers, "Silent Reading of Direct Versus Indirect Speech Activates Voice-Selective Areas in the Auditory Cortex," *Journal of Cognitive Neuroscience* 23 (2011): 3146–3152; Bo Yao and Christoph Scheepers, "Contextual Modulation of Reading Rate for Direct Versus Indirect Speech Quotations," *Cognition* 121 (2011): 447–453; Bo Yao, Pascal Belin, and Christoph Scheepers, "Brain 'Talks Over' Boring Quotes: Top-Down Activation of Voice-Selective Areas While Listening to Monotonous Direct Speech Quotations," *NeuroImage* 60 (2012): 1832–1842; **Christopher I.**

Petkov and Pascal Belin, "Silent Reading: Does the Brain 'Hear' Both Speech and Voices?," *Current Biology* 23 (2013): R155–156.

83   *our familiarity with particular voices:* Christopher A. Kurby, Joseph P. Magliano, and David N. Rapp, "Those Voices in Your Head: Activation of Auditory Images During Reading," *Cognition* 112 (2009): 457–461.

84   *voice they have never heard:* Danielle N. Gunraj and Celia M. Klin, "Hearing Story Characters' Voices: Auditory Imagery During Reading," *Discourse Processes* 49 (2012): 137–153.

84   *they have got the voice of a particular character "all wrong":* Alderson-Day et al., "Vivid Experiences of Reading." One writer told me that he will not listen to the audiobooks of his works for just this reason.

85   *"I've a lover, a lover . . .":* Gustave Flaubert, *Madame Bovary*, Alan Russell, trans. (Harmondsworth, UK: Penguin, 1950), 175.

85   *thought "Burger King" while saying "KFC":* Russell T. Hurlburt, Christopher L. Heavey, and Jason M. Kelsey, "Toward a Phenomenology of Inner Speaking," *Consciousness and Cognition* 22 (2013): 1477–1494. See p. 63.

86   *"It's crash and clatter . . .":* Patrick Ness, *The Knife of Never Letting Go* (London: Walker Books, 2008), 42.

86   *an Urdu speaker, Usman:* Aamer Hussein, *Another Gulmohar Tree* (London: Telegram Books, 2009), 58; Aamer Hussein, interviewed on BBC World Service, *The Forum*, August 19, 2013, www.bbc.co.uk/programmes /p01dyvcm.

87   *"perverted commas":* Joyce made the following remark about the Jonathan Cape edition of *A Portrait of the Artist as a Young Man*: "Then Mr Cape and his printers gave me trouble. They set the book with perverted commas and I insisted on their removal by the sergeant-at-arms. Then they underlined passages which they thought undesirable. But as you will see by the enclosed: They were and, behold, they are not." Letter to H. S. Weaver, July 11, 1924, *Letters of James Joyce*, Richard Ellmann, ed., vol. 3 (London: Faber and Faber, 1966), 99.

87   *"They slipped out of their backpacks . . .":* Cormac McCarthy, *The Road* (London: Picador, 2009), 25–26.

88   *"No. She didn't want anything . . .":* James Joyce, *Ulysses* (Harmondsworth, UK: Penguin, 1986), 46.

88   *the mysterious Man in Black:* Geoffrey Chaucer, *The Book of the Duchess*, ll. 503–506, in *The Riverside Chaucer* (Oxford: Oxford University Press, 2008), 336.

88   *"better than sociable":* Daniel Defoe, *Robinson Crusoe* (Harmondsworth, UK: Penguin, 1994), 135; Patricia Waugh, "The Novelist as Voice-Hearer," *The Lancet* 386 (2015): e54–e55.

89   *"What do I want? . . .":* Charlotte Brontë, *Jane Eyre* (Harmondsworth, UK: Penguin, 1966), 118; Jeremy Hawthorn, "Formal and Social Issues in the Study of Interior Dialogue: The Case of *Jane Eyre*," in Jeremy Hawthorn, ed., *Narrative: From Malory to Motion Pictures* (London: Edward Arnold, 1985), 87–99.

89   *"controlled personality disorder . . .":* "David Mitchell," in John Freeman, *How to Read a Novelist: Conversations with Writers* (London: Constable and Robinson, 2013), 200; Waugh, "The Novelist as Voice-Hearer."

7. Chorus of Me

91   *"Ah if I could only find a voice of my own . . .":* Samuel Beckett, *The Un-namable,* in *The Beckett Trilogy* (London: Picador, 1979), 320.

92   *" . . . The brain has better things to do . . .":* Letter from Samuel Beckett to Georges Duthuit (April–May 1949), *The Letters of Samuel Beckett,* vol. 2, *1941–1956* (Cambridge, UK: Cambridge University Press, 2011), 149. I am grateful to Marco Bernini for drawing my attention to this quotation, which in turn inspired the title of Chapter 11.

92   *"I have never spoken enough to me . . .":* Beckett, *The Unnamable,* 284.

92   *the author, the narrator, and the protagonist:* Marco Bernini, "Gression, Regression, and Beyond: A Cognitive Reading of *The Unnamable,*" in David Tucker, Mark Nixon, and Dirk Van Hulle, eds., *Revisiting Molloy, Malone Meurt / Malone Dies and L'Innommable / The Unnamable, Samuel Beckett Today / Aujourd'hui,* vol. 26 (Amsterdam: Rodopi, 2014), 193–210; Jerome Bruner, "Life as Narrative," *Social Research* 71 (2004): 691–710.

92   *the natural sounds of inner speech:* Marco Bernini, "Reading a Brain Listening to Itself: Voices, Inner Speech and Auditory-Verbal Hallucinations," in *Beckett and the Cognitive Method: Mind, Models, and Exploratory Narratives,* under revision; Marco Bernini, "Samuel Beckett's Articulation of Unceasing Inner Speech," *Guardian,* August 19, 2014.

93   *what I call dialogic thinking:* Charles Fernyhough, "Dialogic Thinking," in Adam Winsler, Charles Fernyhough, and Ignacio Montero, eds., *Private Speech, Executive Functioning, and the Development of Verbal Self-Regulation* (Cambridge, UK: Cambridge University Press, 2009); Charles Fernyhough, "The Dialogic Mind: A Dialogic Approach to the Higher Mental Functions," *New Ideas in Psychology* 14 (1996): 47–62; Charles Fernyhough, "Getting Vygotskian About Theory of Mind: Mediation, Dialogue, and the Development of Social Understanding," *Developmental Review* 28 (2008): 225–262.

93   *The concept of "dialogue":* M. M. Bakhtin, *Problems of Dostoevsky's Poetics,* C. Emerson, trans. and ed. (Minneapolis: University of Minnesota Press, 1984); M. M. Bakhtin, *Speech Genres and Other Late Essays,* C. Emerson and M. Holquist, eds., V. W. McGee, trans. (Austin: University of Texas Press, 1986).

94   *the writings of Plato . . . :* See p. 33.

94   *enacting a dialogue between them:* Michael Holquist, *Dialogism: Bakhtin and His World* (London: Routledge, 1990); Michael Holquist, "Answering

as Authoring: Mikhail Bakhtin's Trans-Linguistics," *Critical Inquiry* 10 (1983): 307–319.

95   *an "open slot"*: Fernyhough, "Getting Vygotskian About Theory of Mind," 242; Ben Alderson-Day and Charles Fernyhough, "Inner Speech: Development, Cognitive Functions, Phenomenology, and Neurobiology," *Psychological Bulletin* 141 (2015): 931–965.

96   *"I have attacked that old giant of a pollard willow . . .":* Vincent van Gogh, *The Complete Letters of Vincent van Gogh*, 2nd ed., vols. 1–3 (London: Thames and Hudson, 1978). The letters quoted are Letter 221 (July 31, 1882), Letter 228 (September 3, 1882), Letter 289 (c. June 5, 1883), Letter 291 (c. June 7, 1883), and Letter 293 (June 15, 1883).

99   *"Though his brother Theo never picked up a brush . . .":* Joshua Wolf Shenk, *Powers of Two: Finding the Essence of Innovation in Creative Pairs* (Boston: Houghton Mifflin Harcourt, 2014), xvii and 70.

101   *this developmental progression:* L. S. Vygotsky, *Thinking and Speech*, in *The Collected Works of L. S. Vygotsky*, vol. 1, Robert W. Rieber and Aaron S. Carton, eds., Norris Minick, trans. (New York: Plenum, 1987 [1934]); Laura E. Berk, "Children's Private Speech: An Overview of Theory and the Status of Research," in R. M. Diaz and L. E. Berk, eds., *Private Speech: From Social Interaction to Self-Regulation* (Hove, UK: Lawrence Erlbaum Associates, 1992).

101   *"new, beautiful, and useful":* Mihaly Csikszentmihalyi, *Creativity: Flow and the Psychology of Discovery* (New York: HarperCollins, 2009), 25.

101   *the "candle" problem:* Karl Duncker, "On Problem-Solving," Psychological Monographs, vol. 58, no. 5, Whole No. 270 (Washington, DC: American Psychological Association, 1945); Fernyhough, "Dialogic Thinking."

102   *"Do our inner thoughts ever show outwardly?":* van Gogh, *Letters*, vol. 1, Letter 133, July 1880.

103   *children who use more self-regulatory private speech:* Martha Daugherty, C. Stephen White, and Brenda H. Manning, "Relationships Among Private Speech and Creativity in Young Children," *Gifted Child Quarterly* 38 (1994): 21–26.

103   *"Suppose I make a break . . .":* Virginia Woolf, *A Writer's Diary: Being Extracts from the Diary of Virginia Woolf*, Leonard Woolf, ed. (New York: Harcourt Brace Jovanovich, 1953), 292–293. The notebook entry relates to Woolf's biography of Roger Fry. Vera John-Steiner, *Notebooks of the Mind: Explorations of Thinking*, rev. ed. (Oxford: Oxford University Press, 1997); Frederick J. DiCamilla and James P. Lantolf, "The Linguistic Analysis of Private Writing," *Language Sciences* 16 (1994): 347–369. Social media provide a modern counterpart to the dialogue with the self that one can have on the pages of a notebook: Charles Fernyhough, "Twittering Out Loud," blog post in The Voices Within, *Psychology Today*, February 20, 2011, https://www.psychologytoday.com/blog/the-voices-within/201102/twittering-out-loud.

104   *I don't have to divert mental resources:* Alderson-Day and Fernyhough, "Inner Speech."

104   *"Have you ever danced with a movie star?":* Daniel C. Dennett, "How to Do Other Things with Words," *Philosophy*, suppl. 42 (1997): 232.

105   *the linguistic act of posing a question:* Ibrahim Senay, Dolores Albarracín, and Kenji Noguchi, "Motivating Goal-Directed Behavior Through Introspective Self-Talk: The Role of the Interrogative Form of Simple Future Tense," *Psychological Science* 21 (2010): 499–504.

106   *"Turn left at the red house":* Linda Hermer-Vazquez and Elizabeth S. Spelke, "Sources of Flexibility in Human Cognition: Dual-Task Studies of Space and Language," *Cognitive Psychology* 39 (1999): 3–36.

106   *search for a particular object:* Gary Lupyan and Daniel Swingley, "Self-Directed Speech Affects Visual Search Performance," *Quarterly Journal of Experimental Psychology* 65 (2012): 1068–1085; Gary Lupyan, "Extra-communicative Functions of Language: Verbal Interference Causes Selective Categorization Impairments," *Psychonomic Bulletin & Review* 16 (2009): 711–718.

106   *"linguistic relativity hypothesis":* Benjamin Lee Whorf, *Language, Thought and Reality* (Cambridge, MA: MIT Press, 1956).

106   *lingua franca in the brain:* **Peter Carruthers, "The Cognitive Functions of Language,"** *Behavioral and Brain Sciences* 25 (2002): 657–726.

108   *the neural basis of dialogic thinking:* Ben Alderson-Day, Susanne Weis, Simon McCarthy-Jones, Peter Moseley, David Smailes, and Charles Fernyhough, "The Brain's Conversation with Itself: Neural Substrates of Dialogic Inner Speech," *Social Cognitive & Affective Neuroscience* 11 (2016): 110–120. If the Dialogic Thinking model is correct, should we be looking for specific centers in the brain that correspond to the different voices that make up who we are? I think that would be both naïve and messy. For one thing, it would require a way of delimiting a set of voices (and thus neural regions) available to internal dialogue, and I think our minds are too open-minded for that. It is overly simplistic to propose, as one neuroscientist has, that one voice in the dialogue of the self is generated in a particular brain region (in this example, the orbitofrontal cortex) while the other is housed somewhere else (the anterior cingulate); Marc D. Lewis, "The Dialogical Brain: Contributions of Emotional Neurobiology to Understanding the Dialogical Self," *Theory & Psychology* 12 (2002): 175–190. Rather, we should be looking for the underlying structure—particularly, a pattern of interaction *among* networks—that makes dialogic inner speech possible.

8. NOT I

118   *When someone reports hearing a voice:* Simon McCarthy-Jones, Joel Krueger, Frank Larøi, Matthew Broome, and Charles Fernyhough, "Stop,

Look, Listen: The Need for Philosophical Phenomenological Perspectives on Auditory Verbal Hallucinations," *Frontiers in Human Neuroscience* 7, article 127 (2013).

9. DIFFERENT VOICES

119 *"I have an illness . . .":* Nathan Filer, *The Shock of the Fall* (London: HarperCollins, 2013), 67.

119 *data from the 2006 US General Social Survey:* Bernice A. Pescosolido et al., "'A Disease Like Any Other'? A Decade of Change in Public Reactions to Schizophrenia, Depression, and Alcohol Dependence," *American Journal of Psychiatry* 167 (2010): 1321–1330.

119 *"schizophrenia" is a highly misunderstood term:* The term first appeared in print in Bleuler's 1911 *Dementia Praecox, or the Group of Schizophrenias* (New York: International Universities Press, 1950). The misuse of the term to refer to split personality is sometimes attributed to T. S. Eliot, who made the mistake in his 1933 essay "Shelley and Keats" in *The Use of Poetry and the Use of Criticism* (Cambridge, MA: Harvard University Press, 1933), 90.

120 *cardinal (or "first-rank") features:* Kurt Schneider, *Clinical Psychopathology* (New York: Grune and Stratton, 1959).

120 *"To know schizophrenia . . . is to know psychiatry":* Roy Grinker, quoted in Roy Richard Grinker, "The Five Lives of the Psychiatry Manual," *Nature* 468 (2010): 168–170.

120 *psychiatry's "sacred symbol":* Thomas Szasz, *Schizophrenia: The Sacred Symbol of Psychiatry* (New York: Basic Books, 1976).

120 *the construct's scientific validity:* See, for example, Richard P. Bentall, "The Search for Elusive Structure: A Promiscuous Realist Case for Researching Specific Psychotic Experiences Such as Hallucinations," *Schizophrenia Bulletin* 40, suppl. no. 4 (2014): S198–S201.

120 *progressive brain disease:* Robert B. Zipursky, Thomas J. Reilly, and Robin M. Murray, "The Myth of Schizophrenia as a Progressive Brain Disease," *Schizophrenia Bulletin* 39 (2013): 1363–1372.

120 *eight genetically distinct disorders:* J. Arnedo et al., "Uncovering the Hidden Risk Architecture of the Schizophrenias: Confirmation in Three Independent Genome-Wide Association Studies," *American Journal of Psychiatry* 172 (2015): 139–153.

120 *the psychiatrist's "bible":* American Psychiatric Association, *Diagnostic and Statistical Manual of Mental Disorders*, 5th ed. (Arlington, VA: American Psychiatric Association, 2013) (*DSM-5* hereafter). "Negative symptoms" involve the loss or lack of typical cognitive processes and emotional responses: for example, poverty of speech or lack of motivation.

121 *only useful up to a point: DSM-5*, 822. Curiously, and despite mounting evidence to the contrary, *DSM-5* makes no allowance for hallucinations

occurring outside of normal experience unless they occur in hypnagogic or hypnopompic states (see first note in Chapter 12).

122 *a whole host of other psychiatric diagnoses:* Frank Larøi et al., "The Phenomenological Features of Auditory Verbal Hallucinations in Schizophrenia and Across Clinical Disorders: A State-of-the-Art Overview and Critical Evaluation," *Schizophrenia Bulletin* 38 (2012): 724–733. It is drearily necessary to emphasize that denying the automatic association of voice-hearing with schizophrenia does not entail denying the reality of severe mental illness. Many people who hear voices find it a very distressing experience. Those people have mental health problems that need serious support; they deserve our sympathy and respect rather than continuing stigma.

122 *"the sacred symbol of the sacred symbol":* Charles Fernyhough, "Hearing the Voice," *The Lancet* 384 (2014): 1090–1091.

122 *Society for Psychical Research:* H. Sidgwick, A. Johnson, F. Myers, F. Podmore, and E. Sidgwick, "Report of the Census of Hallucinations," *Proceedings of the Society for Psychical Research* 26 (1894): 259–394. Note that the reference to the experiences happening "when awake" was intended to exclude so-called hypnagogic and hypnopompic hallucinations, which are very common. See, for example, Simon R. Jones, Charles Fernyhough, and David Meads, "In a Dark Time: Development, Validation, and Correlates of the Durham Hypnagogic and Hypnopompic Hallucinations Questionnaire," *Personality and Individual Differences* 46 (2009): 30–34.

122 *between 5 and 15 percent of ordinary people:* **Simon McCarthy-Jones, Hearing Voices: The Histories, Causes and Meanings of Auditory Verbal Hallucinations** (Cambridge, UK: Cambridge University Press, 2012); Vanessa Beavan, John Read, and Claire Cartwright, "The Prevalence of Voice-Hearers in the General Population: A Literature Review," *Journal of Mental Health* 20 (2011): 281–292.

123 *nearly two hundred newspaper articles:* Ruvanee P. Vilhauer, "Depictions of Auditory Verbal Hallucinations in News Media," *International Journal of Social Psychiatry* 61 (2015): 58–63.

123 *the problem of stigma:* Otto F. Wahl, "Stigma as a Barrier to Recovery from Mental Illness," *Trends in Cognitive Sciences* 16 (2012): 8–10.

123 *"When you say you're a voice-hearer . . .":* Adam was interviewed on BBC Radio 4's *Saturday Live* program, March 2, 2013.

124 *some developmental problem with this process:* I explored this "developmental problem" idea further (and ultimately rejected it) in my "Alien Voices and Inner Dialogue: Towards a Developmental Account of Auditory Verbal Hallucinations," *New Ideas in Psychology* 22 (2004): 49–68.

125 *St. John of the Cross:* Simon R. Jones, "Re-expanding the Phenomenology of Hallucinations: Lessons from Sixteenth-Century Spain," *Mental Health, Religion & Culture* 13 (2010): 187–208. An excellent account of the history of voice-hearing is given in McCarthy-Jones, *Hearing Voices.*

125   *"the interior word":* Thomas Aquinas, *Summa Theologica*, vol. 14 (London: Burns, Oates, and Washbourne, 1927), 1a, 107.1.

125   *"a vividly conceived idea . . .":* Henry Maudsley, *Natural Causes and Supernatural Seemings* (London: Kegan Paul, Trench, 1886), 184.

125   *brain systems that usually monitor which actions are self-produced:* Irwin Feinberg, "Efference Copy and Corollary Discharge: Implications for Thinking and Its Disorders," *Schizophrenia Bulletin* 4 (1978): 636–640.

126   *Frith and his colleagues:* Christopher D. Frith, *The Cognitive Neuropsychology of Schizophrenia* (Hove, UK: Lawrence Erlbaum Associates, 1992); Christopher D. Frith and D. John Done, "Experiences of Alien Control in Schizophrenia Reflect a Disorder in the Central Monitoring of Action," *Psychological Medicine* 19 (1989): 359–363.

126   *monitoring the source of information:* Richard P. Bentall, "The Illusion of Reality: A Review and Integration of Psychological Research on Hallucinations," *Psychological Bulletin* 107 (1990): 82–95; **Richard P. Bentall, Madness Explained: Psychosis and Human Nature** (London: Allen Lane, 2003); M. L. Brookwell, R. P. Bentall, and F. Varese, "Externalizing Biases and Hallucinations in Source-Monitoring, Self-Monitoring and Signal Detection Studies: A Meta-Analytic Review," *Psychological Medicine* 43 (2013): 2465–2475.

127   *A particularly strong demonstration of this bias:* Louise C. Johns et al., "Verbal Self-Monitoring and Auditory Verbal Hallucinations in Patients with Schizophrenia," *Psychological Medicine* 31 (2001): 705–715.

127   *tiny movements in the muscles associated with vocalization:* Louis N. Gould, "Verbal Hallucinations and Activity of Vocal Musculature: An Electromyographic Study," *American Journal of Psychiatry* 105 (1948): 367–372; Louis N. Gould, "Verbal Hallucinations as Automatic Speech: The Reactivation of Dormant Speech Habit," *American Journal of Psychiatry* 107 (1950): 110–119. Similar studies were performed by the pioneering Soviet psychologist A. N. Sokolov, although with a focus on tongue movements rather than electromyographical activations: A. N. Sokolov, *Inner Speech and Thought* (New York: Plenum, 1972). At first glance, these findings fit with John B. Watson's idea that inner speech is simply subvocalized external speech. As we have seen, though, that theory comes with problems. There is stronger support for Vygotsky's model, in which external speech is transformed in the process of internalization. On such a view of inner speech, electromyographical correlates of verbal thinking might or might not accompany the internal experience, but whether they do or not tells us nothing about whether inner speech is happening. Because it is transformed as it is internalized, inner speech might come to rely on different neural systems and have a very different relation to the production of motor actions. See the discussion of the relation between internal and external speech in Chapter 5.

128   *"Miss Jones"*: Paul Green and Martin Preston, "Reinforcement of Vocal Correlates of Auditory Hallucinations by Auditory Feedback: A Case Study," *British Journal of Psychiatry* 139 (1981): 204–208.

128   *asking hallucinating patients simply to open their mouths*: Peter A. Bick and Marcel Kinsbourne, "Auditory Hallucinations and Subvocal Speech in Schizophrenic Patients," *American Journal of Psychiatry* 144 (1987): 222–225.

128   *"The integral will be larger than this sum of the terms . . ."*: James Gleick, *Genius: Richard Feynman and Modern Physics* (London: Little, Brown, 1992), 224. Feynman continued by explaining: "I argue with myself. . . . I have two voices that work back and forth."

129   *"You should get the water"*: Aaron T. Beck and Neil A. Rector, "A Cognitive Model of Hallucinations," *Cognitive Therapy and Research* 27 (2003): 19–52. Another attempt to explain voice-hearing is grounded in a theory known as dialogical self theory, which proposes that our selves are made up of different parts that communicate with each other in dynamic ways. In schizophrenia, the integration of these constituent entities breaks down, and one result is auditory verbal hallucinations. Neither this nor Beck and Rector's account offers a convincing explanation of exactly why and how the anomaly in inner dialogue might happen, partly because of a reliance on a relatively impoverished view of inner speech. Dialogical self theory is valuable as a model of the structure of a dynamic self, but it does not adequately account for the cognitive and neural processes involved in typical and atypical inner dialogue. See G. Stanghellini and J. Cutting, "Auditory Verbal Hallucinations: Breaking the Silence of Inner Dialogue," *Psychopathology* 36 (2003): 120–128; Hubert J. M. Hermans, "Voicing the Self: From Information Processing to Dialogical Interchange," *Psychological Bulletin* 119 (1996): 31–50.

130   *"alien yet self"*: Ivan Leudar and Philip Thomas, *Voices of Reason, Voices of Insanity: Studies of Verbal Hallucinations* (London: Routledge, 2000).

130   *inner speech is "re-expanded"*: Fernyhough, "Alien Voices and Inner Dialogue"; **Charles Fernyhough and Simon McCarthy-Jones, "Thinking Aloud About Mental Voices,"** in F. Macpherson and D. Platchias, eds., *Hallucination* (Cambridge, MA: MIT Press, 2013). If the theory is correct, several specific predictions follow. First, patients who hear voices should not experience regular expanded inner speech, since all such internal utterances should be experienced as voices; however, patients should show ordinary condensed inner speech. Voice-hearing should also be associated with stressful situations and challenging conditions, both of which are thought to increase the likelihood of thoughts being verbalized—in this case, re-expanded into full-blown inner dialogue—in both children and adults. Finally, if conditions are stressful and challenging enough, voice-hearing should happen in psychiatrically healthy individuals. See also Simon R. Jones and Charles Fernyhough, "Neural

Correlates of Inner Speech and Auditory Verbal Hallucinations: A Critical Review and Theoretical Integration," *Clinical Psychology Review* 27 (2007): 140–154.

130   *people who experience auditory verbal hallucinations:* Simon McCarthy-Jones and Charles Fernyhough, "The Varieties of Inner Speech: Links Between Quality of Inner Speech and Psychopathological Variables in a Sample of Young Adults," *Consciousness and Cognition* 20 (2011): 1586–1593; Robin Langdon, Simon R. Jones, Emily Connaughton, and Charles Fernyhough, "The Phenomenology of Inner Speech: Comparison of Schizophrenia Patients with Auditory Verbal Hallucinations and Healthy Controls," *Psychological Medicine* 39 (2009): 655–663; Paolo de Sousa, William Sellwood, Amy Spray, Charles Fernyhough, and Richard Bentall, "Inner Speech and Clarity of Self-Concept in Thought Disorder," *Journal of Nervous and Mental Disease*, in press.

131   *inner speech in patient and non-patient samples:* A challenge for future research is to determine how these variables relate to each other in patient and non-patient samples. In our student sample, more dialogicality was related to increased hallucination-proneness; in de Sousa's study, patients' likelihood of hallucinating was instead linked to their scores on the *evaluative* subscale and the presence of other people in inner speech. Perhaps in the general population a greater volume of dialogic inner speech increases the chance of some internal utterances being mis-attributed as alien. In clinical samples, dialogicality might be less important in triggering voice-hearing than factors such as stress, cognitive challenge, and the emotional quality of inner speech. See McCarthy-Jones and Fernyhough, "The Varieties of Inner Speech."

132   *why isn't* all *inner speech perceived as an external voice?:* This issue has been described by philosopher Shaun Gallagher as the "selectivity" problem: Shaun Gallagher, "Neurocognitive Models of Schizophrenia: A Neurophenomenological Critique," *Psychopathology* 37 (2004): 8–19.

132   *normal in patients who hear voices:* It is possible that something about the condition of schizophrenia makes it difficult for those with the diagnosis to reflect on their inner experience in the way that a semi-structured interview or questionnaire requires. The disorder has previously been associated with problems in understanding other people's mental states, and these might feed into a difficulty in reflecting on one's own thought processes, including one's inner speech and more atypical experiences such as voice-hearing.

132   *particularly developed acoustic properties:* Steffen Moritz and Frank Larøi, "Differences and Similarities in the Sensory and Cognitive Signatures of Voice-Hearing, Intrusions and Thoughts," *Schizophrenia Research* 102 (2008): 96–107; Andrea Raballo and Frank Larøi, "Murmurs of Thought: Phenomenology of Hallucinatory Consciousness in Impending Psychosis," *Psychosis* 3 (2011): 163–166.

132   *voice-hearing is a diverse experience:* Emil Kraepelin, *Dementia Praecox and Paraphrenia* (Chicago: Chicago Medical Book Company, 1919 [1896]); Bleuler, *Dementia Praecox.*

10. THE VOICE OF A DOVE

135   *"Obey the gods . . .":* Homer, *The Iliad*, Martin Hammond, trans. (Harmondsworth, UK: Penguin, 1987), 8.

135   *"There he stood and kept the firelight high . . .":* Homer, *The Odyssey*, Robert Fitzgerald, trans. (London: Harvill, 1996), 359.

137   *"a gigantic vault in mentality":* Julian Jaynes, *The Origin of Consciousness in the Breakdown of the Bicameral Mind* (Harmondsworth, UK: Penguin, 1993), 272.

137   *Jaynes's neuroscientific analysis:* For recent analyses of Jaynes's claims, see Andrea Eugenio Cavanna, Michael Trimble, Federico Cinti, and Francesco Monaco, "The 'Bicameral Mind' 30 Years On: A Critical Reappraisal of Julian Jaynes' Hypothesis," *Functional Neurology* 22 (2007): 11–15; Simon McCarthy-Jones, *Hearing Voices: The Histories, Causes and Meanings of Auditory Verbal Hallucinations* (Cambridge, UK: Cambridge University Press, 2012); Veronique Greenwood, "Consciousness Began When the Gods Stopped Speaking," *Nautilus*, issue 204, May 28, 2015. A modern take on the idea of the two hemispheres having different personalities is presented by the psychiatrist Iain McGilchrist, who has controversially proposed that the two hemispheres of the brain have distinct information-processing "styles": Iain McGilchrist, *The Master and His Emissary: The Divided Brain and the Making of the Western World* (New Haven, CT: Yale University Press, 2009).

137   *conscious, and even verbally-mediated, volition:* Homer, *Iliad*, 353–354, 7–8.

139   *a closet schizophrenic:* For excellent accounts of Socrates's voice-hearing, see McCarthy-Jones, *Hearing Voices*; Daniel B. Smith, *Muses, Madmen, and Prophets: Rethinking the History, Science, and Meaning of Auditory Hallucination* (New York: Penguin, 2007). For an ironic reference to Socrates as a "schizophrenic," see episode 6, season 1, of the TV show *House MD*, December 21, 2004.

139   *ninety-three times:* George Stein, "The Voices That Ezekiel Hears," *British Journal of Psychiatry* 196 (2010): 101; Christopher C H Cook, "The Prophet Samuel, Hypnagogic Hallucinations and the Voice of God," *British Journal of Psychiatry* 203 (2013): 380.

139   *"revelations about the king":* For more on Joan's voices, see McCarthy-Jones, *Hearing Voices*, and Smith, *Muses, Madmen, and Prophets.*

140   *"If a man were to ride here with a sword in his hand . . .":* Margery Kempe, *The Book of Margery Kempe*, B. A. Windeatt, trans. (Harmondsworth, UK: Penguin, 1985), chap. 11. The events described in Kempe's *Book*

have been notoriously difficult to verify historically, and this is the only record of her meeting with Julian of Norwich. However, a letter recently discovered in Gdansk, apparently prepared for Margery's son John in 1431, has been interpreted as confirming at least some aspects of Margery's biography. See Sebastian Sobecki, "'The Writyng of This Tretys': Margery Kempe's Son and the Authorship of Her *Book*," *Studies in the Age of Chaucer* 37 (2015).

143   *the voice of a dove:* Kempe, *Book of Margery Kempe*, chap. 36, 127.

143   *an anchoress who has wisdom in these matters:* Ibid., chaps. 18–20; Grace M. Jantzen, *Julian of Norwich: Mystic and Theologian* (London: SPCK, 1987).

144   *Dame Julian's revelations:* Julian of Norwich, *Revelations of Divine Love*, Elizabeth Spearing, trans. (Harmondsworth, UK: Penguin, 1998). Julian wrote two versions of her book. The first, known as the Short Text, was completed shortly after the events of May 1373. The second, known as the Long Text, represents the results of a roughly twenty-year process of meditating on the meaning of her original experiences.

145   *"Know well now that what you saw today . . .":* Julian of Norwich, *Revelations of Divine Love*, Long Text, chap. 68, p. 155.

145   *Not much is known about Julian's life:* Jantzen, *Julian of Norwich*; David Lawton, "English Literary Voices, 1350–1500," in Andrew Galloway, ed., *The Cambridge Companion to Medieval English Culture* (Cambridge, UK: Cambridge University Press, 2011).

146   *"What can this be?":* Julian of Norwich, *Revelations of Divine Love*, Short Text, chap. 4, p. 7.

147   *three types of visions:* St. Augustine, *De Genesi ad litteram* [On the Literal Interpretation of Genesis], Edmund Hill, trans., book XII, in *On Genesis (The Works of St. Augustine: A Translation for the 21st Century)* (New York: New City Press, 2002).

147   *"beautiful, sweet and low":* The only direct information we have about Joan's experiences comes from the Trial of Condemnation in 1431. Joan's statement here is taken from the fifth public examination, March 1, 1431. The Latin phrase used is *pulchra, dulcis et humilis. Procès de Condamnation de Jeanne d'Arc, Tome Premier*, édité par La Societé de L'Histoire de France, Pierre Tisset, ed. (Paris: Librairie C. Klincksieck, 1960), 84.

148   *"idiopathic partial epilepsy with auditory features":* Giuseppe d'Orsi and Paolo Tinuper, "'I Heard Voices . . . ': From Semiology, a Historical Review, and a New Hypothesis on the Presumed Epilepsy of Joan of Arc," *Epilepsy & Behavior* 9 (2006): 152–157; **Corinne Saunders, "Voices and Visions: Mind, Body and Affect in Medieval Writing,"** in A. Whitehead, A. Woods, S. Atkinson, J. Macnaughton, and J. Richards, eds., *The Edinburgh Companion to the Critical Medical Humanities* (Edinburgh: Edinburgh University Press, 2016).

148   *judge her outpourings as "hysterical":* Barry Windeatt, "Reading and Re-reading *The Book of Margery Kempe*," in John H. Arnold and Kather-

ine J. Lewis, eds., *A Companion to the Book of Margery Kempe* (Cambridge, UK: D. S. Brewer, 2004).

149   *"Also I heard a bodily jangeling . . .":* Elizabeth Spearing translates as follows: "And I also heard a human jabbering as if there were two people, and it seemed to me that both of them were jabbering at the same time, as if they were having a very tense discussion; and as it was all quiet muttering, I could understand nothing they said. And I thought that all this was to drive me to despair." Julian of Norwich, *Revelations of Divine Love*, Long Text, chap. 69, p. 155–156.

150   " . . . *Margery Kempe's inner voices* . . . . Windeatt, "Reading and Rereading *The Book of Margery Kempe*," 15–16; Barry Windeatt, "Shown Voices: Voices as Vision in Some English Mystics," paper presented at *Visions, Voices and Hallucinatory Experiences in Historical and Literary Contexts*, St. Chad's College, Durham, April 2014; Corinne Saunders and Charles Fernyhough, "Reading Margery Kempe's Inner Voices," paper presented at *Medicine of Words: Literature, Medicine, and Theology in the Middle Ages*, St. Anne's College, Oxford, September 2015.

11. A Brain Listening to Itself

152   *What was understood about the anatomy of the brain:* Simon Kemp, *Medieval Psychology* (New York: Greenwood Press, 1990); Corinne Saunders and Charles Fernyhough, "Medieval Psychology," *The Psychologist*, forthcoming; Robert E. Hall, "Intellect, Soul and Body in Ibn Sīnā: Systematic Synthesis and Development of the Aristotelian, Neoplatonic and Galenic Theories," in Jon McGinnis, ed., *Interpreting Avicenna: Science and Philosophy in Medieval Islam* (Leiden: Brill, 2004).

152   *physical movements of the head:* The writer in question is ben Luce; see Kemp, *Medieval Psychology*, 58.

153   *an imbalance in the four bodily humors:* Corinne Saunders, "'The Thoghtful Maladie': Madness and Vision in Medieval Writing," in Corinne Saunders and Jane Macnaughton, eds., *Madness and Creativity in Literature and Culture* (Basingstoke: Palgrave Macmillan, 2005).

153   *"local movement of animal spirits and humours":* St. Thomas Aquinas, *Summa Theologica*, vol. 14 (London: Burns, Oates and Washbourne, 1927), 1a, 111.3.

153   *"hallucination" is a modern concept:* Jean-Étienne Esquirol, *Mental Maladies: A Treatise on Insanity*, E. K. Hunt, trans. (Philadelphia: Lea and Blanchard, 1845). This translation is from German E. Berrios, *The History of Mental Symptoms: Descriptive Psychopathology Since the Nineteenth Century* (Cambridge, UK: Cambridge University Press, 1996), 37.

154   *"you are passive and helpless . . .":* Oliver Sacks, *Hallucinations* (London: Picador, 2012), x.

154   *analogy of a bell-pull:* René Descartes, *Meditations on First Philosophy*, Michael Moriarty, trans. (Oxford: Oxford University Press, 2008 [1641]),

Daniel C. Dennett, *Consciousness Explained* (London: Penguin, 1993). What would be the neural equivalent of hijacking the wire of the bell-pull? If the pulling of the handle in the upstairs room is equivalent to the sound of a genuine external voice, the sounding of the bell in the kitchen is the perception of that voice by the person who is hearing it. If the wire is yanked in an intervening room, a voice will be heard even when there was no one speaking. The idea is that hallucinations can occur as a result of spurious activation within the causal chain that leads from the reception of a stimulus to the perceiving of it. Voices are noise in the system.

154   *Stimulate the machine:* Wilder Penfield and Phanor Perot, "The Brain's Record of Auditory and Visual Experience," *Brain* 86 (1963): 595–696.

155   *random activations of the auditory system:* For a modern take on the "neural noise" theory, see Raymond Cho and Wayne Wu, "Mechanisms of Auditory Verbal Hallucination in Schizophrenia," *Frontiers in Psychiatry* 4, article 155 (2013); Peter Moseley and Sam Wilkinson, "Inner Speech Is Not So Simple: A Commentary on Cho and Wu (2013)," *Frontiers in Psychiatry* 5, article 42 (2014).

155   *inner speech model of voice-hearing:* See pp. 125–133.

155   *activations in the inner speech network:* Simone Kühn and Jürgen Gallinat, "Quantitative Meta-Analysis on State and Trait Aspects of Auditory Verbal Hallucinations in Schizophrenia," *Schizophrenia Bulletin* 38 (2012): 779–786; Renaud Jardri, Alexandre Pouchet, Delphine Pins, and Pierre Thomas, "Cortical Activations During Auditory Verbal Hallucinations in Schizophrenia: A Coordinate-Based Meta-Analysis," *American Journal of Psychiatry* 168 (2011): 73–81.

155   *The earliest brain-imaging studies of the inner speech network:* Broadly speaking, there are two main kinds of brain imaging: *structural neuroimaging*, which aims to map the structure of particular brain regions and pathways, and *functional neuroimaging*, which aims to show brain processes at work as the brain is active: for example, when a participant in the scanner is busy with a particular task. The inner speech studies described here are examples of functional neuroimaging, because they show the brain in action when the participant is, for example, generating inner speech. P. K. McGuire, D. A. Silbersweig, I. Wright, R. M. Murray, A. S. David, R. S. J. Frackowiak, and C. D. Frith, "Abnormal Monitoring of Inner Speech: A Physiological Basis for Auditory Hallucinations," *The Lancet* 346 (1995): 596–600; P. K. McGuire, D. A. Silbersweig, and C. D. Frith, "Functional Neuroanatomy of Verbal Self-Monitoring," *Brain* 119 (1996): 907–917; P. K. McGuire, D. A. Silbersweig, R. M. Murray, A. S. David, R. S. J. Frackowiak, and C. D. Frith, "Functional Anatomy of Inner Speech and Auditory Verbal Imagery," *Psychological Medicine* 26 (1996): 29–38.

156   *the brains of two schizophrenia patients:* Sukhwinder S. Shergill et al., "Temporal Course of Auditory Hallucinations," *British Journal of Psychiatry* 185 (2004): 516–517; S. S. Shergill et al., "A Functional Study of Auditory Verbal Imagery," *Psychological Medicine* 31 (2001): 241–253.

157   *method is flawed:* Remko van Lutterveld, Kelly M. J. Diederen, Sanne Koops, Marieke J. H. Begemann, and Iris E. C. Sommer, "The Influence of Stimulus Detection on Activation Patterns During Auditory Hallucinations," *Schizophrenia Research* 145 (2013): 27–32.

157   *catch the fleeting experience:* This is known as the difference between a *state* methodology (where researchers are interested in activations during a particular experiential state, such as the moment of hearing a voice) and a *trait* methodology (where researchers want to find out whether people who have these experiences also have certain patterns of brain activation as a general trait). A state design will allow researchers to see a hallucination in action—if they can catch one—while a trait design will allow them to establish whether there are any underlying processing differences between people who hear voices and those who do not. See Shergill et al., "A Functional Study of Auditory Verbal Imagery."

157   *asking people to subvocalize in the scanner:* In reviewing the existing neuroimaging evidence, Simon McCarthy-Jones and I argued that researchers needed to pay much more attention to the varied phenomenology of inner speech, along with its developmental course and cognitive functions. Another problem that we identified was that researchers were making an unwarranted assumption that inner speech was not occurring during the baseline phase (when participants were typically fixing their eyes on a cross). That made interpreting comparisons between task and baseline almost impossible. Simon R. Jones and Charles Fernyhough, "Neural Correlates of Inner Speech and Auditory Verbal Hallucinations: A Critical Review and Theoretical Integration," *Clinical Psychology Review* 27 (2007): 140–154. See also the discussion of the validity of methods of artificially eliciting inner speech in Chapter 15.

158   *A "schizophrenic" brain:* A better design would be to use three groups: a patient group with the experience you're interested in; a patient group without the experience of interest; and healthy controls. This is a tougher design to create—as we have seen, most schizophrenia patients hear voices, meaning that a voice-free patient group will be harder to find— but it is feasible and has become the gold standard for studies of this kind.

158   *twenty-one nonclinical voice-hearers:* Kelly M. J. Diederen et al., "Auditory Hallucinations Elicit Similar Brain Activation in Psychotic and Nonpsychotic Individuals," *Schizophrenia Bulletin* 38 (2012): 1074–1082; David E. J. Linden, Katy Thornton, Carissa N. Kuswanto, Stephen J. Johnston, Vincent van de Ven, and Michael C. Jackson, "The Brain's Voices: Comparing Nonclinical Auditory Hallucinations and Imagery," *Cerebral Cortex* 21 (2011): 330–337.

159   *apparent role of the SMA in auditory verbal hallucinations:* Tuukka T. Raij and Tapani J. J. Riekki, "Poor Supplementary Motor Area Activation Differentiates Auditory Verbal Hallucination from Imagining the Hallucination," *NeuroImage: Clinical* 1 (2012): 75–80.

160   *"With voice-hearing . . . the brain pops its head . . .":* Daniel B. Smith, *Muses, Madmen, and Prophets: Rethinking the History, Science, and Meaning of Auditory Hallucination* (New York: Penguin, 2007), 35. For further discussion of the cognitive and neural bases of the sense of agency in voice-hearing, see M. Perrone-Bertolotti, L. Rapin, J.-P. Lachaux, M. Baciu, and H. Lœvenbruck, "What Is That Little Voice Inside My Head? Inner Speech Phenomenology, Its Role in Cognitive Performance, and Its Relation to Self-Monitoring," *Behavioural Brain Research* 261 (2014): 220–239; Simon R. Jones and Charles Fernyhough, "Thought as Action: Inner Speech, Self-Monitoring, and Auditory Verbal Hallucinations," *Consciousness and Cognition* 16 (2007): 391–399.

160   *model of action monitoring put forward by Chris Frith and colleagues:* See p. 126.

161   *Studying the integrity of white matter:* This can be done through an MRI method such as diffusion tensor imagery (DTI). A meta-analysis of five such studies found reduced white matter integrity in the left arcuate fasciculus of schizophrenia patients who heard voices, compared with healthy controls. A meta-analysis is a kind of "study of studies": it pools the results from a number of different studies conducted at different times and places and analyzes them together. Pierre A. Geoffroy et al., "The Arcuate Fasciculus in Auditory-Verbal Hallucinations: A Meta-Analysis of Diffusion-Tensor-Imaging Studies," *Schizophrenia Research* 159 (2014): 234–237.

161   *"dampening" that occurs in Wernicke's area:* Judith M. Ford and Daniel H. Mathalon, "Electrophysiological Evidence of Corollary Discharge Dysfunction in Schizophrenia During Talking and Thinking," *Journal of Psychiatric Research* 38 (2004): 37–46; T. J. Whitford et al., "Electrophysiological and Diffusion Tensor Imaging Evidence of Delayed Corollary Discharges in Patients with Schizophrenia," *Psychological Medicine* 41 (2011): 959–969; Claudia J. P. Simons et al., "Functional Magnetic Resonance Imaging of Inner Speech in Schizophrenia," *Biological Psychiatry* 67 (2011): 232–237.

162   *a "resting state" paradigm:* Debra A. Gusnard and Marcus E. Raichle, "Searching for a Baseline: Functional Imaging and the Resting Human Brain," *Nature Reviews Neuroscience* 2 (2001): 685–694; Randy L. Buckner, Jessica R. Andrews-Hanna, and Daniel L. Schacter, "The Brain's Default Network: Anatomy, Function, and Relevance to Disease," *Annals of the New York Academy of Sciences* 1124 (2008): 1–38; Russell T. Hurlburt, Ben Alderson-Day, Charles Fernyhough, and Simone Kühn, "What Goes On in the Resting State? A Qualitative Glimpse into Resting-State Experience in the Scanner," *Frontiers in Psychology: Cognitive Science* 6, article 1535 (2015); Ben Alderson-Day, Simon McCarthy-Jones, and Charles Fernyhough, "Hearing Voices in the Resting Brain: A Review of Intrinsic Functional Connectivity Research on Auditory Verbal Hallucinations," *Neuroscience & Biobehavioral Reviews* 55 (2015): 78–87.

163   *transcranial magnetic stimulation:* Christina W. Slotema, Jan D. Blom, Remko van Lutterveld, Hans W. Hoek, and Iris E. C. Sommer, "Review of the Efficacy of Transcranial Magnetic Stimulation for Auditory Verbal Hallucinations," *Biological Psychiatry* 76 (2014): 101–110. Among the problems in interpreting these findings is the fact that some of the regions that have been shown to be effective in TMS treatment are not easy to connect to existing cognitive models. Another difficulty is that the technique is not well suited to stimulating auditory regions, partly because applying a current to that part of the skull can cause muscular twitches and other phenomena not relevant to voice-hearing. Peter Moseley, Amanda Ellison, and Charles Fernyhough, "Auditory Verbal Hallucinations as Atypical Inner Speech Monitoring, and the Potential of Neurostimulation as a Treatment Option," *Neuroscience & Biobehavioral Reviews* 37 (2013): 2794–2805.

163   *source-monitoring judgments:* Peter Moseley, Charles Fernyhough, and Amanda Ellison, "The Role of the Superior Temporal Lobe in Auditory False Perceptions: A Transcranial Direct Current Stimulation Study," *Neuropsychologia* 62 (2014): 202–208.

163   *But what kinds of inner speech, exactly?:* An interesting avenue for future research involves asking about the kinds of inner speech that are misattributed in an episode of voice-hearing. As we have seen, inner speech is not just one thing. In the model I proposed, voices are particularly likely to occur when condensed inner speech is re-expanded to form a full-blown inner dialogue. To date, we haven't been able to test whether particular kinds of inner speech relate to particular kinds of voice-hearing experiences, not least because more needs to be learned about the neural underpinnings of these varieties of inner speech in people who are not affected by voices. Another relevant distinction— that between monologic and dialogic inner speech—is also ripe for investigation in people who hear voices, given the initial findings from our lab on how these two kinds of inner speech are instantiated differently in the typical brain. If ordinary inner speech has a dialogic quality, as Vygotsky's theory suggests, then neuroimaging studies of auditory verbal hallucinations should take that into account in their designs, and attempt to elicit dialogic inner speech rather than the more artificial, monologic forms that have been employed in studies to date. Ben Alderson-Day, Susanne Weis, Simon McCarthy-Jones, Peter Moseley, David Smailes, and Charles Fernyhough, "The Brain's Conversation with Itself: Neural Substrates of Dialogic Inner Speech," *Social Cognitive & Affective Neuroscience* 11 (2016): 110–120; Moseley et al., "Auditory Verbal Hallucinations as Atypical Inner Speech Monitoring." See also the note for Chapter 9 for "*why isn't all inner speech perceived as an external voice?*"

164   *area of the cortex around the hippocampus:* Kelly M. J. Diederen et al., "Deactivation of the Parahippocampal Gyrus Preceding Auditory

Hallucinations in Schizophrenia," *American Journal of Psychiatry* 167 (2010): 427–435.

164   *activation of* right-*hemisphere language regions:* Iris E. C. Sommer et al., "Auditory Verbal Hallucinations Predominantly Activate the *Right* Inferior Frontal Area," *Brain* 131 (2008): 3169–3177; Iris E. Sommer and Kelly M. Diederen, "Language Production in the Non-dominant Hemisphere as a Potential Source of Auditory Verbal Hallucinations," *Brain* 132 (2009): 1–2; Simon McCarthy-Jones, *Hearing Voices: The Histories, Causes and Meanings of Auditory Verbal Hallucinations* (Cambridge, UK: Cambridge University Press, 2012).

166   *"stand frozen on the beaches of Troy . . .":* Veronique Greenwood, "Consciousness Began When the Gods Stopped Speaking," *Nautilus,* issue 204, May 28, 2015.

12. A Talkative Muse

167   *children at my bedside:* See the note in Chapter 9 for *"only useful up to a point."*

168   *One fiction writer put it like this:* The quotations from anonymous professional writers in this chapter are from interviews conducted by Jennifer Hodgson at the Edinburgh International Book Festival, August 2014.

168   *You can't tickle yourself:* Sarah-Jayne Blakemore, Daniel M. Wolpert, and Chris D. Frith, "Central Cancellation of Self-Produced Tickle Sensation," *Nature Neuroscience* 1 (1998): 635–640.

168   *connection between madness and creativity:* Thomas O'Reilly, Robin Dunbar, and Richard Bentall, "Schizotypy and Creativity: An Evolutionary Connection?," *Personality and Individual Differences* 31 (2001): 1067–1078; Mark A. Runco, "Creativity," *Annual Review of Psychology* 55 (2004): 657–687.

169   *"to write means having one's voice disrupted . . .":* Peter Garratt, "Hearing Voices Allowed Charles Dickens to Create Extraordinary Fictional Worlds," *Guardian,* August 22, 2014.

169   *"When . . . I sit down to my book . . .":* John Forster, *The Life of Charles Dickens,* vol. 2 (London: J. M. Dent, 1966), 270; James T. Fields, "Some Memories of Charles Dickens," *The Atlantic,* August 1870. Sometimes the voices of Dickens's characters came close to harassing him. An American writer on spiritualism, J. M. Peebles, wrote of how the voice of Mrs. Gamp, the nurse in *Martin Chuzzlewit,* would intrude upon her creator, "whispering to him in the most inopportune places—sometimes even in church—that he was compelled to fight her off by main force, when he did not want her company, and threatened to have nothing more to do with her unless she could behave better, and come only when she was called." Note that Peebles does not give a source for this anecdote. See J. M. Peebles, *What Is Spiritualism?* (Battle Creek, MI: Peebles Institute Print, 1903), 36.

170   *"You know how desperately slow I work . . ."*: Joseph Conrad, letter to William Blackwood, August 22, 1899, in Frederick R. Karl and Laurence Davies, eds., *The Collected Letters of Joseph Conrad*, vol. 2, *1898–1902* (Cambridge, UK: Cambridge University Press, 1986), 193–194. Cited in Jeremy Hawthorn, "Conrad's Inward/Inner Voice(s)," lecture delivered at the annual conference of the Joseph Conrad Society, UK, at Canterbury, July 2014.

170   *"We are in the hands of the Lord . . ."*: Virginia Woolf, *To the Lighthouse* (London: Grafton, 1977 [1927]), 62; Virginia Woolf, "A Sketch of the Past," in *Moments of Being: Autobiographical Writings*, Jeanne Schulkind, ed. (London: Pimlico, 2002), 129; Hermione Lee, *Virginia Woolf* (London: Chatto and Windus, 1996), 756; Leonard Woolf, "Virginia Woolf: Writer and Personality," in J. H. Stape, ed., *Virginia Woolf: Interviews and Recollections* (Iowa City: University of Iowa Press, 1995); Woolf, "Sketch of the Past," 93.

171   *humor as well as tragedy*: Hilary Mantel, *Beyond Black* (London: Fourth Estate, 2005); Patricia Waugh, "Hilary Mantel and Virginia Woolf on the Sounds in Writers' Minds," *Guardian*, August 21, 2014.

171   *relations between voices, illness and writing*: Hilary Mantel, "Ink in the Blood," *London Review of Books*, November 4, 2010; "A Kind of Alchemy," Hilary Mantel interviewed by Sarah O'Reilly, in Hilary Mantel, *Beyond Black* (London: Fourth Estate, 2010), addendum to the paperback edition, p. 8.

172   *voices coming from his radio*: Charles Platt, "The Voices in Philip K. Dick's Head," *New York Times*, December 16, 2011; Philip K. Dick, *The Exegesis of Philip K. Dick*, Pamela Jackson, Jonathan Lethem, and Erik Davis, eds. (Boston: Houghton Mifflin Harcourt, 2011); Philip K. Dick, interviewed by John Boonstra, *Rod Serling's The Twilight Zone Magazine* 2, no. 3 (June 1982): 47–52.

172   *"All writers hear voices"*: Ray Bradbury, interviewed by Terry Wogan, *Wogan*, BBC1, 1990; Ray Bradbury, "The Art of Fiction No. 203," *Paris Review*, no. 192 (Spring 2010).

172   *"automatic writing"*: Siri Hustvedt, *The Shaking Woman or a History of Nerves* (London: Sceptre, 2010), 68.

172   *classical accounts of inspiration*: Daniel B. Smith, *Muses, Madmen, and Prophets: Rethinking the History, Science, and Meaning of Auditory Hallucination* (New York: Penguin, 2007), chap. 7; Eric R. Dodds, *The Greeks and the Irrational* (London: University of California Press, 1951).

175   *Edinburgh International Book Festival*: Jennifer Hodgson, "How Do Writers Find Their Voices?," *Guardian*, August 25, 2014.

175   *their experiences must be of their own making*: Richard P. Bentall, *Madness Explained: Psychosis and Human Nature* (London: Allen Lane, 2003).

175   *"inner speaking" and "inner hearing"*: Russell T. Hurlburt, Christopher L. Heavey, and Jason M. Kelsey, "Toward a Phenomenology of Inner Speaking," *Consciousness and Cognition* 22 (2013): 1477–1494; Simone

Kühn, Charles Fernyhough, Ben Alderson-Day, and Russell T. Hurlburt, "Inner Experience in the Scanner: Can High Fidelity Apprehensions of Inner Experience Be Integrated with fMRI?," *Frontiers in Psychology* 5, article 1393 (2014). Note that it is also possible to innerly hear sounds that are not speech, such as music.

178   *inscribe with the mouth open:* A. R. Luria, *Higher Cortical Functions in Man* (New York: Basic Books, 1966); L. S. Vygotsky, *Thinking and Speech*, in *The Collected Works of L. S. Vygotsky*, vol. 1, Robert W. Rieber and Aaron S. Carton, eds., Norris Minick, trans. (New York: Plenum, 1987 [1934]), 272.

178   *underpinned by spoken language processes:* M. Perrone-Bertolotti, L. Rapin, J.-P. Lachaux, M. Baciu, and H. Lœvenbruck, "What Is That Little Voice Inside My Head? Inner Speech Phenomenology, Its Role in Cognitive Performance, and Its Relation to Self-Monitoring," *Behavioural Brain Research* 261 (2014): 220–239; Cynthia S. Puranik and Christopher J. Lonigan, "Early Writing Deficits in Preschoolers with Oral Language Difficulties," *Journal of Learning Disabilities* 45 (2012): 179–190.

179   *"co-operative and lively" thirteen-year-old:* David N. Levine, Ronald Calvanio, and Alice Popovics, "Language in the Absence of Inner Speech," *Neuropsychologia* 20 (1982): 391–409; Giuseppe Cossu, "The Role of Output Speech in Literacy Acquisition: Evidence from Congenital Anarthria," *Reading and Writing: An Interdisciplinary Journal* 16 (2003): 99–122.

179   *useful tool in the writing process:* James D. Williams, "Covert Linguistic Behavior During Writing Tasks," *Written Communication* 4 (1987): 310–328.

180   *unattended speech effect:* Pierre Salamé and Alan Baddeley, "Disruption of Short-Term Memory by Unattended Speech: Implications for the Structure of Working Memory," *Journal of Verbal Learning and Verbal Behavior* 21 (1982): 150–164.

180   *"90 per cent of the time . . .":* David Lodge, "Reading Yourself," in Julia Bell and Paul Magrs, eds., *The Creative Writing Coursebook* (London: Macmillan, 2001).

181   *"On and on she went, talk, talk, talk . . .":* Louie Mayer, in Joan Russell Noble, ed., *Recollections of Virginia Woolf by Her Contemporaries* (Athens, OH: Ohio University Press, 1972).

181   *"when the children of his brain . . .":* Fields, "Some Memories of Charles Dickens."

181   *engaging with imaginary friends:* Marjorie Taylor, *Imaginary Companions and the Children Who Create Them* (Oxford: Oxford University Press, 1999); Lucy Firth, Ben Alderson-Day, Natalie Woods, and Charles Fernyhough, "Imaginary Companions in Childhood: Relations to Imagination Skills and Autobiographical Memory in Adults," *Creativity Research Journal* 27 (2015): 308–313; Marjorie Taylor, Stephanie M. Carlson, and Alison B. Shawber, "Autonomy and Control in Children's Interactions with

Imaginary Companions," in I. Roth, ed., *Imaginative Minds: Concepts, Controversies and Themes* (London: OUP/British Academy, 2007); Marjorie Taylor, Sara D. Hodges, and Adèle Kohányi, "The Illusion of Independent Agency: Do Adult Fiction Writers Experience Their Characters as Having Minds of Their Own?," *Imagination, Cognition and Personality* 22 (2003): 361–380; Evan Kidd, Paul Rogers, and Christine Rogers, "The Personality Correlates of Adults Who Had Imaginary Companions in Childhood," *Psychological Reports* 107 (2010): 163–172.

182   *often badly behaved or resistant:* Taylor et al., "The Illusion of Independent Agency"; John Fowles, *The French Lieutenant's Woman* (London: Triad/Panther, 1977 [1969]), 86; "Inner Voices: How Writers Create Character," BBC Academy podcast, www.bbc.co.uk/academy/production/article/art20141127135622425.

184   *They became her playmates:* Lisa Blackman, *Immaterial Bodies: Affect, Embodiment, Mediation* (London: Sage, 2012), chap. 6.

184   *"fictional worlds built out of voices":* Patricia Waugh, "The Novelist as Voice-Hearer," *The Lancet* 386 (2015): e54–e55.

185   *convinced that the poet T. S. Eliot:* Martin Stannard, *Muriel Spark* (London: Weidenfeld and Nicolson, 2009), 153.

185   *"With his spirit I converse daily & hourly . . .":* William Blake, letter to William Hayley, 1800. Blake was consoling Hayley, who had recently lost a young son, by recalling the loss of his own brother. There is thus reason not to take his account entirely literally as an account of hallucination. Blake almost certainly had unusual experiences, but this example shows the need to be on guard against taking metaphorical uses of "voice" too literally. See the discussion of the "voice of conscience" on p. 245. Michael Davis, *William Blake: A New Kind of Man* (London: HarperCollins, 1977); Smith, *Muses, Madmen, and Prophets*, chap. 7.

186   *hallucination, delusion, and illusion:* Oliver Sacks, *Hallucinations* (London: Picador, 2012).

186   *effortful imagining:* Charles Fernyhough, *Pieces of Light* (New York: Harper, 2013).

187   *assembling a self:* Waugh, "Hilary Mantel and Virginia Woolf"; Hilary Mantel, *Giving Up the Ghost: A Memoir* (London: Harper Perennial, 2004), 222.

187   *"I often hear voices . . .":* Jeanette Winterson, *Why Be Happy When You Could Be Normal?* (London: Jonathan Cape, 2011), 170; interview with Jeanette Winterson, *Lighthousekeeping*, Harcourt Books, www.harcourtbooks.com/authorinterviews/bookinterview_Winterson.asp.

13. Messages from the Past

191   *"germ of meaning":* Carl Jung, *Memories, Dreams, Reflections*, Aniela Jaffé, ed. and recorder, Richard and Clara Winston, trans. (London: Collins and Routledge and Kegan Paul, 1963), 127.

192   *"She is leaving the building":* Eleanor Longden, *Learning from the Voices in My Head* (New York: TED Books, 2013).

192   *voices are messengers:* Marius A. J. Romme and Sandra D. M. A. C. Escher, "Hearing Voices," *Schizophrenia Bulletin* 15 (1989): 209–216; Marius Romme, Sandra Escher, Jacqui Dillon, Dirk Corstens, and Mervyn Morris, eds., *Living with Voices: Fifty Stories of Recovery* (Ross-on-Wye, UK: PCCS, 2009); Dirk Corstens, Eleanor Longden, Simon McCarthy-Jones, Rachel Waddingham, and Neil Thomas, "Emerging Perspectives from the Hearing Voices Movement: Implications for Research and Practice," *Schizophrenia Bulletin* 40, suppl. no. 4 (2014): S285–S294; Gail A. Hornstein, *Agnes's Jacket: A Psychologist's Search for the Meaning of Madness* (Emmaus, PA: Rodale Press, 2009).

193   *Julian Jaynes's theory:* See p. 136.

195   *"All I know now is that I'm a voice-hearer . . .":* Interview on BBC Radio 4's *Saturday Live* program, March 2, 2013.

195   *"spreading like wildfire":* Interview with Jacqui Dillon, November 25, 2013.

195   *Radiolab:* "Voices in Your Head," *Radiolab,* September 7, 2010.

196   *unresolved emotional problems:* Louis Jolyon West, "A General Theory of Hallucinations and Dreams," in L. J. West, ed., *Hallucinations* (New York: Grune and Stratton, 1962); Simon McCarthy-Jones, *Hearing Voices: The Histories, Causes and Meanings of Auditory Verbal Hallucinations* (Cambridge, UK: Cambridge University Press, 2012).

196   *quality of memories:* Simon McCarthy-Jones, Tom Trauer, Andrew Mackinnon, Eliza Sims, Neil Thomas, and David L. Copolov, "A New Phenomenological Survey of Auditory Hallucinations: Evidence for Subtypes and Implications for Theory and Practice," *Schizophrenia Bulletin* 40 (2014): 231–235.

196   *how they process memories:* Flavie A. Waters, Johanna C. Badcock, Patricia T. Michie, and Murray T. Maybery, "Auditory Hallucinations in Schizophrenia: Intrusive Thoughts and Forgotten Memories," *Cognitive Neuropsychiatry* 11 (2006): 65–83.

196   *childhood sexual abuse:* Richard P. Bentall, Sophie Wickham, Mark Shevlin, and Filippo Varese, "Do Specific Early-Life Adversities Lead to Specific Symptoms of Psychosis? A Study from the 2007 The Adult Psychiatric Morbidity Survey," *Schizophrenia Bulletin* 38 (2012): 734–740. For a recent meta-analysis, see A. Trotta, R. M. Murray, and H. L. Fisher, "The Impact of Childhood Adversity on the Persistence of Psychotic Symptoms: A Systematic Review and Meta-Analysis," *Psychological Medicine* 45 (2015): 2481–2498.

197   *memory for trauma:* Fernyhough, *Pieces of Light,* chap. 10.

197   *Creating a memory is a reconstructive process:* Fernyhough, *Pieces of Light.*

198   *psychological phenomenon known as dissociation:* Pierre Janet, "L'anesthésie systématisée et la dissociation des phénomènes psychologiques,"

Revue Philosophique de la France et de l'Étranger 23 (1887): 449–472; Onno van der Hart and Rutger Horst, "The Dissociation Theory of Pierre Janet," *Journal of Traumatic Stress* 2 (1989): 397–412; Marie Pilton, Filippo Varese, Katherine Berry, and Sandra Bucci, "The Relationship Between Dissociation and Voices: A Systematic Literature Review and Meta-Analysis," *Clinical Psychology Review* 40 (2015): 138–155.

198   *relationship was "mediated" by* dissociation: Filippo Varese, Emma Barkus, and Richard P. Bentall, "Dissociation Mediates the Relationship Between Childhood Trauma and Hallucination-Proneness," *Psychological Medicine* 42 (2012): 1025–1036; Ben Alderson-Day et al., "Shot Through with Voices: Dissociation Mediates the Relationship Between Varieties of Inner Speech and Auditory Hallucination Proneness," *Consciousness and Cognition* 27 (2014): 288–296.

200   *voices take different forms:* Simon R. Jones, "Do We Need Multiple Models of Auditory Verbal Hallucinations? Examining the Phenomenological Fit of Cognitive and Neurological Models," *Schizophrenia Bulletin* 36 (2010): 566–575; David Smailes, Ben Alderson-Day, Charles Fernyhough, Simon McCarthy-Jones, and Guy Dodgson, "Tailoring Cognitive Behavioural Therapy to Subtypes of Voice-Hearing," *Frontiers in Psychology* 6, article 1933 (2015).

201   *Therapy for traumatic memories:* Fernyhough, *Pieces of Light,* chap. 10.

201   *Voice Dialogue:* Dirk Corstens, Eleanor Longden, and Rufus May, "Talking with Voices: Exploring What Is Expressed by the Voices People Hear," *Psychosis* 4 (2012). 95–104

202   *computer-based avatar:* Julian Leff, Geoffrey Williams, Mark A. Huckvale, Maurice Arbuthnot, and Alex P. Leff, "Computer-Assisted Therapy for Medication-Resistant Auditory Hallucinations: Proof-of-Concept Study," *British Journal of Psychiatry* 202 (2013): 428–433. When we visited the Avatar team in June 2014 and tried out the technology for ourselves, the researchers were in the middle of a large clinical trial of the technique, the results of which are due to be published in 2016. If the results from the pilot are confirmed, avatar therapy could become a powerful new addition to the psychotherapist's toolkit for dealing with distressing voices.

203   *"It is about power . . .":* While CBT is supported by scientific evidence for its efficacy, the Hearing Voices Movement has not yet gathered such data, at least to the extent of performing clinical trials. The gold standard for testing the efficacy of a treatment in any branch of medicine is the randomized controlled trial (RCT), a study design in which patients are randomly assigned to a treatment or nontreatment group, without (as much as is possible) them knowing which group they are in, and without that information being known by those who are assessing the outcomes. In reviewing the growth of the movement and the evidence for the efficacy of its practices, Dirk Corstens and his colleagues pointed out that the self-led, organic nature of hearing voices groups does not lend itself to the

formalization that would be needed for an RCT. Another problem is that groups are open, with people free to join and leave as they please; signing up for a course of "treatment" would be anathema. The benefits of the approach, including what must be highly subjective measures of contentment and relative distress, would also be difficult to put numbers to. Although a pilot trial of one-to-one peer support is currently under way in Australia, it is unlikely that there will be a major RCT of the approach anytime soon. The method undoubtedly works for some—I have met many who vouch for that fact—but persuading the world about its effectiveness will be difficult for as long as this gap in the evidence base is there. Corstens et al., "Emerging Perspectives from the Hearing Voices Movement."

204   *one of many mechanisms:* Rachel Waddingham, Sandra Escher, and Guy Dodgson, "Inner Speech and Narrative Development in Children and Young People Who Hear Voices: Three Perspectives on a Developmental Phenomenon," *Psychosis* 5 (2013): 226–235.

205   *"a telephone call from your unconscious":* Jacqui Dillon, interviewed for "Voices in the Dark: An Audio Story," *Mosaic,* Wellcome Trust, December 9, 2014; Jacqui Dillon, "The Tale of an Ordinary Little Girl," *Psychosis* 2 (2010): 79–83.

205   *(hypothetical) drug:* When the scenario was framed as a military one, with the participant cast as a traumatized combatant, the proportion of those saying they would take the drug dropped to around 50 percent. Eryn J. Newman, Shari R. Berkowitz, Kally J. Nelson, Maryanne Garry, and Elizabeth F. Loftus, "Attitudes About Memory Dampening Drugs Depend on Context and Country," *Applied Cognitive Psychology* 25 (2011): 675–681.

206   *therapy can help with traumatic memories:* See Fernyhough, *Pieces of Light,* chap. 10.

207   *"Most of the time they make me laugh . . .":* Jacqui Dillon, interviewed for "Voices in the Dark."

I 4. A Voice That Doesn't Speak

209   *"Once you hear the voices . . .":* Mark Vonnegut, *The Eden Express: A Memoir of Insanity* (New York: Praeger, 1975), 137.

210   *"felt presence":* Tore Nielsen, "Felt Presence: Paranoid Delusion or Hallucinatory Social Imagery?," *Consciousness and Cognition* 16 (2007): 975–983; Gillian Bennett and Kate Mary Bennett, "The Presence of the Dead: An Empirical Study," *Mortality* 5 (2000): 139–157; Ben Alderson-Day and David Smailes, "The Strange World of Felt Presences," *Guardian,* March 5, 2015; John Geiger, *The Third Man Factor: Surviving the Impossible* (Edinburgh: Canongate, 2010); Sara Maitland, *A Book of Silence* (London: Granta, 2008).

210   *"I said nothing to my companions . . .":* Sir Ernest Shackleton, *The Heart of the Antarctic* and *South* (Ware, UK: Wordsworth Editions, 2007

[1919]), 591. The experiences of Shackleton and his team were acknowledged by T. S. Eliot as an inspiration for the "Who is the third that walks always beside you?" section of *The Waste Land*, ll. 359–365.

211 *guarding, motivational function:* Joe Simpson, *Touching the Void* (London: Jonathan Cape, 1998); Peter Suedfeld and John Geiger, "The Sensed Presence as a Coping Resource in Extreme Environments," In J. Harold Ellis, ed., *Miracles: God, Science, and Psychology in the Paranormal*, vol. 3 (Westport, CT: Greenwood Press, 2008).

211 *these additional aspects of the voice-hearing experience:* **Angela Woods, Nev Jones, Ben Alderson-Day, Felicity Callard, and Charles Fernyhough, "Experiences of Hearing Voices: Analysis of a Novel Phenomenological Survey,"** *Lancet Psychiatry* 2 (2015): 323–331.

212 *seminal study of the phenomenology of auditory hallucinations:* Tony H. Nayani and Anthony S. David, "The Auditory Hallucination: A Phenomenological Survey," *Psychological Medicine* 26 (1996): 177–189.

212 *indistinct murmuring:* See p. 149.

212 *"not like those which sound from the mouth of man . . .":* Hildegard of Bingen, *Selected Writings*, Mark Atherton, trans. (London: Penguin, 2001), xx.

213 *". . . 'go and drown yourself'":* Eugen Bleuler, *Dementia Praecox or the Group of Schizophrenias* (New York: International Universities Press, 1950 [1911]), 111.

213 *an assault on all your senses:* See pp. 148–149. Note that, in the modern era, instances of "fused" hallucinations are relatively rare. R. E. Hoffman and M. Varanko, "Seeing Voices: Fused Visual/Auditory Verbal Hallucinations Reported by Three Persons with Schizophrenia-Spectrum Disorder," *Acta Psychiatrica Scandinavica* 114 (2006): 290–293; Flavie Waters et al., "Visual Hallucinations in the Psychosis Spectrum and Comparative Information from Neurodegenerative Disorders and Eye Disease," *Schizophrenia Bulletin* 40, suppl. no. 4 (2014): S233–S245.

213 *A twenty-eight-year-old Danish woman:* Natalia Pedersen and René Ernst Nielsen, "Auditory Hallucinations in a Deaf Patient: A Case Report," *Case Reports in Psychiatry* 2013, article 659698 (2013).

214 *folie circulaire:* Henry Putnam Stearns, "Auditory Hallucinations in a Deaf Mute," *Alienist and Neurologist* 7 (1886): 318–319.

214 *hearing the voice of God:* Kenneth Z. Altshuler, "Studies of the Deaf: Relevance to Psychiatric Theory," *American Journal of Psychiatry* 127 (1971): 1521–1526.

214 *On the skeptical side:* Ibid.; J. Remvig, "Deaf Mutes in Mental Hospitals," *Acta Psychiatrica Scandinavica* 210 (1969): 9–64; Robin Paijmans, Jim Cromwell, and Sally Austen, "Do Profoundly Prelingually Deaf Patients with Psychosis Really Hear Voices?," *American Annals of the Deaf* 151 (2006): 42–48.

214 *seventeen profoundly deaf individuals:* M. du Feu and P. J. McKenna, "Prelingually Profoundly Deaf Schizophrenic Patients Who Hear Voices:

A Phenomenological Analysis," *Acta Psychiatrica Scandinavica* 99 (1999): 453–459.

215 *"How do I know? I'm deaf!":* A. J. Thacker, "Formal Communication Disorder: Sign Language in Deaf People with Schizophrenia," *British Journal of Psychiatry* 165 (1994): 818–823.

215 *This vagueness about the nature of the experience:* Joanna R. Atkinson, "The Perceptual Characteristics of Voice-Hallucinations in Deaf People: Insights into the Nature of Subvocal Thought and Sensory Feedback Loops," *Schizophrenia Bulletin* 32 (2006): 701–708.

216 *nonauditory concomitants of deaf voice-hearing:* Joanna R. Atkinson, Kate Gleeson, Jim Cromwell, and Sue O'Rourke, "Exploring the Perceptual Characteristics of Voice-Hallucinations in Deaf People," *Cognitive Neuropsychiatry* 12 (2007): 339–361.

216 *a version of the inner speech model:* Charles Fernyhough, "Do Deaf People Hear an Inner Voice?," blog post in The Voices Within, *Psychology Today*, January 24, 2014, https://www.psychologytoday.com/blog/the -voices-within/201401/do-deaf-people-hear-inner-voice.

217 *inner speech mediates short-term remembering:* Ursula Bellugi, Edward S. Klima, and Patricia Siple, "Remembering in Signs," *Cognition* 3 (1975): 93–125.

217 *Some descriptions of deaf voices fit this account:* Thacker, "Formal Communication Disorder."

217 *Language processing in deaf people:* Mairéad MacSweeney et al., "Neural Systems Underlying British Sign Language and Audio-Visual English Processing in Native Users," *Brain* 125 (2002): 1583–1593; P. K. McGuire et al., "Neural Correlates of Thinking in Sign Language," *Neuroreport* 8 (1997): 695–698.

217 *a social agent with communicative intentions:* The Canadian psychologists J. Allan Cheyne and Todd A. Girard defined felt presence as "a *feeling* of the presence of a *Being*, and not as a mere existent thing, but an *intentional* Being with a mind or soul": J. Allan Cheyne and Todd A. Girard, "The Nature and Varieties of Felt Presence Experiences: A Reply to Nielsen," *Consciousness and Cognition* 16 (2007): 984–991, 985. A felt presence has a feeling to it; it is not just a belief. And the presence that is felt is not that of any old object: it is an entity with intentionality, in the sense of it having some mental connection to the world. See J. Allan Cheyne and Todd A. Girard, "Paranoid Delusions and Threatening Hallucinations: A Prospective Study of Sleep Paralysis Experiences," *Consciousness and Cognition* 16 (2007): 959–974; Suedfeld and Geiger, "The Sensed Presence as a Coping Resource."

218 *keep track of social agents:* Amanda L. Woodward, "Infants Selectively Encode the Goal Object of an Actor's Reach," *Cognition* 69 (1998): 1–34; Charles Fernyhough, "Getting Vygotskian About Theory of Mind: Mediation, Dialogue, and the Development of Social Understanding," *Devel-*

opmental Review 28 (2008): 225–262; Ben Alderson-Day and Charles Fernyhough, "Auditory Verbal Hallucinations: Social But How?," *Journal of Consciousness Studies*, in press.

218   *In the case of bereavement:* W. Dewi Rees, "The Hallucinations of Widowhood," *British Medical Journal* 4 (1971): 37–41; A. Grimby, "Bereavement Among Elderly People: Grief Reactions, Post-Bereavement Hallucinations and Quality of Life," *Acta Psychiatrica Scandinavica* 87 (1993): 72–80.

219   *"It's a bit like when you're on a bus . . .":* Dolly Sen, interviewed for "Voices in the Dark: An Audio Story," *Mosaic*, Wellcome Trust, December 9, 2014.

219   *"I am spoken to all the time . . .":* Pierre Janet, "Étude sur un cas d'aboulie et d'idées fixes," *Revue Philosophique de la France et de l'Étranger* 31 (1891): 258–287, 274, my translation (with assistance from Sam Wilkinson). For more on Janet's treatment of voice-hearing, see Ivan Leudar and Philip Thomas, *Voices of Reason, Voices of Insanity: Studies of Verbal Hallucinations* (London: Routledge, 2000), chap. 4.

219   *"It's hard to describe . . .":* Woods et al., "Experiences of Hearing Voices."

220   *a rather different way of looking at things:* **Sam Wilkinson and Vaughan Bell, "The Representation of Agents in Auditory Verbal Hallucinations,"** *Mind & Language* 31 (2016): 104–126. The social dimensions of voice-hearing have certainly not received the attention they deserve. One reason for this oversight is probably the dominance of the inner speech model, which, as we have seen, has tended to rely on a conception of internal self-talk that ignores its social origins. Arguably, an account of inner speech that sees it as internalized dialogue is better positioned to explain how voices can represent agents with particular perspectives. The memory model of voices might also be able to explain how voices have these agentive qualities, if voices are in part intrusions from memories of interactions with others. See Alderson-Day and Fernyhough, "Auditory Verbal Hallucinations: Social But How?"

220   *Damage to the temporoparietal junction:* Peter Brugger, Marianne Regard, and Theodor Landis, "Unilaterally Felt 'Presences': The Neuropsychiatry of One's Invisible *Doppelgänger*," *Neuropsychiatry, Neuropsychology, and Behavioral Neurology* 9 (1996): 114–122; Shahar Arzy, Margitta Seeck, Stephanie Ortigue, Laurent Spinelli, and Olaf Blanke, "Induction of an Illusory Shadow Person," *Nature* 443 (2006): 287; Ben Alderson-Day, Susanne Weis, Simon McCarthy-Jones, Peter Moseley, David Smailes, and Charles Fernyhough, "The Brain's Conversation with Itself: Neural Substrates of Dialogic Inner Speech," *Social Cognitive & Affective Neuroscience* 11 (2016): 110–120.

221   *Eleanor Longden's experiences:* See pp. 191–192.

222   *internal self-talk has its origins in interactions between people:* Felicity Deamer, "The Pragmatics of Inner Speech: Reconciling Theories of Linguistic Communication with What We Know About Inner Speech,"

under review; Charles Fernyhough, "The Dialogic Mind: A Dialogic Approach to the Higher Mental Functions," *New Ideas in Psychology* 14 (1996): 47–62.

223   *"There is a feeling of safety to a degree . . ."*: Interview with Adam, BBC Radio 4, *Saturday Live*, March 2, 2013.

15. TALKING TO OURSELVES

226   *"The fact of its insistent indwelling . . ."*: Denise Riley, "'A Voice Without a Mouth': Inner Speech," in Denise Riley and Jean-Jacques Lecercle, *The Force of Language* (London: Palgrave Macmillan, 2004), 8.

226   *One of the aims of our Berlin study*: Russell T. Hurlburt, Charles Fernyhough, Ben Alderson-Day, and Simone Kühn, "Exploring the Ecological Validity of Thinking on Demand: Neural Correlates of Elicited vs. Spontaneously Occurring Inner Speech," *PLOS ONE* 11 (2016): e0147932; Simon R. Jones and Charles Fernyhough, "Neural Correlates of Inner Speech and Auditory Verbal Hallucinations: A Critical Review and Theoretical Integration," *Clinical Psychology Review* 27 (2007): 140–154.

227   *a productive area of research*: Ben Alderson-Day and Charles Fernyhough, "Inner Speech: Development, Cognitive Functions, Phenomenology, and Neurobiology," *Psychological Bulletin* 141 (2015): 931–965.

228   *If the science simply ignores their experience*: Charles Fernyhough, "Hearing the Voice," *The Lancet* 384 (2014): 1090–1091.

229   *the Spider Baby*: "Good Luck, Father Ted," *Father Ted*, series 1, episode 1, April 1995.

229   *reality monitoring*: Marcia K. Johnson, "Memory and Reality," *American Psychologist* 61 (2006): 760–771; Jon S. Simons, Richard N. A. Henson, Sam J. Gilbert, and Paul C. Fletcher, "Separable Forms of Reality Monitoring Supported by Anterior Prefrontal Cortex," *Journal of Cognitive Neuroscience* 20 (2008): 447–457. See also p. 126.

229   *the paracingulate sulcus*: Marie Buda, Alex Fornito, Zara M. Bergström, and Jon S. Simons, "A Specific Brain Structural Basis for Individual Differences in Reality Monitoring," *Journal of Neuroscience* 31 (2011): 14308–14313; Jane Garrison, Charles Fernyhough, Simon McCarthy-Jones, Mark Haggard, The Australian Schizophrenia Research Bank, and Jon S. Simons, "Paracingulate Sulcus Morphology Is Associated with Hallucinations in the Human Brain," *Nature Communications* 6, article 8956 (2015).

230   *resting brains of those who hear voices*: See p. 162.

230   *"hypervigilance" hallucinations*: Guy Dodgson and Sue Gordon, "Avoiding False Negatives: Are Some Auditory Hallucinations an Evolved Design Flaw?," *Behavioural and Cognitive Psychotherapy* 37 (2009): 325–334; David Smailes, Ben Alderson-Day, Charles Fernyhough, Simon McCarthy-Jones, and Guy Dodgson, "Tailoring Cognitive Behavioural Therapy to Subtypes of Voice-Hearing," *Frontiers in Psychology* 6, article

1933 (2015); Guy Dodgson, Jenna Robson, Ben Alderson-Day, Simon McCarthy-Jones, and Charles Fernyhough, *Tailoring CBT to Subtypes of Voice-Hearing*, unpublished manual, 2014.

230   *top-down processes:* Kenneth Hugdahl, "'Hearing Voices': Auditory Hallucinations as Failure of Top-down Control of Bottom-up Perceptual Processes," *Scandinavian Journal of Psychology* 50 (2009): 553–560. Recently, there has been a growth of interest in so-called *predictive processing* approaches to perception, in which top-down prediction dominates the construction of a perceptual representation. In the case of hearing voices, predictive processing accounts propose an imbalance between the predicted sensory state and the signal that cannot be explained in terms of the internal prediction (the "prediction error"). See Sam Wilkinson, "Accounting for the Phenomenology and Varieties of Auditory Verbal Hallucination Within a Predictive Processing Framework," *Consciousness and Cognition* 30 (2014): 142–155.

230   *noise of their breast pumps:* Christine Cooper-Rompato, "The Talking Breast Pump," *Western Folklore* 72 (2013): 181–209.

231   *"shaped by the intellectual, emotional, and imaginative powers of the individual . . .":* Oliver Sacks, *Hallucinations* (London: Picador, 2012), 197.

231   *Cultural beliefs can exert top-down effects:* Frank Larøi et al., "Culture and Hallucinations: Overview and Future Directions," *Schizophrenia Bulletin* 40, suppl. no. 4 (2014): S213–S220; T. M. Luhrmann, R. Padmavati, H. Tharoor, and A. Osei, "Differences in Voice-Hearing Experiences of People with Psychosis in the U.S.A., India and Ghana: Interview-Based Study," *British Journal of Psychiatry* 206 (2015): 41–44.

231   *children from England and Saudi Arabia:* Abdulrahman S. Al-Namlah, Charles Fernyhough, and Elizabeth Meins, "Sociocultural Influences on the Development of Verbal Mediation: Private Speech and Phonological Recoding in Saudi Arabian and British Samples," *Developmental Psychology* 42 (2006): 117–131.

232   *how particular languages confer specific properties on inner speech:* This is a different idea from the one associated with some versions of the linguistic relativity hypothesis (see p. 106). At issue here is not whether the linguistic concepts available to an individual shape the range of thoughts the individual is able to have, but rather, whether certain languages make certain kinds of self-directed speech more powerful or efficient. Alternatively, is there a kind of universal grammar of inner speech that does not vary across languages? As the evidence grows on the varied roles of inner speech in cognition, this question may come more sharply into focus.

232   *keeping track of the mental states of others:* Ben Alderson-Day and Charles Fernyhough, "Auditory Verbal Hallucinations: Social But How?," *Journal of Consciousness Studies*, in press; Ben Alderson-Day and Charles Fernyhough, "Inner Speech: Development, Cognitive Functions, Phenomenology, and Neurobiology," *Psychological Bulletin* 141 (2015): 931–965.

233   *much mind-wandering is verbal:* Alderson-Day and Fernyhough, "Inner Speech"; M. Perrone-Bertolotti, L. Rapin, J.-P. Lachaux, M. Baciu, and H. Lœvenbruck, "What Is That Little Voice Inside My Head? Inner Speech Phenomenology, Its Role in Cognitive Performance, and Its Relation to Self-Monitoring," *Behavioural Brain Research* 261 (2014): 220–239; Pascal Delamillieure et al., "The Resting State Questionnaire: An Introspective Questionnaire for Evaluation of Inner Experience During the Conscious Resting State," *Brain Research Bulletin* 81 (2010): 565–573.

234   *"Life . . . is something of a silent movie . . .":* Boris Eikhenbaum, "Problems of Film Stylistics," *Screen* 15 (1974): 7–32; Norbert Wiley, *Inner Speech and the Dialogical Self* (Philadelphia: Temple University Press, 2016).

236   *the psychology of spiritual meditation:* Corinne Saunders and Charles Fernyhough, "Reading Margery Kempe's Inner Voices," paper presented at *Medicine of Words: Literature, Medicine, and Theology in the Middle Ages*, St. Anne's College, Oxford, September 2015; Barry Windeatt, "Reading and Re-reading *The Book of Margery Kempe*," in John H. Arnold and Katherine J. Lewis, eds., *A Companion to the Book of Margery Kempe* (Cambridge, UK: D. S. Brewer, 2004). See also p. 150.

236   *"pseudohallucination":* G. E. Berrios and T. R. Dening, "Pseudo-hallucinations: A Conceptual History," *Psychological Medicine* 26 (1996): 753–763.

237   *In cases of aphasia . . . :* Alderson-Day and Fernyhough, "Inner Speech."

238   *inner speech in autism:* David Williams, Dermot M. Bowler, and Christopher Jarrold, "Inner Speech Is Used to Mediate Short-Term Memory, But Not Planning, Among Intellectually High-Functioning Adults with Autism Spectrum Disorder," *Development and Psychopathology* 24 (2012): 225–239; Russell T. Hurlburt, Francesca Happé, and Uta Frith, "Sampling the Form of Inner Experience in Three Adults with Asperger Syndrome," *Psychological Medicine* 24 (1994): 385–395; Alderson-Day and Fernyhough, "Inner Speech"; Charles Fernyhough, "The Dialogic Mind: A Dialogic Approach to the Higher Mental Functions," *New Ideas in Psychology* 14 (1996): 47–62.

238   *inner speech as the thread of a necklace:* See p. 106.

239   *"My voices saved my life . . .":* Dolly Sen, interviewed for "Voices in the Dark: An Audio Story," *Mosaic*, Wellcome Trust, December 9, 2014.

239   *"both an attack on personal identity . . .":* Marius A. J. Romme and Sandra Escher, *Making Sense of Voices: A Guide for Professionals Working with Voice Hearers* (London: Mind, 2000), 64.

239   *self-talk . . . into adulthood:* Jean Piaget, *The Language and Thought of the Child*, Marjorie and Ruth Gabain, trans. (London: Kegan Paul, Trench, Trubner, 1959 [1926]), 1–2. See also p. 45.

240   *autobiographical memory:* Katherine Nelson and Robyn Fivush, "The Emergence of Autobiographical Memory: A Social Cultural Developmental Theory," *Psychological Review* 111 (2004): 486–511; Abdulrahman S.

Al-Namlah, Elizabeth Meins, and Charles Fernyhough, "Self-Regulatory Private Speech Relates to Children's Recall and Organization of Auto-biographical Memories," *Early Childhood Research Quarterly* 27 (2012): 441–446; Viorica Marian and Ulric Neisser, "Language-Dependent Recall of Autobiographical Memories," *Journal of Experimental Psychology: General* 129 (2000): 361–368.

240   "*Our inner speech . . . is at least faithful to us . . .*": Riley, "'A Voice Without a Mouth,'" 8.

240   *self-awareness and self evaluation:* Alain Morin, "Possible Links Between Self-Awareness and Inner Speech: Theoretical Background, Underlying Mechanisms, and Empirical Evidence," *Journal of Consciousness Studies* 12 (2005): 115–134; Alain Morin, "Self-Awareness Deficits Following Loss of Inner Speech: Dr. Jill Bolte Taylor's Case Study," *Consciousness and Cognition* 18 (2009): 524–529; Jill Bolte Taylor, *My Stroke of Insight: A Brain Scientist's Personal Journey* (New York: Viking, 2006), 75–76.

241   *think through moral problems:* Mark B. Tappan, "Language, Culture, and Moral Development: A Vygotskian Perspective," *Developmental Review* 17 (1997): 78–100, 88.

241   *angry conversation with himself:* Christopher Isherwood, *Christopher and His Kind* (London: Methuen, 1977), 17.

242   Rumination *refers to an obsessive dwelling:* Susan Nolen-Hoeksema, Blair E. Wisco, and Sonja Lyubomirsky, "Rethinking Rumination," *Perspectives on Psychological Science* 3 (2008): 400–424.

242   *The auditory modality:* I am grateful to David Smailes for making this point.

243   *CBT for voice-hearing:* Smailes et al., "Tailoring Cognitive Behavioural Therapy to Subtypes of Voice-Hearing"; Dodgson et al., *Tailoring CBT to Subtypes of Voice-Hearing.*

243   *obsessive-compulsive disorder:* As with rumination, there has been little attempt to understand the extent to which intrusive thoughts in OCD are specifically verbal. For a recent review of OCD research, see David Adams, *The Man Who Couldn't Stop: The Truth About OCD* (London: Picador, 2014).

243   *Samuel Johnson was likened by his biographer:* Allan Ingram, "In Two Minds: Johnson, Boswell and Representations of the Self," paper presented at *Le moi / The Self in the Long Eighteenth Century*, Sorbonne Nouvelle, Paris, December 2013; Samuel Johnson, *The History of Rasselas, Prince of Abissinia*, Thomas Keymer, ed. (Oxford: Oxford University Press, 2009), 93; James Boswell, *Boswell's London Journal, 1762–1763*, F. A. Pottle, ed. (London: William Heinemann, 1950), 187.

244   "*It's so hard to turn off my brain . . .*": "Make Room for Lisa," *The Simpsons*, season 10, episode 16, February 1999.

244   *via negativa:* Sara Maitland, *A Book of Silence* (London: Granta, 2008); Anonymous, *The Cloud of Unknowing*, A. C. Spearing, trans. (London: Penguin, 2001).

244   *When a thought comes by:* Mindfulness is another area in which the idea of the "inner voice" is sometimes used loosely and without consideration of its sensory-perceptual properties. See, for example, Liora Birnbaum, "Adolescent Aggression and Differentiation of Self: Guided Mindfulness Meditation in the Service of Individuation," *Scientific World Journal* 5 (2005): 478–489. See p. 9.

244   *within a spiritual framework:* S. Jones, A. Guy, and J. A. Ormrod, "A Q-Methodological Study of Hearing Voices: A Preliminary Exploration of Voice Hearers' Understanding of Their Experiences," *Psychology and Psychotherapy: Theory, Research and Practice* 76 (2003): 189–209; Sylvia Mohr, Christiane Gillieron, Laurence Borras, Pierre-Yves Brandt, and Philippe Huguelet, "The Assessment of Spirituality and Religiousness in Schizophrenia," *Journal of Nervous and Mental Disease* 195 (2007): 247–253.

245   *a "voice" of conscience:* Sigmund Freud, "On Narcissism: An Introduction," in James Strachey, ed., *The Standard Edition of the Complete Psychological Works of Sigmund Freud*, vol. 14 (London: Hogarth Press, 1957). Elsewhere Freud argued that hallucinations stemmed from wish-fulfillment that was not kept in check by processes of reality testing: Sigmund Freud, "A Metapsychological Supplement to the Theory of Dreams," *Standard Edition*, vol. 14. David Velleman argued that the "voice" of conscience is not an actual or literal voice, with phenomenological properties, but rather a mode of self-communication. Again, there is a lack of evidence on the extent to which such experiences or intuitions have any specific voice-like properties. David J. Velleman, "The Voice of Conscience," *Proceedings of the Aristotelian Society* 99 (1999): 57–76. See also Douglas J. Davies, "Inner Speech and Religious Traditions," in James A. Beckford and John Walliss, eds., *Theorising Religion: Classical and Contemporary Debates* (Aldershot, UK: Ashgate, 2006).

245   *Sonia Gandhi:* "Gandhi's Rejection of Power Stuns India," *The Times* (London), May 19, 2004, 11.

245   *Mahatma Gandhi:* Richard L. Johnson, ed., *Gandhi's Experiments with Truth: Essential Writings By and About Mahatma Gandhi* (Lanham, MD: Lexington Books, 2006), 139.

245   *the psychology of prayer:* Simon Dein and Roland Littlewood, "The Voice of God," *Anthropology & Medicine* 14 (2007): 213–228; Simon Dein and Christopher C. H. Cook, "God Put a Thought into My Mind: The Charismatic Christian Experience of Receiving Communications from God," *Mental Health, Religion & Culture* 18 (2015): 97–113; Tanya Luhrmann, *When God Talks Back: Understanding the American Evangelical Relationship with God* (London: Vintage, 2012), 233.

247   *"It is entirely a matter of voices . . .":* Samuel Beckett, *The Unnamable*, in *The Beckett Trilogy* (London: Picador, 1979), 325.

Index

Charles Fernyhough is a writer and psychologist. He is the author of the critically acclaimed *Pieces of Light*, shortlisted for many prizes, and of *A Thousand Days of Wonder*. He directs Hearing the Voice, a project on inner voices based at Durham University. He lives in County Durham, United Kingdom.